W9-ARI-343

Theatre, Aristocracy, and Pornocracy

Theatre, Aristocracy, and Pornocracy

The Orgy Calculus

●

Karl Toepfer

●

PAJ Publications
New York

792
T64t

First Edition
All rights reserved
No part of this publication may be reproduced or transmitted in any form or by any means, electronic or mechanical, including photocopy, recording, or any information storage or retrieval system now known or to be invented, without permission in writing from the publishers, except by a reviewer who wishes to quote brief passages in connection with a review written for inclusion in a magazine, newspaper, or broadcast.

All rights reserved under the International and Pan-American Copyright Conventions. For information, write to PAJ Publications, 131 Varick Street, Suite 902, New York, N.Y. 10013.

Library of Congress Cataloging in Publication Data
Theatre, Aristocracy, and Pornocracy
ISBN: 1-55554-055-4 (cloth)
ISBN: 1-55554-056-2 (paper)

Printed in the United States of America

Publication of this book has been made possible in part by a grant received from The Florence Gould Foundation, whose support is gratefully acknowledged. Additional funds were provided in part by the New York State Council on the Arts.

Contents

Acknowledgments

THIS BOOK IS PART of an ongoing research project which examines relations between speech, literary language, and ecstasy. Though pervasively and perhaps supremely desired, ecstasy is a very rare emotion, and the conditions for experiencing it are extremely complex. Orgy strives to signify one category of ecstatic experience. Most research on relations between language and emotion focuses on "accessible" emotions which are not at all difficult to experience: rage, anger, disillusionment, despair, contempt, indignation, fear. But it has been clear to me for some time that understanding relations between language and feelings of injustice, betrayal, or failure cannot adequately empower people with knowledge of these relations if such knowledge does not include a keen interest in understanding relations between language and pleasure, desire, or other categories of "aesthetic" emotions experienced for their own sake. My approach here generally favors a semiotic theoretical perspective, and I am especially grateful to Carlos Tindemans of the University of Antwerp for much guidance regarding the application of semiotic theory to the study of theatrical performance.

Many people made anonymous contributions to the creation of this book; these include persons who operate research libraries at University of California Berkeley, University of California Los Angeles, Princeton University, the New York Public Library, and the San Francisco Public Library and staff of Instructional Resources Center at San Jose State University. The Inter-Library Loan office of San Jose State University (supervised by Jean Meyer) was enormously helpful and persistent in obtaining extremely obscure sources of information. A travel grant from the School of Humanities and the Arts, San Jose State University, enabled me to do some information gathering in Paris. I have benefited greatly from the comments, encouragement, or complexities introduced by various readers, who include Nick Browne (UCLA), Anne Carson (University of Toronto), Henry Goodman (UCLA), Patricia Stanley (Florida State University), and especially Laurence Senelick (Tufts University). But no one should blame these people for whatever theoretical errors or "misreadings" of history other readers may discover. Michael Dempsey of Los Angeles helped me significantly in fulfilling several tasks necessary to complete the book. Howard Burman (Long Beach State University) made available to me slides of eighteenth century engravings for which we are still not able to verify the source. I am also most thankful for the pleasure of my collaboration with Bonnie Marranca, my editor at PAJ Publications, who was always very delightful about maintaining a *modest* sense of scale for the book.

Chapter One
Orgy Theory

Ideologies of Orgy

THE PHENOMENON OF *orgy* awakens complex and strange emotions in
those who contemplate it. Part of the complexity derives from a
peculiar reality: people contemplate orgies far more than they ever ✳
actually participate in them. Moreover, the "contemplation" of orgies
pervasively operates through fantasy, through *images* of orgy which avoid
becoming the object of systematic analysis or theoretical discourse.
Because physical "experience" of orgy is so rare, the meaning of the word
and the conditions to which the word refers remain very fuzzy, and this
fuzziness enhances the rhetorical, metaphorical significance of the word.
Thus, one may speak of a flowery meadow as an "orgy of color"; when
barbarian hordes invade an ancient city, they engage in an "orgy of
destruction." But metaphor mystifies, rather than clarifies; it *conceals* its
component identities within each other, and in so doing, *discloses* only the
complexity of an attitude emanating from the rhetorical choices constructing the metaphor. Suppose, for example, that a person says, "I spent
my summer in an orgy of reading." It is possible that no amount of context
for this sentence could make clear to a listener whether the summer
reading was a good or bad experience: the word "orgy" complicates the
phenomenon of reading to such an extent that the listener's own feeling
about reading becomes complicated. The word inevitably exudes an
erotic aura because it refers to (intense) conditions of sensual, physical
pleasure.

But whatever is orgy also refers to conditions of excess, extremity, and abnormality. An "orgy of reading" always signifies a mood of *danger,* an extravagant risk. Orgy refers to pleasures and desires which are satisfied only by transgressing a limit or norm for their satisfaction. In other words, orgy exposes a conflict between a mode of desire and an ideologically defined norm for the *magnitude* of the desire. Put crudely, orgies signify a *quantitative* dimension for desire, insofar as they are the manifestation of "too much" or "more than enough" pleasure. "Enough" is an ideologically defined condition. However, the power of ideology (norms of pleasure) over the relation between desire and the resources to satisfy desire is such that most people everywhere perceive almost every pleasure (satisfaction of desire) to be "never enough," rather than "more than enough"; and this constant lack of opportunity to reach a threshold and then exceed it means that the phenomenon of orgy exists above all as an object of fantasy, of which metaphor is a category.

But the norms of pleasure which make the physical, sensual "experience" of orgies so rare are not strictly assertions of morality. As this book will demonstrate, any authentic experience of orgy depends on a very complicated set of variables. Establishing the conditions for an orgy requires considerable material resources and "staging" skills, as well as a desire for "more than enough." The complexity of variables controlling the phenomenon becomes evident as soon as we attempt to define orgiastic experience with some rigor. In its original, ancient sense, orgy refers to "secret rites" in honor of Dionysos, and these secret rites involved the impassioned, intoxicated performance of songs and dances. But even in ancient Greece, the identification of orgies with "secret" activities compelled the phenomenon to mean something more precise and complicated:

1) an orgy is a manifestation of *excesses* which therefore must be *hidden* to be experienced.

2) The motives for excess and secrecy have a metaphysical foundation in the desire to get closer to a god, to feel a divine energy within the body.

3) Orgiastic experience entails an *erotic,* carnal pleasure in *worshipping* someone.

4) An orgy involves *groups* of bodies, group eroticism, communal ecstasy. Of course, it is possible that a couple alone may engage in orgies which include only themselves, but I think it is possible only

when the partners "play" numerous roles to construct the idea of many ("too many") bodies in one.

5) An orgy is a type of aesthetic *performance* (such as "singing and dancing") which develops *theatrical* qualities to achieve ecstatic effects.

6) The secrecy associated with orgiastic performance indicates that the dominant function of an orgy is aesthetic, rather than ritualistic or religious. The idea, even when promoted by orgiasts themselves, that an orgy functions to effect some general social benefit for a society lacks credibility when the circumstances of the performance remain secret. Rather, an orgy signifies a current of *exclusivity* within a society, a magnitude of pleasure reserved only for an initiated *class* of persons.

But all these stipulations for the definition of orgy entail further theoretical conditions. Orgy is a category of ecstatic experience. Ecstasy is a category, perhaps the most powerful category, of aesthetic experience, which is emotion felt for its own sake. In its original sense, as *ekstasis*, ecstasy refers to a condition of "standing outside oneself," self-abandonment, a supreme trust in and fearlessness before "otherness." The ecstatic feeling of being "outside" oneself, of being completely "other," seems linked to an impulse toward theatricalization of action, toward the impersonation of "another" through the appropriation ("possession") of another body, an erotic phenomenon. Marghanita Laski observed, however, that ecstasy is not synonymous with orgasm; her evidence suggests that most people never experience ecstasy more than two or three times in their lives and that even those who have never experienced ecstasy at all somehow still *know* that they have never experienced it.[1] Ecstasy is not an "easy" or "accessible" emotion, like anger, despair, or delight; it is an extremely complicated moment; it is a *supreme* and *unique* (unrepeatable) moment of happiness. Ecstasy may recur, but it can never be the same as any previous ecstasy; every instance of ecstasy is always "greater" than any previous instance. Orgy occurs when ecstasy is possible only through an excessive mode of appropriation in which the "other" to whom one has abandoned oneself has "too many" bodies.

Empirical data about orgies is of course very scant. But this lack of information nevertheless has significant theoretical value. Lack of experience with orgies encourages people to *fantasize* them in quantitative terms, as a *large* number of orgasms, number of appropriated bodies, range of perversions, or duration of ecstatic activity. But a focus on the statistical identity of orgies can obscure the importance of *meanings* ascribed to them. An *excess of meaning* is very difficult to quantify and not necessarily equivalent to a threshold number of orgasms, bodies, actions, hours, or costs. The "greatest" orgy may actually require less time and fewer orgasms and bodies than the "usual" (fantasized) orgy. The problem, then, is to identify and "measure" the intensities of ecstatic feeling and meaning produced by orgies. But such analysis depends on disclosing how orgiastic ecstasy operates in relation to myths and ideologically structured perceptions about what constitutes "more than enough" pleasure.

In Disraeli's novel *Lothair* (1870), we find the oft-quoted remark that "the worship of the beautiful always ends in an orgy." From a strictly logical position, we cannot infer from this statement that all orgies result from the worship of the beautiful; but since we have already observed that, at least in its "authentic" sense, an orgy is in itself a manifestation of worship, and since whatever inspires worship is very probably beautiful, Disraeli's statement exerts special theoretical interest. Assuming that beauty is rare and by no means commonplace or readily accessible, we can suppose from the statement that orgies evolve in relation to phenomena that are rare, exclusive, inaccessible, arcane, "difficult," and forbidding as much as forbidden. This point is significant in distinguishing the orgiastic from Mikhail Bakhtin's idea of the "carnivalesque." For Bakhtin, the phenomenon of carnival is a model or metaphor for particular types of "polyvocal" or "dialogic" literature which produce a narrative panorama of social reality. Every sector or class within social reality employs its own voice, its own rhetorical strategies, and the panoramic manifestation of the "carnivalesque" entails the intersection or interaction of these different voices. In the novel, the carnivalesque signifies a subversion of a social order by subverting those linguistic norms of communication by which the social order perpetrates yet conceals class differences within it. Bakhtin perceives carnival as a democratic, inclusive phenomenon wherein all sectors of society celebrate their common liberation from norms which preserve inequities and distances between social classes. From this perspective, carnival provides a critique of social reality and an intimation of an "open," democratic utopia. Carnival signifies a latent revolutionary impulse which surfaces periodically to re-distribute power relations within social reality upon a more equitable ("popular") basis. The re-distribution of power depends on the operation of "polyvocal" modes of discourse; but such discourses blur the "difference" between pleasure (aesthetic motives) and labor (economic motives). This "carnivalesque" conjunction of pleasure and labor gives Bakhtin's view of utopia an aura of theatricality — or rather, utopia implies a social order in which the difference between theatre and reality is considerably less than for a pre-utopian society.[2]

In contrast to the Bakhtinian ideology of carnival, the ideology of orgy, which strives to realize its objectives through secrecy, is consistently the production of an aristocratic impulse, in the sense that desires satisfied through orgy mark those who feel them as members of a *highly privileged class* of persons. An orgy enhances the difference between one *class* of persons (its participants) and "the rest," those excluded from the performance. Orgy culture is subculture or counter-culture, but not a revolutionary culture which posits orgy as a model for the transformation of social reality. Orgy is possible because orgiasts believe either that social reality needs no major changes or that a utopian intersection of desire and necessity embracing an entire society will not happen soon enough, if ever. But this observation does not mean that orgy lacks a utopian dimension. On the contrary, as will appear evident in later pages, orgy culture links the ideal intersection of desire and necessity to a supreme amplification of class difference and exclusivity. Orgy culture supposes that utopia is a "secret," rather than "open," condition of existence. The reason for this supposition is that the orgiast can never escape the inclination to believe that utopia is synonymous with the attainment of ecstasy. But ecstasy, as we have noted, is a dramatic, turbulent, dynamic emotion, based on an exchange, rather than stability, of power between ✳ a sacrificed self and a consuming Other. Of course, the abandoned self is still the Other *to* another. Because ecstasy is an utterly unique (unrepeatable) moment, the basis for its identity is difference and exclusivity, rather than unity and stability (repetition). An orgy is a utopia only for some people (orgiasts) only at particular (ecstatic) moments. And though the orgy is a "secret" phenomenon, it is never a strong assertion of any notion of "privacy," of an attitude toward difference evolved from romantic doctrines of individualism: orgy is always a *communal* event involving "too many bodies" to allow any one body to make "enough" of a difference. The orgiast is not in search of a powerfully unique self; rather, the orgiast seeks to belong to a unique *class* of persons whose collective ecstasy is greater than the happiness of any individual or of an entire society.

Nevertheless, orgy and carnival are similar to the extent that they are theatrical phenomena, that they are "staged" performances which require elaborate signifying codes, intricate aesthetic contrivances, to fulfill their functions. As a category of ecstatic action, orgy "naturally" implies a type of theatrical performance or spectacle in which the performers are not "really" themselves because the pressure of ecstasy compels them to "abandon" themselves. The popular iconography of orgy pervasively incorporates signifiers of aesthetic performance. In the late nineteenth and early twentieth centuries, such images typically associated orgy with (often monumental) "scenes" of luxury and exoticism in archaic, imperial settings. This scenography of luxury entails a variety of signifiers: palatial or temple-like architecture, clouds of incense, the multitudinous presence of bejewelled concubines or ivory-decorated slaves, a stupendous abundance of food, drink, and lurid flowers, the looming, *artistically refined* sculpture(s) of the Idol, a plentitude of expensive decorative details, such as flowing banners of silk, voluptuous pillows, ornate candelabra, exquisitely huge vases, marble or tiled surfaces, glittering, diaphanous garments, plumed headdresses, and of course a panorama of luscious, glowing flesh — all in all a vast symphony of sensual optical delights, which, nevertheless, consistently manages to produce an ambivalent atmosphere of torpidity and languor, as in Fig. 1. This archetypal "vision" of orgy invariably projects a religious message. The emphasis on luxurious details exposes the extravagant *cost* of orgy, which is possible only when the "setting" contains "more than enough" rare and expensive "props." The lavishness of the decor embeds the secondary perception of a monumental magnitude of *waste*. Of course, only a *few people* can ever *afford* pleasure on this scale. Orgy appears coincident with the amassing of tremendous wealth, with the worship of the Golden Calf.

But such a trite critique of materialism merely points to a deeper "view" of the cost of orgy embodied by the archetypal image: one must measure the cost of orgy in terms of catastrophic social pathologies: slavery, concubinage, despotic privileges, monstrous sacrifices, numbness toward human suffering, the worship of false gods (images). The luxurious setting situates orgy within an overly-refined, "civilized" milieu. Moreover, the inclination of the iconography to employ signifiers of torpor, languor, and satiation focuses attention on the *aftermath* of orgy and the knowledge that orgy produces a huge state of *exhaustion,* which the spectator associates with *decadence,* the downfall of civilization, vulnerability to conquest by ambitious barbarian hordes. This point becomes especially clear when the iconography favors a setting ascribed to archaic, vanished civilizations of the Mediterranean and Middle East: Sodom and Gomorrah, the Kingdom of the Sybarites, the Babylon of Nebuchadnezzar, the Carthage of Salammbo, the Imperial Rome of Heliogabulus. The Bible and history "teach" us that orgiastic appetites are self-destructive, manifestations of a powerful death-drive. This quasi-theocratic ideology perhaps achieves its most opulent and accessible expression in cinematic form, in which the peculiar visual capabilities of celluloid technology allow orgy, luxury, despotism, decadence, and paganism to project a compatible set of signs.

Cecil B. DeMille, of course, earned enormous success by titillating the public with glimpses of orgy, in which the screen eventually revealed to the "ordinary," vicarious spectator that even if he or she was not able to "afford" to participate in orgies, the price in the end was really not worth paying [Fig. 2]. But when Stroheim attempted a similar message in a contemporary European setting for *The Wedding March* (1927), the producing studio (MGM) became nervous over the perversity (rather than extravagance) of the orgy scene and ordered it removed from the version of the film offered to the public [Fig. 3]. However, it is in the Babylonian sequence of D. W. Griffith's *Intolerance* (1916) that we find perhaps the most spectacular orgy scene ever filmed [Fig. 4]. No other orgy scene so vividly links Hollywood to Babylon in the public mind — that is, cinema technology disclosed that the whole phenomenology of orgy, luxury, despotism, decadence, and paganism resulted from an expanded power of vision, of new and complicated mechanisms of seeing which, however, made the "ordinary" spectator more conscious of how problematic desires in supposedly vanished civilizations (Babylon) still "live on" in "modern" reality (Hollywood). Advancement toward orgy culture appears as a correlate of technological progess.

But the Western iconography of orgy does not always conform to this popular ideology, even when the artist relies on the Bible for inspiration. Whereas popular mythology tends to associate orgy with the *impending* destruction of civilization, some, rather esoteric, images suggest that orgy culture emerges *after* the destruction of civilization. Consider, for example, images dealing with the theme of Lot and his daughters, the (very brief) Old Testament story (Genesis 19) about how, after God's destruction of Sodom and Gomorrah, the two daughters of Lot decided that the regeneration of the human race depended upon incest with their father, whom they took turns seducing on consecutive nights. However, artists enjoy treating the story in dramatic, spectacular terms in which the regeneration of humanity justifies an orgiastic transgression of taboo. Lucas Cranach's 1530 depiction seems fairly restrained by the modest facial expressions of the women and the sense of drugged unconsciousness ascribed to Lot [Figs. 5-6]. But this signification of innocence is, as usual with Cranach, somewhat complicated by his taste for dramatic effect: Sodom and Gomorrah burn in the background with a hellish red glow which is echoed in the fiery red dresses and hair of the women. For Cranach, the destruction of civilization is a metaphor for the fiery emotions "behind" or clothing the signification of innocence. The destruction is the awakening rather than consequence of orgiastic feeling.

The seventeenth-century artist Joachim Wtewael presents us with a much more voluptuous pair of daughters and a much less drowsy father [Fig. 7]. The spectacle of inflamed civilization recedes to a small corner of the image, where it appears as something incidentally glimpsed beyond the curtain of a great tent. The pleasure of the orgiasts is so obvious that the destruction of civilization has become a distant, almost forgotten memory. The naked flesh glows far more luridly than any hellish flames of destruction. In his 1939 depiction of the subject, Otto Dix discloses an affinity with these earlier versions [Fig. 8]. Indeed, Dix seems to have combined dominant signifying practices from both paintings. As in Cranach, the destruction of civilization assumes a central place in the image. But as in Wtewael, the artist delights in the exposure of flesh. As the flames of destruction rise, so too does the nudity of woman rise and loom over the landscape. However, the brilliant orange of the incinerated cities contrasts dramatically with the soft, creamy glow of the flesh. The orange repeats in the sleeves and belt of the clothed woman, but the green of this figure's blouse and skirt predominate because it connects her to the greeness of the trees, "nature." None of the three figures touches another; the nude woman gazes enigmatically at something excluded from the image, as if she is conscious of someone watching her perform. The father lacks the innocence of Cranach's Lot and the dark potency of Wtewael's; instead, utterly overwhelmed by female beauty, he projects a sly expression (squinting eyes) which suggests that he is congenially resigned to the pretenses the women have devised to strip him of his authority and awaken his hidden, taboo desire for them. It is the very complexity of this image of orgy which gives it a more perverse or disturbing erotic effect than the other two. But all three pictures construct images in which the signification of orgy does not depend on popular signifiers of luxury, oriental despotism, and pagan idolatry.

These artists represent the burning of the sinful cities as simultaneous with the orgiastic transgression of taboo; in doing so, they reinforce the perception that orgy is an aristocratic, exclusionary phenomenon that occurs only to a few apart from "the rest" of humanity. Orgiastic happiness occurs *while* "the rest" of humanity suffers from the obliterating heat of its own corruption and imperfection. In Karel van Mander's *The Garden of Love* (ca. 1585-1595), the apocalyptic element is altogether missing. Here the "old" sign of civilization is the dark, desolate ruin of a castle in the distance, beyond the trees [Fig. 9]. In the foreground of the park-like arcadia blossoms a stunning vision of a communistic-utopian orgy culture. The luminous nudity of the orgy community effaces all class differences between its members. The sky is dark and very dark shadows saturate the landscape, but the unreal (theatrical) radiance of the bodies is such that the spectator may well feel that this communal ecstasy goes on long after "the rest" of the world has gone into eclipse and become a remote ruin. However, the idealization of the bodies implies that membership in the orgiastic community is highly selective, reserved exclusively for those who have attained a high standard of physical perfection endorsed by culture generally but embodied only by the depicted cult. No matter how "big" or encompassing love becomes, it remains a powerfully exclusionary, powerfully differentiating emotion. Of course, the artist more than likely designed this painting for consumption by a wealthy merchant, for whom it was merely a pornographic fantasy rather than the image of a social reality toward which one should seriously, diligently aspire.

Some of the allegorical paintings of Hieronymous Bosch present even more spectacular images of orgy. For example, in *The Garden of Earthly Delights* (1500), perhaps his most famous work, the representation of an orgiastic *world* ("garden") entails the depiction of Paradise and The Last Judgement [Fig. 10]. For Bosch, as for van Mander, the chief signifier of orgy is mass nudity, a plenitude of glowing flesh freed from attachment to luxury or material opulence. But Bosch differs from van Mander in his treatment of the "garden" context for orgy. Van Mander perceives nature as a storm-darkened realm of shadows to which orgy remains oblivious. Bosch sees orgy as a fantastic manifestation of nature — orgy and nature enjoy a "wild" organic relation. The formation of orgiastic society coincides with the weird mutation and bizarre transformation of life forms. Perception becomes distorted by the intricately strange scale of identities in relation to each other. A collage (more than panoramic) organization of perception is at work here: orgy belongs entirely to the world of dreams, to a brilliantly-colored, *hallucinatory* order of perception. In the third panel of the great tryptich, Bosch presents hell itself as a type of orgy. The image as a whole differentiates between an "infernal" or "demonic" mode of orgy and an "earthly" or "paradisial" mode. We cannot see the orgiastic "garden" without being conscious of a *monstrous* capacity for pain and suffering. Fantastic engines of torture link orgy to an anonymous, mechanical manipulation and destruction of bodies. The "delightful" mutation of life forms in the garden "blinds" us, so to speak, to the "demonic" aspect of organic transformation. Indeed, the monstrous otherness of the hell panel reinforces the aristocratic identity of orgy by compelling the spectator to see orgy as coincident with the "eternal" suffering of others.

The collage representation of orgy recurs in a much more "modern" work: Karl Hubbuch's 1922 lithograph *Im Rausch des Irrens (In the Delirium of Madness)* [Fig. 11]. Here the "demonic" aspect of orgy completely prevails. The picture links an ecstatic mass of bodies to the release of criminal or insane impulses. The artist does not idealize the bodies, but makes each body highly distinct from any other, with the result, of course, that the *mass* of bodies does not at all appear synonymous with any *unity* of desire which brings bodies "together." Signifiers of luxury and material opulence are missing, but so too are conventional, gardenesque signifiers of nature. Instead, signifiers of big city culture urge the spectator to see orgy as an *urban* phenomenon or consequence of urbanization, which the artist views from a *critical* perspective. Orgy is a symptom or analogue of a violent, anarchistic social reality dominated by "mad," individualizing lusts rather than unifying love. Voluptuous color disappears from the image of orgy as an entirely linear tension between black and white pressures exposes the inky, imprinting texture of "mad" desire.

But the black-and-white image of orgy is by no means synonymous with a critical, satirical perception. In 1917, a very obscure Russian artist, Sergei Lodygin, published his *Orgy* print [Fig. 12]. Though the image reminds us of the Hollywood view of orgy, with its signifiers of luxury, Mediterranean exoticism, and pagan idolatry, the artist does not complicate the scene with any signs of "warning" for the spectator. Shadows are absent: black serves a purely decorative purpose of making white things dazzle all the more. The geometric precision of the design, the utter lack of uncertainty in the movement of lines, the supreme sense of control over every detail — all these elements link orgy to a "classical" notion of order and "beauty." The artist idealizes the bodies, even if the male figures appear somewhat androgynous. The nude woman standing on the table exudes a luminous pride, a voluptuous confidence in herself and in the moment. The image obviously associates orgy with an exquisitely refined aestheticism, but this aestheticism operates within an exclusive setting of "classical" balance and perfect poise. Orgy is here the creation of a highly refined, delicately controlled civilization which enjoys complete, guiltless confidence in its capacity to experience maximum intensities of pleasure. Orgiastic ecstasy is not "mad"; it is the achievement of a "perfect" (excessive) rationalization of signification.

All these images of orgy embody dramatic, scenographic visual qualities which *fantasy* ascribes to group erotic ecstasy. Theatre of course attempts to bring the imaginary to "life" in a completely literal sense. But in doing so, the theatre constantly makes concessions to the physical reality of the human body (as performer and spectator) and to the material resources of performance. These conditions allow theatre to define orgiastic experience in a much more complex fashion than other modes of representation. Perhaps the most popular theatrical representations of orgy appear in the world of ballet and opera. One thinks of the Venusberg bacchanale from Wagner's *Tannhäuser* (1845), the bacchanale from Saint-Säens' *Samson and Delilah* (1877), the Dance of the Persian Slaves from Mussorgsky's *Khovanchina* (1881), Stravinsky's *The Rite of Spring* (1913), the Dance of the Black Spirits from Prokofiev's *Scythian Suite* (1916), the Orgy and Dance from Florent Schmitt's *Anthony and Cleopatra* (1920), the Orgiastic Dance from Respighi's *Belkis* (1934), or the Orgy of the Golden Calf scene from Schoenberg's *Moses and Aaron* (1929-1952). These constructions of orgy tend to operate as variations on the Hollywood version of orgy: the spectator basks in opulent but "fatal" signifiers of luxury, oriental exoticism, decadence, pagan idolatry, despotic passions. But now it is music which makes these signifiers "live" — or rather, music itself is a signifier of orgiastic desires: orgy results when peculiar tonalities and rhythms urge a group of bodies toward ecstatic dance. Theatre contextualizes such dances within a narrative which "contains" orgy within a non-orgiastic aesthetic ambition. Theatre may present orgy as a "scene" within a narrativized norm of representation, but it does not devote itself entirely or exclusively to orgy or orgiastic narrative. Moreover, theatre's conventional reliance on music to define the orgiastic moment, coupled with its compulsion to "contain" orgy within a non-orgiastic (or "sober") narrative context, is due largely to theatre's effort to resolve an enduring tension between its general social function of "catharsis" and the myth of its orgiastic, "Dionysian" origin. Indeed, the whole tendency to perceive orgy and theatre as intersecting phenomena probably results from a persistent uncertainty (if not outright confusion) regarding the relation between the functions and origins for both theatre and orgy.

Ekstasis and Katharsis

The origin of theatre or, more precisely, of *dramatic language* (for we think of theatre *beginning* with the performance of texts) is very obscure and remains the subject of mythic explanations which propose that the signifying practices developed by Greek theatrical institutions emerged out of ecstatic experience, out of intoxicated submissions to Dionysos, a god of fertility, birth, seed. Certainly the Greeks themselves perceived a link between the theatre and the rituals of the Dionysian Mysteries, but they did not produce any coherent theory for explaining the nature of the link. Such a theory requires a historical perspective which takes into account variables which the evidence of Greek cultural life infers rather than declares. The thesis here is that dramatic language and what we call theatrical signifying practice emerged in Greece in the early fifth century BC as a response to a set of complex social problems which the Greeks sought to resolve by shifting the ideological foundation of Greek (or at least Athenian) consciousness from a ritually-ordered relationship to reality to a "civilized" condition in which representations, such as drama, ordered human relationships to the world. Drama functions to represent dialogic interactions of voices. Theatre, as a public cultural event, functions to institutionalize, objectify, and control the phenomenon of impersonation, the human capacity to change one's identity at will. The origin of drama seems synchronous with the origin of theatre, and therefore it is easy to suppose that drama and theatre have a common origin in ritual, where extreme ambiguity of language and symbolic action inhibit the formation of a fundamental difference between representation and reality.

A coherent explanation of the mythic origins for the Greek theatre in the Dionysian Mysteries assumes that a particular ideological (rather than historical) reality was in place to motivate specific attitudes and the strategies for representing them. Such an ideology proposes that for a long and unspecified time, before the Greeks had established the "civilized" institutions of the city-state, "primitive" Greek communities or tribal societies experienced, presumably on an annual basis, departures of many women from their homes. These women disappeared into remote mountain enclaves, where, under conditions of extreme secrecy which forbade the presence of any men, they turned into *maenads* or *bacchantes* [Figs. 13-16], and conducted orgiastic rites to signify their worship of Dionysos [Fig. 17], who, by some mysterious, ecstatic fertilizing process, suffused their bodies with divine energy and empowered them to produce children of extraordinary strength or destiny. Orgasmic intoxication coincided with the performance of extremely violent sacrifices and displays of tremendous physical strength. After about two weeks, the women returned home to fulfill their sexual and domestic functions in a mood tinged with a divine aura[3] The Dionysian rites codified the belief that human (i.e., female) happiness and salvation depends on ecstatic erotic unity with a god from the earth.

But from a male perspective, these rites served to perpetuate the "mysterious," unstable, mutant identity of woman. The rites can only have exacerbated tensions, not only between men and the gods, but between men themselves. For to obtain favor in the eyes of women and the world, a man must always strive to project the "heroic" qualities of a god, a being above and apart from other men. The mythic treatment of the Trojan War in the Homeric epics and in tragedy indicates the catastrophic consequences of men fighting each other over Woman (Helen), the authenticity of whose erotic desires is simultaneously a question of international political concern and a problem compelling the "advancement" of language to produce more "civilized" forms of communication and modes of "understanding." The rites thus helped to inhibit the unity of purpose and identity that the Greeks needed (by the seventh century) in order to prosper in a mountainous landscape, which, due to population pressures, was becoming increasingly inhospitable to agriculture and the sort of rural economy that the Dionysian cult seemed to celebrate.[4]

Of course, the cult of Dionysos was only one of many cults which the Greek patriarchy had to demystify if the Greeks were to achieve a "civilized" consciousness and an economy founded on trade, maritime activity, and interaction with foreigners rather than on the internal, soil-bound, and fundamentally secluded mechanisms of agrarian culture. The patriarchy saw the necessity of directing communal attention toward human rather than divine sources of happiness. In general, this shifting of perception from divine to human concentrations of power implied an expansion of confidence in public institutions (e.g., the courts, the military, the city commissions, the theatre) to shape human destinies and a corresponding loss of confidence in the priesthood to "speak for" the gods. This confidence reached maturity after the Persian War (from 475 BC), which confirmed for the Greeks the existence of a unique, European identity that the vast, amorphous domain of Asia, the home of Dionysos, would never absorb. The Eleusinian Mysteries endured for centuries precisely because its secret celebrations of female deities (Demeter, Kore, Persephone) never distressed the architects of public policy, and indeed, the administrators of those Mysteries came from prominent ruling class families who regarded the cult as a kind of elite society comprised of both sexes.[5] The Eleusinian Mysteries functioned to channel elitist impulses into a public institution under the control of the same forces charged with maintaining the ideology of democracy in most other institutions, such as the theatre.[6] Meanwhile, the evidence amassed by Joseph Fontenrose indicates that the cryptic language emanating from the Delphic Oracle, where a female official purported to transmit the messages of a god, had no relation to ecstatic experience; in any case, the Pythia was a representative of Apollo, and as such, her credibility, which nevertheless was an object of considerable Athenian skepticism, depended on her remoteness from any maenadic identity.[7]

Of course, religion continued to flourish among the Greeks, and with it an elaborate schedule of mysteries, festivals, ritual occasions, temple consecrations, and commemorations of mythic events. But as Otto Kern observed, religious feeling never achieved dogmatic intensity among the Greeks, who could not construct an attitude of certainty regarding the fundamental source of power in the universe.[8] Religious life was fragmented into numerous cults and sects until Byzantine times. Even then, the conflicts generated by the Monophysites, the Iconoclasts, and the continuously uneasy relationship between the Emperor and the Patriarch all suggest a nagging sense of doubt about the authority of any doctrine. In the more wholly European West, such doubt enjoyed far less respect. The Greeks, however, simply had no confidence in religious feeling and institutions to produce political and social unity. By tolerating a plethora of cults, they actually reinforced the notion that unity of experience depended on human rather than divine manifestations of power. Yet the Dionysian cult could not escape a persistent stigmatization which succeeded in representing it as a form of decadent obscurantism; the sinister secrecy defining variations of the cult in Greece, Asia Minor, and Italy (though not, apparently, North Africa) until the third century AD indicates an increasingly obscure and in some cases criminal status for the initiates. Indeed, the extraordinary complexity of paganism in general reveals the failure of any cult to establish a unifying presence in the imagination of ancient peoples.[9]

The Greeks saw in the Dionysian cult the heart of the problem regarding the failure of religious feeling to create a unified public identity. The Dionysian cult linked religious feeling with ecstatic experience. But ecstatic experience derived from unity with a god rather than with humans. The pursuit of ecstasy therefore had the effect of estranging one from social and public life; and of course, it negated the salvational power of public institutions and the men who governed them. Consequently, the Dionysian Festivals, out of which theatre evolved, did not constitute an institutionalized accommodation of the Dionysian cult; rather, they functioned to *transform* the psychic and emotional energies that produced the myth of Dionysos into an institutionalized context which objectified the myth through representation and thus distanced the spectator from it.[10] The Festivals created conditions which stressed the pursuit of catharsis over the pursuit of ecstasy in forming a sense of public identity. But the shift from an ecstatic to a cathartic realization of identity meant, for the Greeks, that a sharp distinction must exist between ritual and representation and that the citizen/spectator must rely more on representations than rituals to understand conditions of power and the nature of reality.

Rituals blur distinctions between performer and spectator. Moreover, in rituals, the emotion of the performer/spectator is incidental or in any case subordinate to whatever emotion pleases the god. Since the pleasure of the gods invariably depends on sacrifices of varying magnitude offered by humans, and since any sincere sacrifice entails suffering, we must assume that ritual in general implies a repression or at least devaluation of emotional expression in its human agents. Thus, the ecstasy the maenads derived from their violent rituals depended on their success in repressing other emotions, such as compassion, curiosity, or devotion, which extend human relations outside the cult. The situation is analogous to that of drug-users whose search for a "high" tends to anesthetize them to other emotions which "get in the way" of their objective. In ritual, cryptic, hieratic sequences of sounds and gestures (which almost anyone can perform given basic instructions) function to provoke emotion in an "absent" being, the god, in whom the logic of emotional response must necessarily be incomprehensible to the relatively weak, sacrificing humans.

As an art, however, representation operates, through complex technical procedures which only specialized members of the community can execute, to differentiate the spectator from the representation. The "distance" between spectator and representation functions to produce exchanges of power between them — that is, the value of both the representation and the spectator depends on the difference between them, so that the *meaning* generated by a representation expands according to the degree to which it expands the *identity* of its consumer. The signifier of power is no longer a "real" manifestation of sacrifice and suffering. Because he cannot enter the representation, the spectator cannot become whatever is represented, and the sense of safety secured through distanciation implies that intense emotions, otherwise suppressed in daily life as in ritual (i.e., in "reality") can arise in the spectator without fear of displacing the emotional logic of some absent god; they can even become ends in themselves. A developing tension between ritual and representation indicates that the emotional focus of the world is shifting from gods to humans: happiness and other signs of destiny depend on conditions that are as much internal as external to the spectator.

But representation in this "civilized" sense, as an objectification of reality rather than a production of it, also means that intense emotion arises, not in response to the "real," but to the imaginary, in which case it is a consequence of a kind of misperception or, more precisely, of a perception *of* reality that is inaccessible to us *in* reality. The representation is the manifestation of a consciousness that is greater than that which results when objects and identities signify only themselves. In rituals, objects and identities assume metonymic rather than distinctly symbolic properties, and for that reason, rituals function within a lower state of consciousness than representations.

Theatre, then, emerged among the Greeks as the public institution for controlling the Dionysian myth. The orgiastic mysteries of the maenads indicated that a social order dominated by ritually organized sacrifices failed to allow an adequate outlet for emotional energy, particulary erotic feelings. An enigmatic circumstance preceded the theatre: ritual practices entailed the repression of emotions unique to the participant, yet the pursuit of ecstasy (unity with the god) entailed involvement with ritual practices. Such a circumstance does not favor the cultivation of social unity. The problem confronting those (men) seeking to transform Greek consciousness was to determine what sort of representations effectively transformed volatile, disunifying erotic energy into a unifying social feeling, as manifested by the phenomenon of catharsis. Remember: the Greeks sought to instill a *feeling* of social unity; they distrusted the imperial ideas of unity operating in Asia and Egypt because the Greek landscape did not offer the economic conditions to support a centralized despotism that could afford to adopt a remote, god-like indifference toward the feelings of its subjects. In fact, for the Greeks, imperial ideas of unity (Alexander's Empire, the Byzantine Empire) materialized only in relation to a "civilizing" Greek presence in Asia.

The very early phases in the development of Greek theatre are perhaps forever obscure. But we can recover some events. The satyr plays, for example, which preceded the appearance of tragedy, seem to have functioned as crude parodies of the Dionysian cult. Men impersonated half-man-half-goat creatures who distanced the spectator from the god and from sexual excess generally by suggesting that sexual feelings linked humans to animals rather than to the gods. These actors wore *phalloi* to indicate their ideological objectives. But it is possible that originally these *phalloi* were erect [Figs. 18-19] and that these erections, in spite of their bestial, "ridiculous" context, still had an inciteful effect on spectators.[11] At any rate, by the time the satyr plays had become subsidiary appendices to monumental tragic productions, the *phalloi* had become limp and grotesque accesories to essentially impotent, laughable buffoons. For many centuries afterward, figures on stage were comic because the grotesquely exaggerated *phalloi* they wore indicated how ludicrously inappropriate and impotent any celebration of the phallus was for the situations in which the characters found themselves. Comedy worked to devalue ecstatic experience that was dependent on phallic (i.e., erotic) energy. Orgy, however, is a *serious*, even monumental, pursuit of sensual pleasure.

Meanwhile, tragedy became the genre which linked ecstatic experience with heroic action; but this "tragic" linking of the ecstatic with the heroic meant that inflammatory and erotically suffused desires for unity with the gods had been transformed into a more abstract and diffuse feeling of unity with humanity. One achieves this unity of social identity when one is able to feel compassion for imaginary human identities ("characters") in a drama. Compassion is the name for a condition of identification which exists between identities that cannot "possess" each other in any physical sense. But compassion arises only when these imaginary identities, such as Oedipus, strive to be more than what the community, the chorus, humanity expect them to be or expect themselves to be. It is the nature of the constraints or limitations on human action which determine the "heroic" qualities of this striving, of the choices made to achieve an identity that is "greater" than that which makes one the same as the spectator. Compassion is a strange emotion which produces identification ("sameness") between identities without dissolving a fundamental distinction between one who feels compassion (spectator) and one who deserves compassion (a spectaclized identity). Aristotle believed that the strength of one's compassion depended upon the extent to which one was able to bestow it upon strangers, of which the imaginary identities encountered in a representation are a category.[12] Ritual, with its focus on revealing "infinite" conditions, with its blurring of distinctions between performer and spectator, between representation and reality, acknowledges only arbitrary rather than moral (intelligible) limitations on human action and therefore inhibits the cultivation of compassion. Where identity and communal unity arise primarily out of the difference between sacrificer and victim, compassion will remain a "weak" and even dangerous emotion.[13] Carl Niessen claimed that tragedy can only emerge within a culture which places equivalent high values on the concepts of the individual and the state.[14] It is, however, limitations, finite qualities, which define individuality. A consciousness of the limitations on human action evolves out of an aesthetic (pleasurable) contemplation of the power of the human body to move in time and place. This pleasure in the body may have deepened from an appreciation of the physical prowess, the muscular dexterity, displayed by Greek warriors, particularly in the Persian War. But the pleasure became an objectifiable, cultural activity only through the process of theatrical representation that proceeded from the satyr plays to choric dances to the individual, characterizing gestures of an actor. As Anne Carson remarks in relation to the refinements of Greek poetic language: "The poets record this struggle [for identity, an accommodation of desire and destiny] from within a consciousness — perhaps new in the world — of the body as a unity of limbs, senses and the self, amazed at its own vulnerability."[15]

Rather quickly the Greeks comprehended that the transformative, unifying power of dynamic (theatrical) representations depended more on linguistic than on iconographic properties. After centuries of convoluted, "mysterious" evolution in the Aegean world, language was understood (ca. 480 BC) to be the chief resource or technology for constructing perceptual unity within culture, and the voice easily emerged as the dominant signifier of those represented emotions which produced catharsis. But the "Greek" language had to achieve a fairly pervasive level of standardization for this function of representation to occur, and the evidence presented by Eric Havelock suggests that drama did not exist because a standardized language was in place to facilitate "communication" to large audiences; on the contrary, particularly in Athens, drama appeared as a medium which created a pressure for standardization.[16] Standardization remained an ideal rather than a reality until literacy was able to penetrate all zones of Greek culture.

Epic poetry was an appropriate mode of communication for aristocratic societies in which a single speaker controlled all voices within a myth and its narration. Of course, the epic narrator, as a kind of ambassadorial visitor to cities and courts, contributed to the standardization of Greek dialects. But as public institutions expanded and social processes became more complicated, the concept of unity as consensus ripened into more overt forms of public *dialogue*. The centralization of mythic language in the single, aristocratic voice of the epic narrator gave way to a "democratic" distribution of mythic language among the voices of a citizen chorus. Even before any actual enacting of mythic scenes took place, the Greeks glorified the word through elaborately mathematical combinations of voices in the chorus.[17] However, the obsession with unity of perception prevented the Greeks from ever producing a polyphonic sound-mass from the chorus; though voices within the chorus might alternate according to numerous complex and mystical combinations (*strophes* and *antistrophes*), the Greeks never abandoned the notion that language in the theatre must always be spoken in unison.[18] Contrapuntal organization of speech avoided polyphony of voices and concentrated on relations between words and speakers, i.e., on the *alternation* of word-sounds and voices, the consequence eventually being the production of highly complex dialogues. By contrast, the conventional musical signification of orgy or "bacchanale" in the modern theatre is extravagantly polyphonic and instrumental (rather than vocal); but this difference actually reinforces the Greek effort to put controls on the power of music to strengthen orgiastic impulses.

However, it was only after the Persian War that the Greek patriarchy and proud citizenry enjoyed the confidence necessary to produce an even bolder distinction between ritual and representation, between religion and state. The chorus no longer recited mythic events; it functioned as a component in a dramatic *enactment* of a myth. The hero, the protagonist, was one who stood outside the communal voice, which could not contain the language constructing his identity and the conflict that separated him from the community. The introduction of the antagonist simply reinforced the recognition that a reciting communal voice could never establish the *presence* of an imaginary identity as fully as *that identity which speaks for itself.*

Of course, the Greeks were so conscious of the radical nature of enactment that they applied a large number of constraints or "conventions" on representation to insure that the spectator would not mistake representation for reality and thus lapse into ritual identification with the action. Masks, cothurni, the total exclusion of women from the stage, the total exclusion of violent action from the stage, taboos on touching, an almost exclusive focus on archaic mythic subjects as the material for tragedy, the "rule" of having only three speaking characters on stage at once, the rigorously inscribed boundary separating the *orchestra* (playing area) from the *theatron* (viewing place), the confinement of public performances to "dramatic festivals," the very cautious and highly stylized introduction of scenic effects (*periaktoi, eccyklema, deux ex machina*), the treatment of performances as "contests" between performers rather than as pageants which turned spectators into participants, the amateur status of the performers — all these conventions and more served to indicate the anxiety of the Greeks toward the process and consequences of theatrical representation. Nevertheless, it was said that people died of fright when, during a production of the *Oresteia* (458 BC), the Eumenides made their appearance.[19] Eventually, however, anxiety toward the phenomenon of representation achieved its clearest and most reflective manifestation in the writings of Plato, who implied that no human being could ever get into the habit of treating representations *as* representations and not incarnations of the "reality" represented.

Indeed, the unifying emotion, the cathartic reaction, which representation functioned to provoke, sanctify, and control, was impossible without at least some concession, not perhaps to reality as defined through ritual, but to a condition of "semblance." At any rate, the monumental task of transforming ideology from a ritual to a representational mode of transmission entailed the formation of a complicated theatre culture in which a deepening or intensification of a cathartic emotional condition resulted from the power of the representation to complicate perception without complicating the relationship between the subject and the object of representation.

This self-conscious cultivation of ambiguity occurred in spite of, or perhaps even because of, the Greeks' confidence in the power of humans to control their destinies, for that confidence had as its corollary a persistent uncertainty regarding the distinction between humans and gods. For this reason, the city-state could not eclipse religion altogether; it simply superseded religion as the *governing* power in social life. Temples remained attached to the theatres in a rather subordinate manner, and even when the Parthenon was built (438 BC), the great goddess Athena appeared *contained* within a structure which glorified the authority of men to define completely the identity of the gods. Human beings impersonated the gods on stage. An oracular figure like Teiresias, almost inhuman in the ambiguity of his identity and his knowledge of the gods, could fascinate audiences as much as the tragic heroes themselves. Sophocles enjoyed a dual career as a dramatist and priest. His Oedipus eventually becomes a sort of god or unearthly spirit at Colonus, and the heroes of his other plays strive for some superhuman identity that elevates them above a stigmatized or stigmatizing community. With Euripides, the gods possess great, destructive powers, but their motives in exerting these powers are never more than human and often petty (e.g., the jealousy of Aphrodite, the vanity of Dionysos).

But it was above all speech which complicated distinctions between gods and humans — or more precisely, the relation between speech and action. Divine power speaks through prophetic voices. Whoever is divine knows the future and can describe it. Prophetic language, the mysterious, emblematic voices of the oracles, implies a language in which actions conform to the word (if not the will or desire) of the speaker. Truth is never clearer than when this conformity, this unity of speech and action occurs. The production of ecstatic experience through prophetic language implies a rhetoric of riddles, predictions, and commands. Moreover, ecstasy results from speaking rather than hearing prophetic language, for the ecstatic moment constitutes a union of god and human that allows the human to speak *for* the god. Because the prophetic speaker has little concern with whether his language is "understood," he tends to regard the listener as incidental to the utterance itself. The cryptic and obscure often characterize the prophetic statement precisely because to know the future

future means to allude to conditions which the listener can never foresee. The future constitutes something given rather than constructed through an exchange of signs, meanings, and values. Thus, dialogue is not an ideal medium for the transmission of prophetic language. Although prophetic statements frequently emerge in response to questions, the relationship between the prophet and the questioner is not dynamic. Dynamic interaction of voices (dialogue) occurs when the relationship between word and action is *open* to interpretation — i.e., when a tension exists between intended and perceived meanings which cause words to become sources of unpredictable actions. The concept of change has reality only when actions undermine the authority of prophetic statements. As long as they remain bound up with the release of prophetic language (knowledge of the future), states of ecstasy cannot function as sources or activators of transformative energies within society. The Greeks therefore understood dialogue, as represented by democratic political debate, the drama, and the symposium, as an organization of language that moved speakers away from ecstatic detachment from listeners and toward cathartic assimilation into a community of interactive wills in which a consensus of desires rather than a unity of identity has any reality. Indeed, since the Greeks, the drama has only very rarely attempted to use dialogue to represent a state of ecstasy, while monologue (often of a lyrical character) remains the preferred device for dramatizing the power of language to provoke ecstasy. And usually this power operates only within the speaker, not within any listeners (or spectators).

But even if prophetic authority disappears from it, the dialogic language of human interaction must be no less powerful or "mysterious" than the language of the gods. Indeed, human language is "mysterious," not because it "speaks for" the gods, but because it is the manifestation of a cosmic intelligence which constructs the enigmatic phenomenon of identity for both the gods and humans. In the *Oresteia,* Aeschylus associates prophetic language with female being, with Cassandra, who knows the language of birds, Greeks, foreigners, and gods, and whose knowledge of ecstasy derives from her intimate attachment to Apollo. But in establishing these connections, he also associates prophetic language with a monumental doom for the one who speaks it, for this woman enters as the captive of Agammenon and exits as the sacrificial victim of Clytemnestra. Justice comes, of course, not from the language of sibyls and prophets, but from the language of Law. In Clytemnestra, prophetic language operates in an ironic mode, as a language which deliberately deceives those to whom it is addressed (Agammenon) yet accurately defines the relation between speaker and addressee to those who happen to overhear it (the spectator). Irony, however, is altogether lacking in Athena's speeches which conclude *The Eumenides,* and perhaps her protracted stream of statements belongs more to the overly fertile rhetoric of hope (prayer) than to the spare, cryptic language of prophecy. At any rate, her language dramatizes a liberation, not only from the chthonic values that dominated the beginning of the tetralogy, but from an ironic level of consciousness which prevents any unity of feeling between speaker and addressee ("discover that road where speech goes straight," ll. 988-989, Aeschylus, *The Eumenides*). The language that concludes the *Oresteia* may prophesize a utopian state, but it is not ecstatic, for it projects a moral code for defining a basic, unifying humanness — it does not drive its speakers and listeners to transcend or "abandon" the identities they construct for others and for the sake of preserving modes of perception which unify people into a society.

In *Oedipus the King,* Apollo has no image, nor does the oracle ever appear. The messages of the god are given entirely through messengers, modest human interpreters. For Oedipus, as already for Teiresias, the world as image becomes in the end an illusion; the heroic figure is one who lives without illusions — reality is what the voice creates, reality is that which the misperceptions of human vision cannot contain. Such knowledge, though it always comes too late to prevent suffering, and though it may exile one from home and society, is that which marks a person as heroic. But unlike Aeschylus, Sophocles did not detach himself from ironic modes of thought, and it is doubtful that any serious representation of heroic identity is possible without introducing an element of ironic intelligence (the blind man "sees" more; the investigator of the crime is himself the criminal). In the Aeschylean worldview, "civilization" results from the sacrifice, the vanquishment of heroic types (Clytemnestra, Agamemnon, Cassandra) and produces instead a modest, anxiety-ridden "citizen" (Orestes) who is far less certain than his ancestors of his relation to others and the gods. In the Sophoclean worldview, this self-effacing modesty which unifies "civilized" humanity, this compromising sense of doubt, is precisely what motivates *individuals* to construct identities which set them above or beyond "the rest." In both views, the formulation of Civilization and the Hero entails a supreme control over speech. But neither Civilization nor the Hero appear as manifestations of or pointers toward ecstatic experience.

For the Greeks, expansion of the maritime economy depended on understanding the world as voice, as a language-resource harnessed through knowledge, not only of foreign languages, but of the more subtly categorized languages of negotiation, diplomacy, and indoctrination — the art of Persuasion (*peitho*), as Athena calls it in *The Eumenides* (l. 885). But persuasion requires a process of calculation no less complex than the ritual formulas that give authority to prophetic statements. Words and numbers possess a mystical affinity with each other as emblems of fate and heroic consciousness, as emblems of a metaphysical order in tension with arbitrary nature and the imagery of myth.[20] The agreement of perception that results from persuasion is understood in practice as the consequence of the "right" combination of words, inflexions, timbres, rhythms, and dynamics. Even before the drama appeared as a literary form and civic institution, formulaic control of language had already achieved a sophisticated mathematical precision in the epic.[21] Havelock explained how the habit of formularizing experience was incorporated into dramatic language for ideological purposes (such as the indoctrination of illiterate spectators through rhetorical devices which make ideas, images, and relations easy to remember). I have already mentioned the complex combinations of sound and meaning at work in strophic distributions of choral voices. Bernd Seidensticker has investigated the formal properties of that most dramatic yet most artificial mode of speech, the stichomythia, and classified types of stichomythia according to rhetorical function rather than intentions ascribed to the authors or speakers.[22] Meanwhile, others have explored the intricate metrical subtleties of Greek dramatic language, although none of these studies has revealed any great, overarching system at work, such as we find in Senecan or French classical drama. Greek dramatic language tends to be formulaic rather than systematic because system unfolds in conjunction with a centralization of political power, the realization of which continued to elude the Greeks until the encroachments of the Romans.[23]

All these calculations and subtleties of speech may indeed be efforts to link ecstatic states to the enunciation of some elusive, "mysterious" combination of words and sounds. George Thomson seems to suggest as much when, as a Marxist, he argues that the achievements of Greek literature arise organically out of the language of anonymous people, whose struggle against various oppressions urges them to integrate labor and poetry, so that life itself no longer consists of work and rapture divided against each other.[24] Ecstasy from this perspective is that work which produces no surplus value, no tensions between supply and demand, no inequalities of wealth, whereas from almost any other perspective, ecstasy, whether it is "work" or not, is the consequence of a surplus, is in some sense a condition of giving away, giving away identity (the self). Thomson sees literature as a manifestation of the will to ecstasy, which operates unconsciously, even subversively, within the contradictory pressures defining civilization. But this theory underestimates the power of consciousness to treat *choices* as signifiers of inequalities. The elaborate calculations the Greeks invested in poetic language were attempts to render as consciously as possible the choices of perception controlled by language in forming identities and destinies. This obsession with control also asserted itself in the study of music and geometry. The Greeks strove to achieve a calculated rather than arbitrary (prophetic) unity of word and action. Havelock contends that dramatic language began to decay when its poetic density increasingly failed to satisfy the demand of an educated elite for the self-consciously analytical and philosophical dialogues cultivated by the Socratic circle of intellectuals at their symposia and other such semi-private forums, where a general disillusionment with the mythic foundations of public institutions and ideology prevailed.[25] Not even catharsis had much interest for this circle, which looked at language as if it were a kind of map of the universe. In spite of its mathematical complexities, tonal subtleties, and intricate music, poetic language seemed merely a system for mapping memory, and, from the standpoint of the Socratics, such memory-laden, formulaic language embodied too many formal constraints upon what could be thought and spoken.

Aeschylean drama features convoluted and monumental masses of words which saturate the spectator with a sense of awe at the sheer scale of human voices in a public context. Sophocles, however, understood that expressive power depended as much on economy as on scale of representation, and so his dramas feature a reduction in choral forces at the same time that they introduce greater dramatic weight within individual lines: stichomythic interactions rather than choral masses become the high points of dramatic action (e.g., *Antigone*, ll. 508-526, 536-576, 726-760, 1048-1064, 1098-1106, 1171-1179). Indeed, by reducing the scale of dramatic effects, Sophocles achieves a concentration of dramatic energy which reveals an even greater confidence in speech to represent heroic identity, even if it is language which separates the hero from the community rather than places him at the summit of communal power (as in Aeschylus).

But of course, with Euripides, we encounter a skeptical perception of the power of language to create either social unity or heroic identity. In *Hippolytus* (440 BC), to take the most obvious example, speech invariably produces catastrophe or some tragic misperception. Yet when characters such as Phaedra and Hippolytus choose to remain silent rather than risk being misunderstood or damaged by their words, their silences have no less tragic consequences. Though it is the great objectifier of human will and identity, language is ultimately a tragic phenomenon, because its consequences betray the intentions that release it. The power of language (speech) to create unity between desire and action is an illusion. For Euripides, ecstasy, utopian feeling, as dramatized most overtly in *The Bacchae* (407 BC), is a response to illusions, and these illusions are strongest when the language that projects them has become a doom-saturated apparatus for satisfying a logic, "pure" combinations of sounds, meanings, beliefs, that do not derive from any observed experience of the world, but from mythic configurations of the utopian status of either "civilization" (the state) or "nature" (some "realm of Dionysos").

And yet this disillusionment with the power of language to create utopian unity between speakers perhaps reaches its most intellectual manifestation in *The Birds* (414 BC), in which Aristophanes contrives a ludicrous utopia, where the "natural" world of birds appears as an idealized alternative to the trivial irritations and discomforts (rather than tragedies) contaminating the "civilized" world of humanity. But a basic feature of the bird utopia is a complicated choral-lyrical language; indeed, with the birds as representatives of utopia, this lyrical language emerges virtually as an end in itself, the major signifier of communal ecstasy. In a huge and spectacular Chorus of the Birds, at the center of the play, Aristophanes appears to be exploring every nuance, every rhythmic and tonal possibility within the Greek language. A luxurious and fantastic music overwhelms the spectator:

> Such was the music
> (*Tio tio tio tiotinx*)
> Made by the swans for Phoebus' greeting
> Quire of voices and pinions beating
> (*Tio tio tio tiotinx*)
> Wafted afar from the moors above Maritza's bed
> (*Tio tio tio tiotinx*)

To the clouds of high heaven the melody sped.
Beasts of the wilds were crouching in wonder;
Breathless, the billows were quenching their thunder.
(*Tototo tototo totototinx*)
Gods were awed. Olympus' portal
Rang, when the Muses and Graces immortal
Sang, to the birds replying,
Hail! Hosanna! crying
(*Tio tio tio tiotinx*).[26]

But this lyricism, this ecstatic speech, constructs a utopia in which nature is no longer a source of ecstasies, exuding some erotic "mystery." For Aristophanes, language does not create unity between people and gods, nor between people and nature, nor even between nature and the divine. It creates unity only between, as Pisthetaerus later remarks (277), certain "transported" spirits who transcend the species classifications ascribed to nature. The bird utopia is neither of the earth, where "beasts of the wild" crouch "in wonder" at its ecstatic lyricism, nor of Olympus, where the gods respond with "awe" to a greater paradise than their own. Utopia is actually *between* nature and the gods, a state of suspension, flight, music; and language, when it achieves the intricate musico-mathematical complexity of the huge bird chorus, is the mechanism which "transports," "uplifts," or "elevates" (277) trivial and comic humanity to this neither/nor happiness.

In the Old Comedy of Aristophanes, with its preference for episodic (revue) over narrative modes of action, it was possible to link ecstatic experience with a comic spirit. But this ecstatic comedy betrayed symptoms of a peculiar aesthetic decadence, for it could only thrive in a culture in which the very concept of utopia was approaching the status of an absurd fantasy, a ridiculous impossibility, a subject demanding comic treatment. A sense of orgiastic excess pervades the language of the bird chorus, but such excess is now a component of a grand joke and successfully obscures any allusion to the tragic origin of choral voices in a heroic hunger for ecstatic unity with the gods. For Aristophanes, ecstasy is at best merely the catharsis which results from the spectator's recognition that myth is another name for the absurd fantasies that reduce humanity to a comic condition.[27]

In any case, the comic ecstasies of the Old Comedy enjoyed only a short life in the theatre and did not survive long after the advent of the fourth century. As Socratic and Platonic thinking gained new adherents, as the consequences of the Peloponnesian War eroded public confidence in mythically-justified institutions, such as the theatre, Greek high culture (Hellenism) became less preoccupied with transforming ecstatic energies into cathartic representations, less obsessed with the formation of heroic consciousness, less fascinated with the prophetic power of the word. Instead of the monumental task of converting disunifying erotic ecstasy (a corollary of tribal economy) into socially unifying catharsis (a precondition of empire), Hellenistic culture concentrated on determining the relation between pleasure and virtue, or, as Aristotle seems to propose, on the perfecting of perception.[28] The major Greek intellects focused on philosophical rather than political questions. The attempt during the fifth century to uncover the prophetic power of language, the unity of speech and action, was transformed, during the Hellenistic period, into a highly self-conscious critique of language, an elaborate analysis of the ways in which language fragments perception. In the realm of aesthetic representation, the concept of "imitation" (*mimesis*), which valued observation over prophetic intimation of the invisible, operated to reduce the tension between nature and the heroic ideal (the looming tension within fifth-century consciousness), until, eventually, Hellenistic culture reached "an awareness that naturalistic imitation is not only an irrelevant goal but also an unattainable one".[29] Indeed, the whole process of "perfecting perception" and the knowledge we derive from the senses depended on reducing the presumed, dramatic tension between nature and the ideal to a more subtle and less presumable tension between appearance and essence. Hellenism produced beautiful theatres and marvelous actors, but nothing to match the dynamic world of *drama* offered by the previous century.

The Greeks developed tragic theatrical representations as a "civilized" method for containing the suffering resulting from ritual sacrifices; imagined (enacted) actions deepened yet controlled the emotional life of the detached spectator to a far greater extent than ritual actions which confused the distinction between performer and spectator. This concern for the emotional condition of humans rather than gods encouraged the spectator to extend greater confidence (than Asian culture permitted) in human institutions and fellow spectators to determine the destiny of the community.[30] To build such confidence, ideology and its apparatus of myths unveiled a profound tension between two contradictory emotional values: *ekstasis* and *katharsis*. Catharsis, the assimilation of the spectator into the system of norms governing the perceptions and desires defining social reality, operates in the public sphere, with theatre carefully functioning to objectify and institutionalize it; *ekstasis,* the release of the spectator from social norms, operates in the secret sphere of the cult, where theatrical artifices function to complicate the difference between ritual and representation. In the all-pervasive cathartic mode, theatre works to "contain" orgy within signifying practices ("bacchanale" scenes) which transform impulses toward orgy into cathartic accommodations of social reality, of "the rest" of us.

The Greek preoccupation with ecstatic experience stemmed in large part from an intense fear of death, which was perceived as a condition of complete negativity and meaninglessness: for the Greeks, "death is not a power," not a redemptive phenomenon.[31] The fear of death stimulated the formation of a philosophical consciousness centered on the problem of meaning and what fills life with meaning. Ecstasy always signifies that moment when one's existence feels most saturated with meaning, even if, as dramatists and Platonists alike suggested, the meaning is only the projection of an illusion. The Greeks sensed that such meaning, which is after all as much a matter of chance as cultic communication codes, is possible to the extent that it depends on the exclusion or sacrifice of "the rest," on the denial of ecstasy for someone else. But ecstasy is also possible to the extent that life has *another,* equally intense, public meaning than that which is ecstatic. Only a profound fascination with the "mysterious" authority of language to mediate the relation between feeling and action could invent a mode of representation, theatre, that objectified meaning above all through dialogue, through tensions between voices, which emerge out of a more obscure tension between the mythic origin ascribed to theatre and the actual function theatre assumes within social reality.

Thus, the reason I have devoted so much space to Greek theatre is that a failure to differentiate between the origin and the social function of theatre in Western society can lead to confusion (and illusion) regarding the relation between theatre and orgy. In modern times, some artists have proposed that an enhanced value for theatre depends on developing a new, non-cathartic, orgiastic function for theatre. Others have suggested that an orgiastic function for theatre depends on recovering an "original," Dionysian dimension which entails amplifying the musical aspect of performance and depressing the authority of language, speech, and dialogue to control the meaning of performance. Friedrich Nietzsche's famous essay on *The Birth of Tragedy* (1872, 1886) is probably responsible for some of the confusion regarding the relation between orgy and theatre. According to Nietzsche, the "rebirth" or "gradual awakening of the Dionysian spirit in our modern world," which the marriage of Christian morality and Apollonian (logocentric) aesthetics has emasculated and trivialized, depends on a "dangerous" rebirth of tragedy, such as Wagner attempts in his music dramas. "In the total effect of tragedy, the Dionysian [musical communication] predominates," for "tragedy closes with a sound which could never come from the realm of Apollonian art." From this perspective, the "awakening" of the Dionysian spirit easily becomes confused with the operation of catharsis: "We cannot begin to sense [tragedy's] highest value until it confronts us, as it did the Greeks, as the quintessence of all prophylactic powers of healing."[32] But this proposed dichotomy between Dionysian and Apollonian aesthetics obfuscates the historical reality, initiated by the Greeks, that orgiastic theatre is not public theatre. Nevertheless, the idea or myth of a great, salvational "return" of an "original," orgiastic theatre to civilization has held considerable appeal for some very ambitious artists, and their strategies for achieving this "return" are useful in exposing the "real" (as opposed to mythic) relation between orgy and theatre.

Pseudo-Orgy

A famous propagandist on behalf of the confused notion of an orgiastic public theatre in which the ecstatic moment lies "beyond" the speaking of words is Antonin Artaud (1896-1948). His radical and poetic treatise, *The Theatre and Its Double* (1938), first appeared as journal articles in the 1930s, but because, during the next three decades, the Western theatre successfully insulated itself from the volatile, invigorating influence of all the "isms" that had invaded it during the 1920s, few took his ideas seriously until the 1960s. Though Breton excommunicated him from the surrealist movement in 1929, Artaud's ideas about "healing" the theatre by creating a healing theatre owe much to the theory of surrealism, which is a type of realism, a realism of the unconscious, achieved through the incongruous "juxtaposition" of realistically formed images. In densely metaphorical language, he promoted perceptions of speech and the body which one could interpret as calls for an orgiastic mode of performance. The body was for him the site of disease, "an unprecedented organic upheaval," which the theatre, in a violently cathartic manner, may purify through the performance of actions which produce a convulsive, visceral, pre-conscious response in the spectator.[33] The cause of the disease, the "gigantic abcess" that is modern human identity, is the "social disaster" of Western civilization and its institutions, which use language to "translate" — and thus misrepresent — what is untranslatable.[34] "All true feeling is in reality untranslatable," because

> All powerful feeling produces in us the idea of the void. And the lucid language which obstructs the appearance of this void also obstructs the appearance of poetry in thought. That is why an image, an allegory, a figure that masks what it would reveal have more significance for the spirit than the lucidities of speech and its analytics.[35]

Since for him "the domain of the theatre is not psychological but plastic and physiological," Artaud could regard the theatre as place where the body was the dominant signifier of feeling. But in his ambition to restore theatre to a primal ritual function, he does not make a clear distinction between the body of the performer and the body of the spectator. The distinction collapses because language no longer operates as an apparatus for "communication" between discrete bodies. Artaud, however, is not very clear about the nature of the speaking body in "the theatre of cruelty"; he seems to have in mind a voice that is free of language (or at least writing) and creates incantatory, hypnotic sounds ("No one in Europe knows how to scream anymore") which intensify the "hieroglyphic" signification generated by the body. Ecstatic experience, which situates one "between dream and events," which constitutes above all a *therapeutic* condition, results from this juxtaposition of this "snake-charming" voice and the pathological body. Artaud treats language (dialogue) as a kind of germ or virus which invades the human organism and pollutes it; ecstasy occurs through a process of purification. But this process, like the processes of surgery or the taking of powerful drugs, entails the infliction of convulsive, even "cruel" physiological sensations upon both the performers and the spectators (the spectacle should surround the audience and then assault it). Ecstasy thus emerges out of masochistic violence, and the chief signifier of this masochism is the incantatory voice which puts the body into a trance and transforms it into a hieroglyphic signifier of "the Void," an indecipherable nothingness.

Artaud was himself too sick to realize any of these ideas for restoring the "Dionysian" spirit to modern theatre. But one of his disciples from the early 1960s has spent thirty years staging this salvational synthesis of therapy and orgy. The "Orgies-Mysteries Theatre" produced by the Austrian Hermann Nitsch, which began in 1961, perhaps presents an extreme, rather than typical, realization of Artaud's ideas, but of course orgy loses all meaning unless it is the manifestation of an extreme. Nitsch stages what he calls "actions," which he presents in a variety of environments, such as galleries, warehouses, auditoriums, studios, amphitheatres, and, most recently, a castle which he owns in Lower Austria, where the "actions" unfold in various rooms or "crypts" on six levels above and below the earth.[36] The "actions" often last for many hours; one project, which so far he has been able to stage only in fragments, is supposed to last six days. Nitsch conceives of the "actions" as ritual "symphonies" of considerable aural and physical complexity. His purpose is to materialize "the concept of the Dionysian" (240) by awakening in the spectator an intoxicated sense of being which results from participation in an orgy, the most extreme form of communication with divinity: "Communication with god can be understood as communication with the unconscious/Die kommunication mit der gottheit lässt sich als kommunikation mit dem unbewussten begreifen" (239-240). For Nitsch, then, orgy is a system of communication. However, such "communication" entails the performance of actions which are "excessive" and reveal the "most extreme zones" of pleasure (240). These actions are not only sadomasochistic; they involve the "destructive" dissolution of distinctions between god, human, and animal. The theatre becomes a "slaughterhouse" of desires, drives, and dreams (521).

But Nitsch does not confine himself to a metaphorical use of the word "slaughterhouse." His productions have aroused hostile responses from spectators and public authorities because the action involves the "sacrificial" employment of animal cadavers, embryos, entrails, and enormous quantities of blood.[37] "In the form of an animal, Dionysos is torn apart by the furious cult participants/ Dionysos wird in gestalt eines tieres von rasenden kultteilnehmern zerissen" (240, 656). The ecstatic moment is simultaneously the moment of tearing apart the (animal) body by the cult (e.g., 536-544). But in order to reach this moment, one must pass through a vast assortment of excesses, over which Nitsch himself presides as a sort of grand priest. He "scores" these "actions" in incredible detail, like cosmic operas which indeed push the concept of realism into the "most extreme zone" of aesthetics in a manner that bears some affinity to the monstrously naturalistic dramas (1903-1913) of Arno Holz, an author whom Nitsch apparently admires. The symphony of actions results from a complicated polyphony of excesses: Nitsch calls for the orchestration, not only of often large musical resources, but of non-musical sounds, light (including sun-and moonlight), colors, smells, tastes, and materials (esp. 334-388). This orchestration of the senses accompanies an enormous and minutely calculated repertoire or sequence of ritual actions: mixing and pouring of numerous fluids (363), enactments (or solemn parodies) of liturgical rites (637-638), washing of bodies (533), movements of animals (650-653), eating and drinking (548), processions (243), crucifixions (64), fornications and perversions, often unapologetically obscene (445-468), and of course, a considerable amount of activity devoted to the tearing apart of animal bodies, a wallowing in blood. Nudity constitutes a pervasive element of performance, because for Nitsch ritual action is inseparable from sustained sexual activity. In his projected six-day "mystery," he envisions hundreds of nude bodies engaged in an almost continuous state of sexual excitement which depends on an increasingly complex polyphony of excesses to sustain it. But although Nitsch describes in great detail the operation of particular body *parts,* especially the sex organs, he really does not have much to say about the body as such. The body has significance for him only as *part of a mass of bodies;* living or dead, the body is something *fragmented through action* (see esp. 742). Indeed, ecstasy within this aesthetic is simply the supreme moment of bodily and psychic fragmentation, quite in contrast to the sense of unity with a powerful Other usually associated with ecstatic self-abandonment (818: ecstasy is the "atomization" of heavenly and carnal bodies).

Throughout the performance of these complicated "festivals of psycho-physical naturalism" (255), language assumes a negative or at least highly constrained role, except insofar as Nitsch continues to publish, as a manifestation of excess in itself, hundreds and hundreds of pages of theoretical text and documentation concerning the "Orgies Mysteries Theatre." Although the performance occasionally includes the utterance of non-dramatic texts by famous authors such as Novalis, Goethe, F. Schlegel (308), and Mallarmé (661), as well as pseudo-liturgical chants composed by Nitsch himself (787, 795), the voice is not a part of the body upon which Nitsch lavishes much in the way of complex attention. Words merely prescribe and document at great length actions in which no one speaks. The voice is important to the extent that one recognizes ecstasy when "THE WORD IS TRANSFORMED INTO A GUT-

TURAL SCREAM/DAS WORT WIRD ZUM GUTTERALEN SCHREI VERWANDELT" (153). Consequently, Nitsch orchestrates the action with an assortment of screams produced by animals, humans, "scream choirs," and instrumental ensembles. Indeed, the only example of dialogue that appears in the vast documentation is the exchange of ecstatic screams between "scream choirs" and instrumental ensembles in the 1961 *1. Abreaktionspiel* (242-243); otherwise the screams resound according to an overall tonal pattern, choric in character, which hardly dramatizes tensions between perceptions of speakers. Yet this unifying power or "harmony" of the scream actually functions as a mode of violence which accelerates the fragmentation of the body. The speech of individuals is virtually non-existent, except when, as in the six-day project, they emerge from cells, from isolation, to deliver fragmented statements *in* isolation:

I HAVE SLEPT WITH MY MOTHER
ICH HABE MIT MEINER MUTTER GESCHLAFEN

I AM ALWAYS AFRAID IN THE DARK MY LOWER BODY
WILL BE WOUNDED BY SOMETHING SHARP

ICH HABE IMMER ANGST IM DUNKELN MEIN UNTERLEIB
WIRD MIT ETWAS SCHARFEM VERLEZT WERDEN (566)

The most complex spoken syntactic constructions in the entire documentation consist of hymn-like verses sung by choirs in the *Harmating* production of 1971 (702-705):

o that i had a thousand tongues
and a thousand-fold mouth!

o dass ich tausend zungen hätte
und einen tausendfachen mund! (702)

maria wanted to go to church
then she came to a deep lake
then she came to a deep lake

maria wollt zur kirche gehen
da kam sie an ein' tiefen see
da kam sie an ein' tiefen see (703)

It is clear, however, that Nitsch imposes severe constraints on speech within his aesthetic because he perceives that dialogue imposes severe constraints on the "excessive" physical conditions necessary to achieve ecstasy. After all, language is dramatic only to the extent that speakers, in dialogue, are acutely conscious of particular listeners who also wish to become speakers; this consciousness attached to dialogic conditions kindles a mood of urgency which urges the speaker to compress or maximize the meaning of a spoken statement "in time" to yield to the listener's desire to become a speaker.

The importance of Nitsch's work derives in part from the attention it calls to time as a variable defining the relationship between language, the body, and ecstasy. Although he designates very precisely the duration (often only seconds) of many actions in his projects (e.g., 241-245), the conglomerate perception provoked by the performance is that "communication" with the unconscious requires a vast amount of time. One needs this almost suspended sense of time, this temporal architecture of eternity (and death), in order to achieve the "total" orchestration of the senses which results from the polyphonic performance of an ever-expanding list of excesses. The concept of excess undermines the constraints of time. Moreover, as the documentation for the six-day project makes especially clear, once one has experienced ecstasy according to this aesthetic, one must escalate the scale of excess before experiencing it again — i.e., one needs more time, more bodies, more blood before achieving another moment of ecstasy because the next moment is possible only to the extent that it is "greater" than the last. A quantitative principle, characteristic of realism, governs the aesthetic, and it is not at all strange that Nitsch includes in the documentation cryptic excerpts from mathematical treatises on the gravitational powers of celestial bodies (824, 834-836, 852-867). But as the time of performance expands, the range of actions performed remains constant and narrow, for excess comes to mean the protracted *repetition,* by a larger and larger set of performance elements, of a basic set of ritual actions involving the fragmentation of bodies. The cosmic consumption of time required for "communication" with the unconscious indicates the enormous number of *material conditions* needed to achieve a moment of ecstasy. Ecstasy is not a response to anything as obvious as a body or the language which issues from it; ecstasy is a response to a great mass, an amorphous galaxy, of stimuli which expands through the repetition of its elements.

It is this "destruction" of time which negates the body and introduces the "ecstatic" phenomenon of amorphousness. For Nitsch, time is unable to contain the form which produces ecstasy. Form is synonymous with body, which implies that consciousness of time intensifies consciousness of the body. Since language is what produces consciousness of any sort, the body emerges as a construction of language — i.e., as a signifier, a repository of meaning. Nitsch and his followers perceive the unconscious, which seems to *secrete* ecstasy (as the inundation of the action with "formless" fluids — blood, sperm, water, etc. — indicates), as a void empty of language, body, and time, the origin of death. The idea that language creates only the illusion of identity, that it conceals within itself contradictions which amplify rather than resolve tensions within the body is by now so well-known as to seem banal. With Tristan Tzara's *The Gas Heart* (1917) and Georges Ribemont-Dessaignes' *The Emperor of China* (1917), the "impossible" Dadaist theatre presented "plays" which featured parts of bodies talking ("nonsense") to each other to dramatize the perception that the body was nothing more than an arbitrary complex of contradictory, even unconnected, desires, drives, motives, and significations. For Dadaism, it is above all language which "tears apart the body," but unlike Nitsch, Dadaism does not equate the fragmentation of the body with ecstatic experience. For Dada, in its quite scientific determination to "believe" in nothing, does not believe it is possible to get "beyond" language. What Nitsch and Artaud ignore, and Dadaism and psychoanalysis do not, is that language constructs the unconscious as much as it constructs consciousness. Psychoanalyst Jacques Lacan even asserts that the unconscious is itself an "organism," which has a body "structured like a language" and which manifests itself primarily through language.[38] The fantastically elaborate system of excesses, fetishes, and resources employed by Nitsch to reach a moment of ecstasy that exists, inhumanly, "beyond" language, and the apocalyptically metaphorical theory devised by Artaud to explain the therapeutic violence of the system, arise out of a profound fear of the body which neither science nor "civilization" are as yet able to transform, as the Greek notion of "catharsis" proposed, into a heightened awareness of a social body that allows the body to signify not only itself but another body, that "organism" of the unconscious, which we might call the "invisible" body of the Other. This atavistic, "timeless" fear of the body spawns a family of subsidiary fears: fear of form, fear of language, fear of time, the collective energy of which works to "destroy" bodies by destroying difference, by collapsing distinctions between reality and representation, between performer and spectator, between catharsis and ecstasy, between human and animal, between god and death. Indeed, only death offers the possibility of really getting "beyond" language, time, and the body. But perhaps this possibility is the greatest illusion of all, for even if the unconscious is the amorphous "body" of death, as Nitsch supposes, it nevertheless assumes the form of language, because although we cannot say (yet) that language is an organism, neither can we say that it is indifferent to its own existence, to its fragmentation or negation.

Mysticism, a quasi-religious, therapeutic (cathartic) ideology suffuses the efforts of the "Orgies Mysteries Theatre" to fragment the diseased or impure body into a formless, translucent ecstatic ether. Nitsch's endless theorization, as well as the *objet d'art* marketing of artifacts from his productions (923-929), work to ensure the perception that his ideas function as solutions to, rather than sources of, suffering, corruption, and repression in Western civilization, even though, of course, forces representing the Law or Ethics (of aesthetic experience) periodically question and sternly discredit this perception. But the assumptions about language and the body controlling the Artaudian performance aesthetic merely reach an extreme manifestation in Nitsch's productions; in their "normal" forms, they pervade the myth-saturated realm of popular culture. Rock concerts, for example, consistently offer the promise of an orgiastic mass of ecstatic bodies, and the fulfillment of this promise depends on linking a powerful (but usually simple) rhythm, a hypnotic throbbing vibration, to a monumental apparatus of high-tech "supplements" to perception of the performing body. Voice in this context is quite abstract in the Artaudian sense, an often "unintelligible" signifier of a quasi-hallucinatory mode of communication. But this pervasive relation between "simple" rhythm (heartbeat, pulse) and "mysterious" technology ("shattering" fields or waves of sensation) perpetuates the archaic myth that ecstasy (including orgy) is a "communication" with the unconscious, and as such is "beyond" the power of language, words, to construct it. And because this relation remains mythic and insulated from rigorous critical and theoretical inquiry into the "real" conditions of orgy, the Dionysian aesthetic of the rock concert tends to confuse orgy with therapy, *ekstasis* with catharsis, and mass ecstasy with mass hysteria delirium. The confusion is necessary to conceal the well-founded observation that orgy is not a popular event at all; only the *promise* of orgy is popular, never the reality.

Romantic Orgy

Richard Wagner was deeply aware of the problems (rather than pseudo-solutions) produced by mythically-defined (Dionysian) relations between speech, music, and ecstasy. Wagner looms over the nineteenth century because he more than anyone else linked the attainment of ecstasy with a supreme synthesis of perceptions. In a theatrical context, this concept of synthesis implies the inclusion, rather than exclusion, of meanings constructed by language, by voiced words "themselves." Wagner does not repudiate the basis of ecstasy in a mythic order of perception, but his work makes this order of perception so complicated that myth begins to expose itself as such, as a signifying practice which embodies ideological controls over perception and feeling. From Wagner's perspective, an ecstatic synthesis of perceptions (through the *Gesamtkunstwerk*) occurs only when performance connects the spectator to mythic and archetypal forms of identity. But the operatic role of language in achieving this synthesis is much more ambiguous than it is for either Artaud or Nitsch and has much more complex implications for an understanding of relations between theatre and orgy. In *Tristan und Isolde* (1859), perhaps the most complete disclosure of Wagner's attitude toward the relation between myth and ecstasy, a crude, but nevertheless intricate, model of orgy emerges insofar as we can accept that orgy arises out of a *dialogue* between two ecstatic lovers, the archetypal Couple (orgy is not necessarily "more than enough" bodies, but a body which is "more than enough" for whomever desire it). Act II, Scene 2 consists of a monumental love scene between the lovers, Tristan and Isolde, which defines the romantic *yet dramatic* conditions that permit a couple to produce orgiastic significa-tion. But though Wagner seeks a "primal" level of economy in terms of the actual *bodies* in performance which "feel" the ecstasy signified, the scale of the signification is immense, requiring a multitude of "invisible" bodies to produce.

To begin with, movement toward ecstasy consists of a suspenseful, protracted development of themes or tonal motifs, whose structures mutate under the pressures of different rhythms, instrumentations, dynamics, and harmonic complexes. The operatic context allows themes to develop in parallel rather than serially, so that orgy entails the production of sensations within and without speech that the listener/ spectator processes simultaneously. Parallel development of themes ac-commodates the phenomenon of the "endless melody," whereby a theme (or *leitmotiv*) is subjected, by orchestra, singer, and scenography, to continual variation and re-statement without ever reaching a decisive formulation which signifies the end of development and the onset of synthetic transformation (ecstasy). Movement toward ecstasy seems to be a release of power to control time by filling it as densely as possible with meanings and variations of meanings. The Wagnerian concept of ecstasy depends heavily on parallel exploitation of energies outside of speech and language to produce, so to speak, a *crescendo* of feelings which those who feel them do not want to resolve or transform, but to "develop," intensify, and protract. A seductive statement, a statement which embodies a promise of ecstasy, is a melodic line which attracts by its power to be repeated constantly while it develops a subtly different meaning (variation) with each repetition.

For Wagner, the cosmic synthesis of male and female (ecstasy) results from a synthesis of elements external to the bodies of the lovers themselves, a synthesis, for example, of language and music, a synthesis of the solo voice on stage and the anonymous, "hidden" orchestral sound mass. The lovers "speak" within a web of sound that is greater than any voice. As Leo Spitzer suggested, in discussing this work, movement toward ecstasy depends on cultivation of the ear, not the eye.[39] But the passionate feelings which "produce" or motivate the immense sound web arise from the will of the sound web itself to become emancipated from tonal centers that constrict the combinations of tones that may be heard. The music is highly chromatic; the key is unstable, the scene beginning in E-flat major (Wagner 1906: 132), then shifting to C major (133), D-flat major (147), F-sharp major (148), D-flat major (153), D major (153), D-flat major (154), C major (155), D-flat major (156), C major (157), D-flat major (162), C major 166), D-flat major (167), G major (170), D-flat major (172), f-sharp minor (173), F-sharp major (173), D-flat major (175), E major (176), D-flat major (177), F-sharp major (180), E-flat major (182), a-sharp (b) minor (183), c-sharp minor (184), a-flat minor (185). Numerous changes in rhythm and tempo also contribute to the highly dynamic condition of the sound mass. The complex "coloration" of mood provided by the proliferation of accidentals dramatizes the perception that the whole process of seduction is a business of releasing the lover's feelings, not only from the constraints imposed upon them by the social context, but from constraints imposed by "nature" itself, as embodied in the concept of tonal centers. The nocturnal setting of the scene emphasizes the idea that a movement toward ecstasy heightens the speaker's sense of *infinity* and the infinite condition of a will outside any particular identity, a will, so to speak, within "nature." Infinity is the dissolution of difference, the "loss" of identity, as the text itself makes clear:

Ohne Nennen	No more naming
ohne Trennen	no more parting,
neu' Erkennen	newborn knowledge
neu' Entbrennen;	newborn ardors
ewig endlos,	ever endless,
ein-bewusst:	both one mind:[40]

Movement toward orgy entails a kind of rhetorical architecture (sound structure) which attempts to release the speaker and listener from the communicative "norms" embedded in the architecture. The scene contains within it the assumption that heightened ambiguity occurs, not through complex semantic relationships within and between statements, but through an increasing abstraction of language to the point that speech ("naming") no longer has referential significance and "meanings" result from purely tonal relationships. But these relationships are nevertheless mathematical and belong to an ordering of time and space "beyond" the control of the Word.

The text equalizes the distribution of language between the dialogue speakers. Moreover, this equality of distribution, unfolds according to a three-part structure. The scene opens with Tristan and Isolde enjoying a kind of stichomythic exchange of brief lines and phrases (66-69). The size of the individual units of exchange escalates from one to two to four lines each to the point (68-69) that the speakers begin to exchange entire monologues with each other. The third part of the distribution structure consists of having both speakers speak the same lines together, a device which first occurs 35 bars into the scene, recurs intermittently, and eventually brings the scene to its conclusion. However, these passages are never really sung in unison. Rather, the effect is of an echoing of feelings, a reproduction of one speaker in the Other. But all of the exchanges, including the monologues, can be perceived as echoings or segments of a continuous strand of thought:

Isolde:	Ewig!	Endless!
Tristan:	Ewig!	Endless!

Isolde:	Ungeähnte,	Never dreamed of!
	nie gekannte!	Never known of!
Tristan:	Überschwenglich	Exaltation
	hoch erhabne!	never equaled!
Isolde:	Freudejauchzen!	Joy-exulting!
Tristan:	Lustenzucken!	Raptured pleasure!
Both:	Himmelhöchstes	Heaven-high
	Weltenrucken!	above all earthly!
		(68-69)

****

Isolde:	Ohne Wahnen —	No illusions, . . .
Tristan:	sanftes Sehnen;	. . . tender yearnings!
Isolde:	ohne Bangen —	All fear ended, . . .
Tristan:	süss Verlangen	. . . sweet desiring!
	Ohne Wehen —	No more sorrow, . . .
Both:	hehr Vergehen.	Noble surcease!
Isolde:	Ohne Schmachten —	No more pining . . .
Both:	hold Umnachten.	. . . night-encompassed.
Tristan:	Ohne Meiden —	No more parting . . .
		(90-91)

The irony here is that unity of perception derives from a fragmentation of language. The lovers speak in phrases rather than complete sentences; some phrases lack nouns, others verbs. A few phrases consist only of an adjective or adverb. As words become isolated, feelings become synthesized. The speakers do not adhere to any rigid metrical scheme (although, of course, their voices are locked into the "cosmic" rhythms and tempos of the music). Some lines contain only two syllables. But the music protracts and contracts them according to rhythms that are independent of those linked to language. Still, it is difficult to avoid the suggestion that the narrow line length is a signifier of repression — a repression of Language. A repression of Language is a repression of meanings which can never be released through more complex tonal (mathematical) relations, only through more complex grammatical relations or *choices*. So: despite the controlling concept of synthesis, the ambiguity of meanings produced by the ecstatic voice depends on preserving the notion of things which "can't be said."

Wagner links the equal distribution of speech with a blurring of differences between (or synthesis of) numerous identities: male and female, music and language, day and night, sleep and consciousness, etc. But the process of synthesis and equalization of language also entails confusion regarding the distinction between the seducer and the seduced. Tristan and Isolde seduce each other. One identity does not absorb the other; rather, they both give up their "separate" identities to achieve together some sort of indivisible infinite being that is "nameless." The confusion of the seduced with the seducer means that neither seducer nor seduced has to deal with the problem that troubles anyone seeking to initate movement toward ecstasy (or orgy): how to mask the loss of innocence produced by the normative notion of seduction. For the romantic Wagner, equalized distribution of language *is* a condition of innocence which connects the speakers to the innocence of nature, music, and the cosmos, all of which lack consciousness; "No more wakening/Nie erwachen" (84-85) is the ecstatic objective of the seduction. But even if the seduction, the promise of and movement toward ecstasy, is a release of mutually innocent feelings, it nevertheless remains subject to pressure from the notions of guilt and "fraudulent" identity (such as the threat of "daylight," 78-79). "No more wakening" is synonymous with "no more fearing" (86-87). The iteration of "no more . . . ," "never," and "forever" links ecstasy with a threshold of satiation. But the speakers do not reach this threshold. Wagner tries to synthesize innocence and ecstasy much as he synthesizes music and language. But in this respect he is perhaps less successful (convincing) for the obvious reason that thresholds of satiation cannot be identified. The dramatized desire of the lovers for "more" of each other, more words, more music, more time, more night, conflicts with their stated desire for the infinite "never," a boundless void, filled not with "more" but with nothing. Innocence is probably incompatible with feeling contradictory desires, for the pursuit of one desire betrays the other, and in the betrayal is the seed of guilt. The scene does not end because its objective has been reached, but because of the unwelcome intrusion of another person, Kurvenal, whom the ecstatic dialogue does not accommodate. The desire to protract the present in order to derive "more" from it means that ecstasy is always something "more" than what is now. It is really "beyond" even life itself: only in death can one "know" the infinity of being that constitutes the authentic ecstatic state:

So stürben wir,	But should we die
um ungetrennt,	we would not part,
ewig einig	joined forever,
ohne End',	without end,
ohn' Erwachen,	never waking,
ohn' Erbangen,	never fearing,
namenlos	nameless there,
in Lieb' umfangen . . .	in love enfolded . . .
	(86-87)

This "final" synthesis of the ecstatic moment and ecstatic infinitude is as obscure (or "mystical") as the synthesis of life and death pursued by the speakers. I suppose it means that "total" ecstasy is always a future, deferred condition, always "beyond" the bodily, voice-defined present, when one is compelled to extract "more" from the present.

But this reluctance to admit a clear distinction between moment and eternity simply disguises the intimation that ecstasy is beyond dramatic representation itself. Death is the threshold between the orgiastic appetite for "more" and the ecstatic infinite. Death is the liberation of being from representation, from the desire to signify, from that which is "between" identities, between desire and its objects. Wagner, who persistently saw a revolutionary political objective for his art, also saw the whole phenomenon of performance as a densely intricate but nevertheless mesmerizing model of utopia. The ecstatic utopia of the love scene is a world which distributes language equally and sonorously between speakers. In this scene, however, dialogue does not imply any *tension* between speaker perceptions; utopian dialogue as embodied in the love scene simply echoes or mirrors the perceptions of speakers. Nor of course does Wagner encourage, as Nitsch does, the idea of an ecstasy which results from transforming the dialogic relation between performer and spectator such that the difference between them becomes blurred. Whether Bayreuth, the utopian site of representation, really functions to initiate social transformation or only exists as a haven or temple to which the spectator turns in order to escape confrontation with unhappy social realities is a question that requires more space to answer than we have at our disposal.

Yet even if Wagner assumes that the "synthetic" theatre can "only" represent ecstasy, but not produce an ecstatic, orgiastic "synthesis" of performance and audience, his power to complicate the relation between voice and ecstasy is so great that it undermines confidence in the cathartic function of dramatic representation as defined by classical aesthetics. Performance by no means "frees" the spectator from a powerful identity with the mythic world represented; yet neither does it work entirely to assimilate the spectator into the value system defining the social context, for the mythic world is the revelation of an unconscious reality which the social context represses. Ecstasy implies a perpetual, unresolved suspension of the *individual* spectator between moment and eternity. The aesthetic of synthesis works to produce a non-orgiastic ecstasy in this or that spectator; it does not produce mass catharsis, because in reality synthesis does not involve a "final," culminating resolution of tensions between voice and music, between body and abstraction — it keeps them perpetually suspended in relation to each other. The "synthesized" relation between performance and spectator actually encourages tensions between spectators, very "controversial" receptions which neither Wagner nor his disciples anticipated. The love scene does not purge or satisfy desires which put the spectator in tension with the social context; it objectifies and memorializes them, as grand motivations for sacrifice and "greatness" of action. Yet the unresolved tension between language and music nevertheless contains a pressure toward orgy, insofar as perpetual suspension itself (rather than synthesis) signifies, though it never satisfies, the orgiastic demand for "more" of itself, "more" of the moment (the now), rather than the "end" of anything.

The strategy pursued by the Russian composer Alexander Scriabin (1872-1915) was spectacularly radical in both the aesthetic and political senses. Scriabin imagined a world-orgy created by a Wagnerian-type *Gesamtkunstwerk* (or monumental synthesis of perception) that would dissolve all distinctions, including those accepted by Wagner, between the representation of ecstasy and the awakening of that emotion in the spectator. In the *Poem of Ecstasy* (1908), Scriabin used an enormous, abstract (voiceless) orchestral sound mass as a metaphor for "ineffable" vibrations of ecstasy which he assumed could be experienced universally, by a humanity unified through a cosmic tonality. Subsequently, however, as he drifted toward atonality,[41] he became preoccupied with the relation between sound and color, and his understanding of the source of ecstasy became less abstract, more theatrical. Or rather, he began to think that ecstatic experience could derive only from explicitly ritual action, from the production of trance states, through which world ecstasy becomes synonymous with the effacement of all difference, all relevant distinctions between classes of identity:

> What does it matter if two million or a thousand million people experience the state of ecstasy, when a single soul remains excluded from universal light [. . .] Such a partial consummation cannot be imagined; either all mankind and nature undergo transformation or none do. Scriabin understood very well that the transfiguration of a single individual [. . .] had no validity, for universal consummation must perforce be total. In other words, cosmic ecstasy is not the sum of single ecstasies, but individual ecstasies are manifestations of the cosmic ecstasy [. . .] An individual ecstasy [. . .] constitutes a temporary suspension of time, a momentary break in the linking chain of multiple states of being. Only universal ecstasy can grant absolute freedom, all the little "I's" transfigured in a single moment in the Unique.[42]

To achieve this ecstatic "suspension of time," which nevertheless involves a rather revolutionary political aspect insofar as it incorporates "an erotic and sexual element incompatible with Christianity,"[43] it is necessary to dissolve boundaries between reality and representation, art and life, to the extent that theatrical resources actually work to "overthrow theatre"[44] and, for that matter, the notion of ecstasy as a *dramatic* condition: "But the idea of cosmic ecstasy must by necessity exclude the roles of actor and spectator, for it can be realized only as a collective act drawing everyone into the circle without opposing anyone to anyone else."[45]

With the never-realized *Mysterium* (1906-1915), Scriabin contemplated a vast synthesis of sensations, cosmic symphonies of light, sound, and color, comparable in scale to a great engineering project, for which there was "no longer a public,"[46] no spectator, only an infinite multitude of performers. The gigantic orchestral sound mass would merge with the sounds of nature, the rustle of trees, the undulation of waves; the voices of the chorus would merge with the cry of nature, hums, shrieks, hisses, chirps; the symbolic colors of the costumes, torches, and light media would merge with the colors of sunsets, sunrises, the light of the stars. The movements of animals would be integrated into an enormously intricate rhythmic structure. Scriabin seems to have had in mind a series of concentric stages which placed the Prophets (including himself) at the center and the Profane at the periphery. But he also seems to have considered a multi-site performance, since he did not make clear whether the event takes place entirely beside a river in India (or Kashmir) or at times on the slopes of the Himalayas. At any rate, after seven days, the great mass of rhythms would congeal into an orgiastic dance, leading finally to collective ecstasy. The contagious effect of this ecstasy would give birth to a "new race."[47] The composer, however, died before he had even sketched out most of the scheme, and this fact is not without relevance to the concept. When the conditions for ecstasy become so complex and "cosmic" in their political ramifications and material demands, so distrustful of mere words, so detached from the semantically grounded sound-world of speech itself, ecstasy then entails such "infinite" dimensions that only the infinitude of death can give it any reality.[48]

Orgy, then, as a monumental theatrical "synthesis" of language and music, is probably as much a myth as the "Dionysian" identity of theatre itself or the Hollywood-Babylon conjunction of signs. Consequently, the next step in understanding the relation between orgy and theatre is to suppose that an anti-mythic idea of orgy is not somehow "beyond" language, but a type of "excessive" deployment of language. But because such an anti-mythic idea conflicts severely with the general cathartic function of theatre, examples of orgiastic theatre speech (in the "bacchantic" sense) are extremely scarce.

Of course, Euripides opens *The Bacchae* (407 BC) with a spectacular chorus (100 lines) of maenads, who "raise the old, old hymn to Dionysos." The language is highly irregular in rhythm and permeated with repetitions of simple syntactic structures. The speakers rely on only a few rhetorical devices, such as commands ("Let ever mouth be hushed"), instructions ("crown your hair with ivy"), fragmented allusions to the story of Dionysos ("So his mother bore him once"), inventories of emblems associated with the god ("and the squeal of the wailing flute"), descriptions of the god ("He is sweet upon the mountain . . . he delights in raw flesh"), and a mere couple of fragmented descriptions of the actual divine power of the god ("With milk the earth flows!"; "Flames float out of his trailing wand").[49] The speech as a whole, as a combination of all these devices, is the strongest evidence of the god's power over the *speaker*. Metaphor, however, is not a prominent device in this orgiastic speech.[50] But Euripides' purpose is satiric: after Dionysos' prologue speech, it is clear that the bacchae are in the grip of a frenzied delirium. Orgy appears as a response to monstrous illusions, from which the text rigorously distances the spectator. The subject of the play is the tragic consequences of this insanity, of this inclination to perceive fantastic phenomena as "real," rather than as metaphorical constructions. The chorus ends the play with a pathetic wimper, a platitudinous hush: "But god has found his way/for what no man expected." The play therefore conforms to the cathartic model of theatre by "containing" orgy within a larger moral design of warning the spectator about the frailty of human vision. Orgy "ends" in violent disillusionment.

This containment strategy also applies to the numerous enactments of the medieval Walpurgis-Night revels, of which the most famous is perhaps Scene XXI of Goethe's *Faust: Part I* (1808). It is a huge scene (388 lines). Faust and Mephistopheles, wandering through the Harz Mountains, encounter will-o-the-wisps, a chorus of naked witches, a chorus of wizards, various voices of invisible bodies, Lilith, phantasmal caricatures of literary and social types (such as the Prokophantasmist), and even reference to the "Dilettante" author (Goethe himself) responsible for the text. Mephistopheles metamorphoses into an old man to dance with an old witch. Orgy appears synonymous with the nocturnal transformation of the natural into the supernatural, but the spectator perceives this transformation as *grotesque,* as an extravagant mode of hallucination. An enormous quantity of speech fills the scene, much of which is sung (using very *regular* metric forms). But for the most part, speakers confine themselves to descriptions of fantastical, magical phenomena ("there sprang/A red mouse from her mouth"), as if, indeed, none of it could really be "seen" until it is spoken. Speech which does not revel in this extravagant descriptive mode is merely "chatter" and "gossip": orgy does not involve any "serious" level of communication such as prevails nearly everywhere else in the text. In fact, the orgy comes to an end only when Faust turns "serious" again (pervaded with guilt) upon seeing the phantasmal image of Margaret, whom he has abandoned to a gloomy fate. He "wakes up" as if from an intoxicating dream.

But post-classical containment of orgy in the theatre does not necessarily assume this grotesque form. *Bacchanterna eller fanatismen* (*The Bacchantes; or Fanaticism,* 1822), by the Swedish romantic author, Erik Johan Stagnelius, contains a very "serious" construction of orgiastic speech.[51] The play dramatizes the ambition of the bacchantes, worshippers of Dionysos, to hunt down and destroy Orfeus, whose melancholy songs unwittingly threaten the unity of the maenad community by luring individual members (Euridyke) away from it. The isolated, lyric voice of the lone human male is in competition with a kind of "ventriloquized" voice of the divine male, although in fact Dionysos never appears or speaks anywhere in the play (he "speaks" through the female chorus or the Chorus Leader). The bacchantes accomplish their grim task, and the Ghost of Orfeus appears at the end to warn his male "adepts" that the longing for ecstasy embodied by song reaches fulfillment only in death, not in the heroic isolation of the masculine Orphic poet nor in the feminine, orgiastic, communal worship of the god.

In the center of this large one-act tragedy is an immense (342 lines), orgiastic chorus of the bacchantes. The language is far more complex than even that of the bird-chorus devised by Aristophanes. Chorus and Chorus Leader shift between ten different rhyme schemes and seven different scansion rhythms; large chunks of speech contain the quoted or impersonated speech of persons talked about. It is as if the chorus as a whole as well as the individual speaker (Chorus Leader) contains different "voices" within it/her, voices in dialogue within the body of the speaker(s). But the complexity is yet more manifold. At one point, the Chorus Leader falls asleep, while the chorus thunders on about the glory of Dionysos. When the Chorus Leader wakes, she proceeds to describe her dream, in which Dionysos spoke to her and commanded the destruction of Orfeus. In other words, orgiastic speech entails speech which is not *heard* at the moment of utterance (the Chorus Leader did not hear part of the chorus's speech and the chorus did not hear what Dionysos "said" in the dream). Orgiastic speech reveals the ecstatic operation of two simultaneous or concurrent realities which are "invisible" to each other: the dreamt, individual "voice" of the unconscious and the communal voice of consciousness. Moreover, it is.extraordinarily ironic that these highly intricate and specific signifying practices create a monumental anonymity of speech: no one in the chorus has a name and even the Chorus Leader remains "separate" from the mass by virtue of her power to speak *for* the mass rather than for herself. Thus, movement toward orgy implies an increasing complexity of signification that is concurrent with an increasing anonymity of the speaker. Ecstatic self-abandonment becomes synonymous with the anonymity of the signifying body.

All these strategies for expanding the role of speech in constructing (and "containing") the orgiastic moment still retain a strong attachment to music, to tonal and rhythmic complexities of voice, and indeed it seems doubtful that any speaking or listening that does not pay attention to intricacies of *voice* can produce orgy. But this obsession with voice by no means implies that words themselves are irrelevant to the production of orgy. On the contrary, these strategies for signifying orgy through a conjunction of language and music suggest that orgy involves a very complicated "communication" between bodies which requires the simultaneous transmission and exchange of signs by different systems of signification. Orgy is not a "freedom" from system, from complex rules, devices, and structures of signification; it is an "excessive" manifestation of system. The "freedom" of orgy is synonymous with an ecstatic pleasure in complexity of signification. But the examples of the representation of orgy that we have examined so far associate such complexity with monumentality of *scale.* The "more than enough" peculiar to orgiastic appetite means a "panoramic" or "collage" mode of vision, spectacular signifiers of luxury, masses of bodies, huge chunks of speech, giant sound webs (opera and ballet), or immense theatrical resources (Wagner, Scriabin). To represent orgy requires a *big* exertion of energy and labor.

But these exertions work on behalf of conventionally mythic (and very "public") ideas about orgy. While it does seem impossible to detach orgy from some form of monumental communication and action, it is not at all impossible to detach the concept of monumentality from conventional perceptions of its scale. Not everything monumental is "big" in a physical or material sense. Monumental intensities of feeling or intimacies of signification do not necessarily depend on the appropriation of large spaces, many bodies, or multitudes of sensations, but they do depend on reaching "excessive" magnitudes of complexity in communication. Such magnitudes consist, not of big or many signifiers, but of many relations between signifiers. It is a monumentality of meaning that emerges out of an intricate (rather than "big") economy of signification. Of course, such an economy should not imply that orgy means "more" or constructs "more" meaning(s) than other forms of communication; rather, for the orgiast, meaning which is ecstatic depends on "more" complexity of signification. And it is above all this complexity of signification, rather than the size or quantity of either signifiers or meanings, that assures the "secret," exclusive, aristocratic identity of the orgiastic moment. We need only examine some of the "excessively" complex activities pursued by the so-called "clandestine" theatres of pre-Revolutionary Paris to affirm the validity of these assertions.

Fig. 1—Orgy as an "Oriental" sign of decadence, the end of civilization, and exhausted world. Georges Rochegrosse, *The Death of Babylon* (1891).

Fig. 2—Cinematic perpetuation of the nineteenth-century popular view of orgy: a scene from Cecil B. DeMille's *Manslaughter* (1922).

Fig. 3—Still from an omitted scene of orgy in Erich von Stroheim's
The Wedding March (1927).

Fig. 4—An archetypal Hollywood image of orgy as a multitude of pleasure-loving bodies
overwhelmed by a gigantically ''excessive'' scale of luxury and materialism: still from the
Babylonian sequence of D. W. Griffith's *Intolerance* (1916).

Fig. 5—Between 1528 and 1530, Lucas Cranach did several paintings on the theme of *Lot and His Daughters.* Discussion of this figure (1530) appears on pages 15 and 16.

Fig. 6—Alternative versions by Cranach on the theme of
Lot and His Daughters (1528-1530).

Fig. 7—Joachim Wtewael, *Lot and His Daughters* (early seventeenth century).

Fig. 8—Otto Dix, *Lot and His Daughters* (1939).

Fig. 9—Karel van Mander, *The Garden of Love* (1590s) (Hermitage, Leningrad).

Fig. 10—Detail of Bosch, *The Garden of Earthly Delights,* central panel (Prado, Madrid).

Fig. 11—Karl Hubbuch, *Im Rausch des Irrens* (1922).

Fig. 12—Classical form in tension with orgiastic content: Sergei Lodykin's *Orgy* (1917).

Figs. 13-15—Ancient Greek images of maenads performing
ritual actions (early fifth century B.C.).

Fig. 14

Fig. 15

Fig. 16—Maenads performing for Dionysos (early fifth century B.C.).

Figs. 17-18—Maenads and satyrs with erect phalloi (early fifth century B.C.).

Fig. 18

Fig. 20

Figs. 19-21—Orgy as violent, Artaudian ritual: images of Hermann Nitsch's
Mariä Empfängnis-Aktion, Munich, 1969.

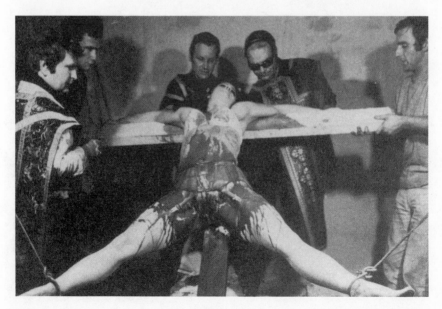

Fig. 21

Fig. 22—One of Fragonard's portraits of Mlle. Guimard (1770s).

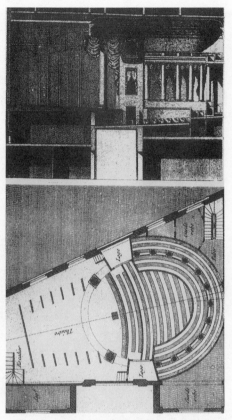

Fig. 23—Interior views of Mlle. Guimard's
first theatre, at Maison Pantin (1768).

Fig. 24—Exterior view of Mlle. Guimard's
second theatre (1772).

Fig. 25—An enchanting reconstruction of an eighteenth-century public theatre performance in Paris. This still from Marcel L'Herbier's film *Adrienne Lecouvreur* (1938) shows the separation of aristocratic spectators in loges from bourgeois spectators in the orchestra section, a distinction not rigorously observed in the clandestine theatres.

Fig. 26—Before the Revolution, the public theatre was, for members of various aristocratic circles, the scene of highly privileged, private erotic pleasures. Eroticism was a motive for extending the world of the salon into the world of the theatre.

Fig. 27—The loge was a separate theatrical milieu within the public theatre which, from an aristocratic perspective, signified an entirely different moral realm on stage than it did offstage.

Fig. 28—The left side of Fragonard's huge painting *The Fete at Saint-Cloud* (ca. 1775) depicts a fairground type theatre performance in which distinctions between aristocratic, bourgeois, and "common" spectators are difficult to discern. This portion of the painting carries the name "The Charlatans."

Fig. 29—Fragonard's engraving *The Ring Biscuit (La Gimblette,* 1783) treats bed, feminine nudity, and erotic gesture as elements of a curtained theatrical scene.

Fig. 30—Orgy as theatre in an
eighteenth-century French engraving.
But the image illustrates a fantasy
rather than documents a clandestine
performance.

Fig. 31—Here the fantasy of orgy as
theatre assumes a vaguely "oriental"
quality, but the sense of audience is
missing except for the solitary spectator on the left, a black eunuch, who
is in fact part of the scene rather than
"outside" of it.

Fig. 32—This image theatricalizes male fascination with the female body; the "scientific" examination of woman masks an orgiastic impulse behind the "costumes" of medical practice, scholarship, education. The figure in the lower right hand corner indicates that the spectator of this fantasy is someone who writes it down.

Au carnaval il faut se réunir.
Toujours folie nouvelle
Mais sans l'amour point de plaisir.
Arlequin, Pierrot, Scanarelle,
Aux Porcherons allaient se divertir
Ils emmènent leurs maitresses
Et sur une table à loisir
Ils enfilent les doucettes.

Fig. 33—A "popular," rather than aristocratic, fantasy of orgy as a comic, complicated acrobatic spectacle, performed in a *commedia* style which, unlike aristocratic fantasies, does not emphasize scenographic complexity.

Fig. 34—A nineteenth-century image of Sophie Arnould giving a
clandestine salon performance.

Fig. 35—Clandestine dance performance, with spectators presented as outside of the action.

Fig. 36—A pornographic theatrical perform-ance of the sort attempted by *Les Plaisirs du cloître*, the image treats the spectator of the performance as synonymous with the spectator of the image.

Fig. 37—This image depicts a clandestine version of the postmodern orgy described in Chapter Four. But in this case, the performers apparently want to deflate the perversity of their actions by wearing comic costumes, whereas the postmodern performance, favoring total nudity, does not seek to disguise its perversity. This image is also interesting because it does not make clear whether we should view the masturbating figure in the foreground as a spectator or performer.

Fig. 38—Even though in clandestine performance genitals are exposed and masturbated for the pleasure of an audience acknowledged by the kneeling boy, the wearing of masks and costumes suggests that the audience views the most intimate contacts between bodies as highly theatrical actions.

Fig. 39—Participant snapshot of an orgy in a middle-class apartment living room. Los Angeles, 1970. Here signifiers of decadence, "excessive" luxury, and theatre are absent or highly recessed; instead, signifiers of comfort and casualness predominate.

Chapter Two
Orgy Salon

IN 1905, GUSTAVE CAPON AND ROBERT YVE-PLESSIS privately published 530 copies of their book *Les Théâtres clandestins*. Though these authors were not the first to publish data about this theatrical phenomenon,[1] their use of the term "clandestine" has been effective, enduring, and provocative in characterizing the evidence they presented. In 1963, when Arthur Maria Rabenalt published his luxurious and very expensive *Voluptas ludens*, which relies heavily upon Capon and Yve-Plessis, he referred to the "secret" theatre culture in France (*Geheimbühne*).[2] But "clandestine" is a more appropriate term, because, as will soon become apparent, this theatre culture was by no means secret in the sense that it was known only to those who participated in it. This theatre did not "hide" from the world; it observed conventions which preserved its exclusivity and inaccessibilty, but not its secrecy. Yet Rabenalt's use of the term "secret" is accurate in a metaphorical sense, which refers to a form of theatre which *theatre history*, not the participants of this theatre, has kept secret, confined to discussion in very rare books and excluded from the "dominant" discourses on theatre that have prevailed since the French Revolution and which focus almost entirely on theatre as a great, accessible, *public* institution.

A good deal of research on "libertine" literature has appeared throughout this century, but virtually none of it explores the orgiastic performance cultivated by the clandestine theatres.[3] Although audiences for clandestine performances may well have included some of the audience for libertine literature, clandestine performance and libertine literature do not exactly embody the same values. Research on French libertine literature inevitably views this phenomenon in relation to the culminating significance of the prodigious mass of "subversive" writing produced by the Marquis de Sade, and this view of the phenomenon suggests that libertine literature is orgiastic to the extent that it involves an "excess," not of erotic activities, but of *writing*. With Sade as its grand master, the value of libertine literature derives from its power to expose magnitudes of desire and imagination which culture, ideology, and religious doctrine constrain, repress, or marginalize. Monumental descriptions of orgy disclose a mighty *potential* in "rational" humans for "evil," perversity, or pleasure — a potential which *only writing* (sometimes reinforced with accompanying illustrations) can objectify. Libertine literature constructs an "impossible" realm of fantasy insofar as it is a vigorous *critique* of a moral system which sets (or "inscribes") limits on the range or magnitude of the "possible," of the desires defining "nature." As Jean-Pierre Dubost observes in relation to Sade's writing, libertine literature emerges out of a profound sense of loneliness.[4] Though it revels in dialogue and theatricalizing rhetoric, libertine literature is pleasure for people who are alone. The writing and reading of it has more to do with solitary masturbation than with orgy.

By contrast, clandestine performance is passionately communal. Writing is never "enough" for the orgiast, for whom performance is always the test of the "possible." From this perspective, clandestine performance is less a *critique* of morality than a *critique* of "nature," of the physical, material constraints on desire. For this reason, it is not quite accurate to propose that libertine literature constitutes a theoretical perspective on desire which clandestine performance attempts to apply or test in an "experimental" fashion. The libertine and the orgiast possess different sensibilities which perhaps can exist in the same person but not simultaneously. The libertine sensibility, moreover, seems largely the creation of men, whereas the orgiast sensibility belongs as much to women as to men. This distinction is perhaps why clandestine performance is such a disturbing or intimidating subject for research: it does not reinforce any "dark" or "critical" vision of society; rather, clandestine performance promotes the perception that happiness depends exactly on "excessive" performance and not on the writing down of what is otherwise "impossible" to perform. Research on libertine literature tends to link this writing to the emergence of a modernist sensibility which finds its ripest expression in the "transgressive" works of such authors as Breton, Bataille, and Klossowski.[5] But clandestine performance is not "modern" in any sense applied to theatre, which is "modern" to the extent that it claims for itself the task of imbuing performance with a moral seriousness calculated to challenge "traditional" (institutionalized) modes of perception. Yet through its aesthetic perversity and complex, collaborative modes of production, clandestine performance was perhaps more radical than theatre since the French Revolution has *dared* to be. Our inclination to associate modernity with an expanded condition of freedom begins to pause when we consider the freedoms signified by modern theatre (rather than modern writing) in relation to the freedoms embodied by clandestine performance (rather than libertine literature).

The clandestine theatre was an invention of the Parisian aristocracy; its audience was very largely aristocratic, and even many of the performers were aristocrats. Sponsors of the theatre regarded it as a type of manor-house entertainment closely related to the giving of lavish suppers, balls, and masquerades. The amateur element of production was necessary in complicating the distinction between spectating and performing, but it did not preclude professional actors of considerable stature, such as Le Kain and Mlle. Raucourt, from appearing in numerous entertainments, though their more than occasional willingness to perform without fee somewhat complicated their professional status. The scale of production varied according to the sponsor's particular social ambition of the moment. Plays were written with particular sponsors, audiences, and performers in mind, and so the repertoire included full-scale comedies and operas as well as farces, *parades,* revues, dance pieces, *vaudevilles,* burlesques, historical travesties, and mythological parodies.

However, plays in a tragic mode appeared only rarely. Apparently Alexis Piron (1689-1773) attempted, on the eve of his death at the age of 84, a pornographic tragedy with his *Vasta, reine de Bordelie* (1773), but the result, possibly performed by Raucourt and Le Kain, was a confused monstrosity which only reinforced the belief that, in the theatre at least, tragedy and pornography are antithetical and irreconcilable aesthetic domains.[6] Earlier (ca. 1750), the actor Charles-Francois Grandval (1710-1784) had written a one-act verse tragedy, *La Nouvelle Messaline,* in which the Empress Messalina exhausts the sexual potency of numerous men without suffering the slightest waning of her own appetite. But this play was never performed. Grandval, however, persisted in trying to give a tragic dimension to pornographic theatre. In 1770, he wrote and produced

La Temperament, a one-act "tragic-parade, translated from the Egypt-ian," in which the intersection of tragic and pornographic aesthetics results from weaving the themes of impotence, incest, and morbid jealousy into a story of foreign royalty. Grandval concluded his career as a dramatic author with yet another attempt at tragedy, *Sirop-au-Cu ou l'Heureuse deliverance* (ca. 1760?), "tragedie heroi-merdifique," in three acts, which Capon and Yve-Plessis suggest is "not obscene, but simply disgusting and hopelessly boring."[7] Here Grandval combines the speaking of elegant Alexandrine verse with continuous discourse on and performance of intolerably repulsive scatalogical actions. It is not clear if the work was ever performed.

What is clear is that in the clandestine theatre the tragic spirit was never anything more than a mood of extreme cynicism. For pornography to achieve a tragic dimension, it is necessary for speech and action to explore a wider range of emotional regions and intensities than either a cynical or a comic sensibility cares to acknowledge. Pornographic tragedy entails the sexual excitement of the performer or spectator through the representation of a melancholy grandeur associated with a monumental (rather than merely obsessive) meditation on the power of the body to construct, transmit, and fulfill desire. Franz Blei once remarked: "Characteristic of pornographic literature is strict seriousness, which does not drift into either the tragic or the comic, but instead fixes itself completely within a sexual mechanism of functions whose motive is nothing but a never exhausted libido and whose capacity to enjoy this libido knows no limits except impotence."[8] For these reasons, Blei contended that pornography is a category of idealism. Yet every category of idealism, because it is vulnerable to profound disillusionment, also seems vulnerable to a tragic manifestation. Thus, the failure of the clandestine theatres to achieve much in the way of tragic pornographic performance is due, not to inherent limitations of pornography itself, but to limitations on the perception of pornography within the clandestine cultural milieu.

Capon and Yve-Plessis uncovered about a hundred published and unpublished texts for the clandestine theatre. That the authors of a few of these works remain anonymous is not surprising, but that some authors, anonymously or not, should publish them at all is somewhat more puzzling. Nevertheless, in 1780, Delisle de Sales (1741-1816), to take perhaps the most prolific of these authors, published his collected works for the pornographic stage, *Théâtre d'amour,* four volumes "composed of Greek, Assyrian, Roman, and French pieces." All these plays are comedies, or at least de Sales thought of them as "comédies érotiques," and they bear such titles as *Juno et Ganymede, La Vierge de Babylon, Cesar et les Vestales, Anacreon, Heloyse et Abeilard,* and *Ninette et Finette.* A *Jugement de Paris* occupies the whole of the third volume and requires, as Capon and Yve-Plessis put it, a lead actor of "Herculean temperament" to perform all the perversions prescribed by the text. By publishing these lewd plays (with detailed commentaries on the circumstances of their performance), de Sales perhaps hoped to document the power of theatre to function as an ultimate encyclopedia of lust, perversion, and depravity. Each play offers opportunities to realize a new set or combination of perversions, and the aim of the dramatic author is to discover the limit of possibilities and thereby at last satiate both himself and his audience. The monstrously interminable writings of the Marquis de Sade indicate that pornographic fantasy may never reach its end or limit. But de Sales and his ilk wrote their plays because they were not content to fantasize; they wanted theatre to make their fantasies "real," for only in the reality created by theatre could one determine the true "limit" of the pornographic imagination and the most "complete" disclosure of erotic desire.

For these writers, neither Law nor Morality asserted itself as a limit on their capacity to envision erotic pleasure as a theatrical performance. The police did not interfere with the productions of the clandestine theatres, though they did file numerous reports about its activities and participants, for high-ranking inspectors themselves were spectators. A bizarre exception to this indifference on the part of the police involved the ingenious Nicolas Audinot (1732-1801), a tirelessly innovative entrepreneur who supplied entertainments for both the suburban fairground theatres and the clandestine theatres. He apparently ran afoul of the police around 1770, when he staged clandestine erotic (though not overtly pornographic) plays featuring children. The .police responded to complaints from professional actors, who saw the child performers as competitors for lucrative engagements within the clandestine sphere. Audinot was a master of devising ways to stage plays outside the authorized public sites, and the use of child performers was one such device; however, this device, successful in relation to public performance, proved costly when transferred to the clandestine sphere of performance, a very strange irony indeed.[9]

Delisle de Sales' theatre pieces suggest that writers for the clandestine theatres had to accommodate a very demanding, if not especially "sensitive," audience. These authors felt little pressure to reach different types of audience, only an obsessive compulsion to satisfy that one aristocratic audience whose appetite for pleasure far exceeded that defining the mix of audience types for public entertainments. The total number of potential spectators of clandestine theatre in all Paris was probably no more than several hundred. Audiences for particular performances might number as few as six or as many as two hundred; it was therefore no small matter for authors and performers to determine the appropriate theatrical resources. De Sales, for example, wrote several charming miniature dialogues for the opera singer Sophie Arnould and her lover the Chevalier de Grammont (included in the *Théâtre d'amour*); they sang these as pornographic duets lasting no more than a few minutes. By contrast, in the 1750's, the Count de Clermont staged theatrical *soirées* that included as many as twenty separate speaking roles and continued over consecutive evenings. Nearly all clandestine performances augmented other entertainments: banquets, balls, garden parties, salon gatherings, fireworks displays.

Perhaps the most lavish sponsor of clandestine theatre was Marie-Madeleine Guimard, the so-called "goddess of the dance," adored star of the opera ballet. She built three "temples de Terpsichore" over a twenty year period. The first of these appeared in 1768, with very generous financial contributions from her lover, Marechal Prince Benjamin de la Borde and Prince Soubise, who asserted great influence over the affairs of the opera. This theatre, built into one of Soubise's mansions ("maison Pantin"), was a masterpiece of classical refinement: blue-marble ionic columns, luxurious rose and cream-colored wall panels, voluptuous vases of flowers: tulips, lilies, violets. The stage was about twenty-one feet wide and nearly fifty feet deep. Its lush blue curtain was a little more than fifteen feet high; the orchestra pit, however, rested twenty-two feet below the stage! The theatre could accommodate about 240 spectators in a kind of pre-continental (or "demi-elliptical") auditorium. Grilled loges and curtained vestibules provided space for erotic activity when spectators became excited by the marvelous "orgies which often celebrate[d] this nymph," La Guimard.[10]

But after a few years, Soubise began to feel that Guimard's theatricals exerted too much appeal for Parisian society — or at least, her orgies created unspecified difficulties for him in shaping the destinies of other opera personnel. Guimard therefore embarked on a new alliance with the Bishop of Orleans, who paid for an even more lavish theatre nearer the heart of the city (1772). Le Doux was the architect, Fragonard painted the wall panels. Again a marble colonnade established the elegant classical atmosphere, but now the ornamentation was even more exquisite: a sculpted fresco of Apollo crowning Terpsichore, "gallant but not indecent" tapestries, silver ropes, a salon opening onto a small winter garden, a dining hall with terrace, a bathing apartment, and grilled loges that were "delicious boudoirs." The theatre apparently could accommodate up to five hundred persons. Metra raved about it in his *Correspondance* (1782), and no one at the time appears to have raised a critical voice. The Revolution, of course, put an end to such extravangances. Nevertheless, Guimard proceeded to build a third theatre. With her husband, the dancer Etienne Despreaux, she moved to apartments in Montmartre; and there, because she was not in good health, she staged, through the inexhaustible mechanical ingenuity of her husband, marionette performances for a very small circle of old acquaintances.

Guimard's capacity for extravagance and excess never seems to have reached its limit. The anonymous *Memoires secrets* observes that she was in the habit of giving three suppers a week (with theatrical entertainments). One supper was for highly placed members of the court and government; the second supper was attended by artists, writers, and scholars; the third was a "veritable orgy, where one found the most seductive and lascivious women and where luxury and debauchery attain their zenith."[11] (See Figs. 22-24.)

Yet such extravagance always remained subordinate to the demand for *intimacy* of atmosphere. Moreover, the degree of licentiousness fluctuated according to the taste (if not the morality) of the sponsor. It is difficult to say that any theatre or group of participants, including Guimard, established a "standard" for clandestine performance, although the constant involvement of professional artists seems to have assured a generally high quality of enactment. Indeed, some private theatres never staged pornographic plays at all. The "success" of a theatre performance depended on the success of a *sponsor* in competing against social rivals. From a formal perspective, the clandestine theatre was highly conservative and completely devoted to preserving classical aesthetics of theatrical signification. Hybrid genres such as parades, revues, vaudevilles, "Assyrian" tragedies, and ballet comedies all had their origin in the *public* theatre. It is significant, however, that although the theatre inclined heavily toward burlesque, travesty, and parody for its comic base, it did very little to accommodate satire, the aggressive critique of social and political institutions. It was a theatre that did not associate comedy (or ecstasy, for that matter) with powerful laughter, which always has a stigmatizing effect upon its target. Laughter is the release of aggressive feeling toward a subject that deserves desecration. The clandestine theatre permitted indecency, perversion, even obscenity, but never anything its audience would call vulgar.

The origin of the clandestine theatre is obscure. Capon and Yve-Plessis point to a "tradition" of "private" theatricals dating back well into the Middle Ages, but the *clandestine* theatre — as they use the term — was a distinctly eighteenth-century phenomenon. They quote Edmond de Goncourt, who believed that the social ambitions of upper class women after the death of Louis XIV (1715) created this theatre, wherein "an environment of applause" and highly cultivated appearances accommodated Woman's perception of identity as synonymous with playing a role, with simulation and pretense. Women obviously assumed great importance in the development of this theatre culture, and the diversity of their contributions is in itself significant.

Between 1780 and 1785, the Queen herself, Marie-Antoinette, maintained a beautiful private theatre (Trianon), upon whose stage she often performed. As a spectator at least, she occasionally enjoyed pornographic entertainments. But by that time, the Queen was perhaps following fashion rather than initiating it. Besides the sensational Guimard, the Comédie Française and the opera spawned a number of high-powered women participants in the clandestine theatre: Mademoiselles Gaussin, Le Duc, Lamothe, Lafond, Dervieux, Dumesnil, Raucourt, Dangeville, Arnould, Drouin, to name but a few. In the two decades before the Revolution, Madame de Montesson became the lover, then wife and princess, of the Duke of Orleans in part because of the elegant theatre she operated in the mansion adjoining the Duke's; her theatre troupe consisted of herself, the Duke, and several other aristocrats, all directed by Mademoiselle Drouin of the Comédie Française. But unlike other sponsors, Montesson favored the performance of serious, morally edifying dramas which often bored those who were not performing them. She was fond of having an audience of ecclesiastics, but the Duke himself sponsored entertainments which appealed more to the princes, ambassadors, soubrettes, and courtesans.

By contrast, an atmosphere of frivolity and gaiety constantly prevailed for a dozen years (1740-1753) in the very suave theatre of the rich widow, Madame de Rochefort. She had a rather large troupe consisting almost

entirely of her aristocratic friends, including, among many others, the
Duchess of Luxembourg and the Count de Forcalquier, who performed
comedies, ballets, and operas, with a wide range of settings and opportunities for scenic delight. In a single evening, she could appear, pictur-
esquely costumed, in a play about an exotic Queen Zayde, then reappear
in a second play in the role of an amorous male. In 1753, she withdrew
from theatre and society when her close collaborator, Forcalquier, died.

Following her (1757-1775), the Verrier sisters, Genevieve and Marie,
sustained the attention of the Paris elite with their lavish productions of
musical comedies in two theatres; one theatre, in Auteuil, was a luxurious
garden pavilion, expensively ornamented with statues, colonnades, facades,
huge plumes, terraces, richly upholstered seats, horticultural decorations,
and a rotunda, all of which "placed the arts and voluptuousness side by
side." The other theatre, in Paris, though smaller, was equally glamorous,
distinctly Roman in complexion, and especially alluring on account of its
seven ornately veiled loges. The Verrier sisters were mediocrities as
professional dancers in the opera, but in their amorous relations with men
their theatrical sensibilities were powerful and incredibly complex. Their
benefactors included in succession the mighty Count Maurice de Saxe,
the financier d'Epinay, the poet Colardeau, and the actor La Harpe, each
of whom seems to have loved both women at the same time. D'Epinay
apparently lived with the women long after he had been replaced as a lover
by Colardeau and then La Harpe. Yet the sisters had distinctly different
personalities (they registered all their property in Genevieve's name).
When Marie died in 1775, Genevieve retreated into seclusion with
d'Epinay and Dupin de Francueil, who had been the lover of Madame
d'Epinay.[12]

Stranger yet was the theatre created by the Duchess de Villeroi, an
apostle of libertine freedoms (bisexuality). She produced two kinds of
shows in her gilded theatre. The first were operas, ballets, and dramas
which made brilliant use of elaborate scenery machines that far surpassed
in technical sophistication those of any other private theatre. The second
consisted of lewd plays glorifying lesbian love and setting the scene for
huge sapphic orgies involving women from the opera and the Comédie
Française (Villeroi was a benefactor of the great actress Clairon). Because
men were rigorously excluded from performance or attendance of these
latter enterprises, Villeroi was one of the very few women to assume
complete responsibility for some of the texts she performed. The actress
Raucourt, another flamboyant lesbian, also conducted theatrical *soirées*

celebrating her bacchantic "cult."[13] A number of other women were responsible for promoting the clandestine theatre, in addition to various men whom we have not mentioned at all (such as Voltaire and the Prince de Conde). But by now it is clear that women exerted considerable influence in defining this subculture and that the motives and methods through which the women made their contributions were by no means uniform. But because even the fantastic lesbian theatre of the Duchess de Villeroi functioned through complex partnerships with men, it is necessary to examine the larger ideological context which encouraged such an elaborate subculture to flourish.

In his *Correspondance secrete* of 1782, Metra asserted that when the whole of society constitutes a complex network of dissimulations, theatre becomes the most objective representation of that society.[14] Certainly the presence of a luxurious theatre within the home did much to certify the wealth of its owner and establish his/her reputation for bestowing pleasure upon those invited to the soirées. Owners competed with each other, not only in the ingenuity of the theatrical entertainments they presented, but in the glamor they could infuse into the theatre architecture itself. The Roman theatres of Mlle. Guimard appear to have been models of elegance and refined atmosphere. In any case, the clandestine theatre was an elaborate extension of the *salon* and to some degree a point of intersection between the *salon*, the *boudoir*, and the court.

In the *Salon de 1767*, Diderot observes that the artificialities of a dissimulated style ("maniere") governed above all by the *salons* is the "vice" of a highly policed, regulated, and controlled society. And Marian Hobson remarks, in regard to the *salons*, that "even when spontaneity ["le spontan" promoted by Diderot] is invested with consciousness, the distinction between the secret and the manifest, the private and the public, perhaps even between nature and art, is lost."[15] One might say that both the *salon* and the clandestine theatre occupied an ideological terrain that was "between" the socially defined categories of secret and manifest, private and public, nature and art, and this between-ness constituted for those in it a superior condition of freedom.

However, it is not quite right to suggest that the *salon* functioned as the theory and the theatre functioned as the praxis for the ideology of between-ness, because distinctions between *salon* and theatre themselves were not very clear. The "rules" governing conversation in the *salon* contained a strongly theatrical (rehearsed) component, and the theatre never operated independently of an intricately conversational milieu prior to and after the performance.

But these features of Parisian *salon* culture prevailed because the Parisian aristocracy had so little interest in the middle-class values that had dominated the public theatre from at least the time of Neville de la Chaussèe (ca. 1735). Middle-class theatre stressed an ideology of self-improvement: the "virtues" of one's "character" entitled one to rise to a higher status within society; material prosperity, so essential for any upward mobility, was treated as a reward for virtue, if indeed it was not actually a sign of it. The middle class domesticated the theatre, so that the characters on stage and the people in the audience performed in a manner that celebrated the triumph of Virtue, a concept that was as useful (as a mechanism of power) to the aristocracy as to the bourgeoisie. Since the time of Louis XIV, public theatre had come to mean state theatre (as embodied by the Comédie Française, 1688), and the bourgeois cult of respectability had gradually succeeded in linking state interests with a particular idealization of family life. A public theatre was an institution which encouraged the presence of families in the audience; it was a theatre in which a middle-class merchant did not have to fear any "corruption" of his presumably very vulnerable wife or daughter (i.e., he didn't have to worry about competition from predatory aristocratic males).

A public theatre had a *didactic* function: to teach the appropriate modes of action that embody Virtue. In his essay "On Dramatic Poetry" (1758), Diderot remarks that "it is always necessary to have virtue in mind when one writes." And Marmontel, in his *Encyclopedia* article from around the same time, observes that "it is undoubtedly very useful to expose the follies of man in their true light, but would it be less useful to offer examples of honest dealings, of noble sentiments, of decent behavior, of all the virtues of social life, so that these examples could touch us, move us, and make a lasting impression on us?"[16] A didactic function, as opposed to a process of indoctrination (propaganda), implies the stimulation of a critical attitude toward the spectator's own society, and this critical attitude coloring the representation implies that theatre is deviating, delicately, from the cathartic indoctrinations of the previous century, when the aristocracy dominated theatrical taste. A didactic impulse carries with it the concept of reform within the public sphere. For Diderot, Marmontel, Voltaire, Mercier, Rousseau, and other reformers, the power of theatre to reform social reality depended above all on the reform of dramatic *texts*. The creation of a virtuous society depended primarily on "enlightened" authors writing about virtuous persons in a wider variety of contexts than the classical drama generally permitted. Virtue was not the property of monumentally "heroic" figures nor the result of "tragic" sacrifices; it was the product of "enlightenment," of responsible, concerned *writing* about people who embodied theories of virtue.

Only the eccentric Restif de la Bretonne seems to have proposed a different relation between virtue and theatre. In an enormous book, *La Mimographe* (1770), he contends that only a vast reform of theatrical production practices can elevate theatre to a high level of art which adequately represents the values and aspirations of the state and its citizens. Presented as the "ideas of an honest woman," the book describes in exhaustive detail Restif's program for revising nearly every aspect of theatrical life: actor education, scenography, theatre administration, theatre architecture, performance style, genre categorization, repertoire, public relations, finances, audience development. Restif perceives the authority of an institution to embody Virtue as resulting, not so much from the efforts of *literary* interests to introduce into the institution *dramas* depicting the value of particular virtues, but from the success of the institution in "correcting" the lives of those who work within it, rather than those who attend it (spectators).[17]

However, with Restif's theatre treatise, the concept of Virtue achieves such immense complexity that no one can hope to realize it by sitting alone at the writing desk. The focus on reform of the drama and the spectator, rather than on reform of the theatre and the performer, made Virtue seem an easier, more attainable, and more individual condition than Restif's program acknowledged. Moreover, for much of the middle-class, a critical attitude tends to measure the imperfections of a society in relation to a sanctified idea of family life. The health of a society depends upon the vigor with which it preserves the power structure defining the family. An assumption of the middle-class theatre is that the spectator learns by seeing or recognizing himself in the representation. When the representation produces this condition of recognition, we have the phenomenon of identification. The clandestine theatre also operates on the principle of identification.

But, as Hobson has explained in considerable detail, in the public theatre, the principle of identification became entangled in theories of illusion, wherein representation strives to conceal itself, producing a level of consciousness that is somehow independent of the signs that construct it: "The reform of drama [. . .] tries to make meaning and play coincide:

signs are to be eliminated in favor of the thing signified" (179).[18] Theatrical representation conceals itself when it signifies, not so much a world, but a set of values endorsed by the audience well before it enters the theatre: the perfectibility of humans; the authority of modesty, prudence, and sobriety over rationality, artifice, and grand ambition; the necessity of "honesty" and "naturalness" in intimate as well as public affairs; the priority of respectability over honor; personal labor (work) rather than inherited position as the measure of human worth; capital rather than land as the strongest sign of wealth; the formation of power through legal ("natural") rights rather than through "customary" privileges; the assumption that desire is good so long as the Good is desired; the suspicion of any pleasure that is not morally edifying ("good"). Values such as these do not encourage an impulse toward orgy; they encourage notions of ecstasy and utopia that can be achieved "at home," so to speak, within the family rather than within a mysterious cult.

But these values, embedded in an idealized image of family life, entail heroic "situations," as Diderot called them, in which the *range* of characters is wider and the *status* of characters lower than prevailed in aristocratic tragedy. It was a matter of producing narrative contexts which accommodated social types (merchants and judges, fathers and daughters, priests and gamblers) rather than emblematic figures of political power and relationships (queens and princes, generals and servants). These narrative contexts established conflicts between the social types which put the values to a test. Marriage was an obsession with the reform dramatists as a problem and a solution to the attainment of happiness. In marriage and the desire for marriage was the key to grasping the utopian relation between "nature" and society. Play after play prescibes a cosy, attractive domestic milieu threatened by obstacles to marriage, forced marriage, bored marriage, splenetic marriage, adultery, marital deceptions, debauchery, prodigal or wayward children, and misfortunes of "character" (bankruptcy, alcohol, gambling).

In this milieu, to be heroic often meant little more than being able to express love or compassion or remorse or some other emotion that sustained identification merely because it signified vulnerability. The material prosperity pursued by the middle class depended to a large degree on an indifference to human suffering, and of course this indifference contradicted the whole ideology of virtue as the justification for wealth. The public theatre functioned to resolve the contradiction by contriving representations that disclosed the large reservoir of feeling deposited in the middle-class spectator.

The most peculiar example of such representations was perhaps the *comédie larmoyante,* an invention of the aristocrat Pierre-Claude Nivelle de La Chaussèe (1692-1754), in which the spectacle of characters weeping moved the spectator to weep as well. By weeping in the theatre, the middle-class spectator assured himself as well as other spectators (if not those, generally absent from the theatre altogether, who were victims of his desire to "rise" within society) that he was aware of his own vulnerability in a world governed by cruel choices; his tears became a sign of his own capacity to be victimized. The virtuous display of "sentiment" situated the spectator within "nature," which was now synonymous with a state of innocence. Innocence in turn implied a receptivity to representations which concealed themselves, a receptivity to the theory of art as a cult of illusions, with illusions becoming a technical term for processes of seduction, as Maillet Duclairon observed in 1751: "We are moved only to the degree that the illusion seduces us."[19]

When representation seeks to *disguise* itself (as "nature"), it is not long before moods of secrecy and exclusivity begin to suffuse one's taste for representation. But the process of disguising the representation included more than expanding the range of character types and dramatic "situations"; it also included various formal innovations. The *comédie larmoyante* was only one of several middle-class dramatic "forms" which escaped easy classification within the traditional categories of tragedy and comedy: the *genre serieux,* the *drame,* the *mélodrame,* the *drame sentimentale,* and all sorts of plays, spectacles, and "pieces" which refused to designate at all their genre affiliations. The business of domesticating and "liberating" the theatre was a grandiose project that included waves of convoluted theoretical contributions from the Encyclopedists and the intellectual *salons* (Diderot, Mercier, Voltaire, Rousseau, Riccoboni, to name only a few), great strides in the particularization of scenic detail by engineers and technologists (Servandoni looms large in this respect), and above all the production of dramatic texts in which Language gained its "freedom" through prosaic structures. The state, ever-dependent on middle-class money to sustain its sprawling apparatus, assisted considerably in the domestication process. Public theatre was in fact "official theatre," an extension of the state. The government rigorously inhibited any competition with its own theatres, and the theatres themselves operated in accordance with complicated administrative procedures and standards. State centralization of theatre culture facilitated the application of theory, as it developed within the *salons*, to production, for the *salons*, even before the epoch of Louis XIV, were ceremonial occasions in which the rhetoric of national destiny and policy was transformed into an intimate, cultivated mode of discourse.

The police, too, assumed much responsibility for "reforming" the theatre, not only through the influence exerted by the heavy, moralizing hand of the police censor on the content of public theatrical representations, but in continuing the tradition instituted by Louis XIV of "inspecting" the theatres, of conducting surveillance of theatre performances, and of maintaining elaborate networks of informants and detailed dossiers on theatre artists and spectators.[20] In short, the public theatre functioned simultaneously as a school, a model, and an objectification of the middle-class perception of state, nation, and society as macrocosmic embodiments of familial feelings and relations.

Of course, the aristocracy tended to view any notions of social mobility and dynamic society with deep skepticism, even hostility. It viewed the structure of society primarily in terms of class, rather than family, relations and therefore cultivated a sharper distinction between familial and public values. Yet it is too simple to say that the middle class systematically excluded the aristocracy from the public theatre, for the aristocracy never ceased to exert its "influence" over the public theatre, especially backstage, where "theatre" signified an almost completely different moral realm than it signified onstage. Rather, the aristocracy, growing *disinterested* in public manifestations of art, vaguely relaxed its grip on the mechanisms which institutionalized the theatre and thus created opportunities for a different, emerging audience. The reason for this indifference has been difficult to explain. The advent of rococo ideology, which coincided with a lessening of state demands upon the resources of the aristocracy, allowed the aristocracy to accumulate more wealth than ever. Committed to far less grandiose political and international ambitions than was the case under Louis XIV, the aristocracy could well afford to establish its own set of institutions, its own "culture," which operated independently of the state ideology as long as it, too, remained domesticated, confined to a "private" context.

As a profoundly social institution even within this context, the clandestine theatre functioned as a monument to the aristocrat's power to reduce life itself to a play staged according to his or her taste and authority. Indeed, the whole justification of an aristocracy now appeared in its ability to function as the ultimate embodiment of the privatization and domestication of passion so earnestly pursued in the public sphere of culture. It is therefore wise to accept that the cult of exclusivity surrounding the clandestine theatre was not something imposed upon the aristocracy by some official ideology, nor was it a reaction to any moralistic rhetoric of virtue and self-elevation pervading the public theatre. It was a cult initiated by the aristocracy for the purpose of linking the most perfect (ecstatic) domestication of passion with the most refined and blasé assertions of privilege.

But these statements do not explain why the clandestine theatre focused so obsessively on the representation of erotic feeling without ever introducing a serious attitude toward marriage. Obviously the clandestine theatre was not an "alternative theatre," as we understand the term, in relation to the "official," public theatre, for even if it projected an uncompliant attitude toward middle-class values, it was never a serious critique of any social or political condition. In fact, the clandestine theatre conformed to most of the formal conventions and fashions prevailing in the public theatre, and then added all sorts of implicit "rules" peculiar to its context, so that it was in no sense "freer" than the public theatre in terms of production choices. As for subject matter, the exclusive concentration on erotic scenes completed the sense of a totally regulated emotional environment which insulated the spectator from a wide range of dramatic conflicts or violent moods.

Yet it is true that within this exclusive concentration the clandestine theatre enjoyed far greater freedom, in the sense of explicitness, accuracy of perception, and experimentation, than perhaps any public or "offical" theatre has ever permitted. Apparently the value of erotic representations increases with their exclusion from the public sphere, with the degree of privilege linked to their accessibility. Not so apparent is that exclusion from the public sphere operates in relation to the power of the public sphere to *extend* greatly the range of subjects appropriate for representation. As the range of subjects expands, it forms a hierarchy of subjects. A subject is "appropriate" because it has a place within a hierarchy of subjects, in which some subjects are "more" or "less" appropriate than others in relation to a controlling value for representation. But an expanding hierarchy of subjects appropriate for representation inevitably encourages the perception that there is always "something else" worth representing than that which is "appropriate." Power consists of annexing "something else" to the "appropriate."

When representation concentrates on the erotic, rather than on sexuality,[21] the whole concept of representation, as a phenomenon which is or encourages "imitation," becomes entangled in passionate controversy, for nothing is really erotic if it does not inspire imitation — if by imitation we mean a desire to possess the erotic object or movement, not just its representation. Imitation is a mode of possession (appropriation). The erotic refers to the power of a body to construct a desire to possess it. Pleasure, aesthetic experience, then depends on some form of possession, of rightful or privileged access to the object of desire, not to the representation of the object (which is also, to complicate matters somewhat, the subject of representation).

Representation is perhaps never so ambiguous as when it becomes erotic (which usually, though not always, means when it takes the erotic as its subject), because erotic representations produce such intense identification with the subject of representation at the same time that they create an acute awareness of representation as a barrier between the spectator and the subject itself. In the sense that it maximizes the identification between the spectator and the subject of representation, erotic theatre constitutes a form of representation which disguises itself more completely than anything in the public theatre, with its technology of illusions and rhetoric of "natural" actions. Pornographic theatre encourages its spectators to "imitate" its performance . . . as part of the performance. And in this notion of imitation, this mode of identification, this theatre which refuses to define itself wholly as an illusion, is the will to orgy.

The choice of the erotic as subject matter must therefore arise from a powerful desire to deepen, rather than negate, the concepts of imitation and possession. The erotic amplifies the aesthetic dimension to the phenomenon of disclosure. It is an "unveiling" of an aesthetic response to another body, to a production of nakedness. And this condition of disclosure or unveiling constitutes a supremely materialistic definition of reality. The theatre provides the ideal context for this materialism of bodies, flesh, and desire. Orgy theory, as a category within a general theory of the erotic, provides the logic for possession of the materials. We must remember, however, that this preoccupation with the theatrical representation of the erotic, this fascination with the equation of the erotic and the theatrical, flourishes above all in an atmosphere of material satiation and stupefying, torpid luxury, in which the possession of *things,* no matter how numerous or precious, nevertheless fails to establish the "true" value of one's identity.

Instead, one must penetrate all sorts of illusions, all sorts of representations, in order to possess that which finally constructs the "true" identity of human "subjects": bodies, voices, nakedness, perverse desires "hidden" within the glamorous mask of the flesh itself. Ecstatic, orgiastic nakedness of being implies that supreme possession of "more than enough" which only theatre can offer. The erotic "subject" (body) is a spectacle, a text, even a machine authored by the "enlightened," suavely rational, and consummately materialist aristocrat. For this reason, we should observe that the orgiastic hunger for ecstasy creating the clandestine theatre *stems* from a profound sense of boredom and satiation, whereas, for most people, satiation is the "end" of ecstasy. And this hunger implicitly involves the clandestine theatre in a critique, not of social or political institutions, but of life itself, so that utopia is never anything more (or less) than this "monumental" intersection of theatre and the erotic.

However, the atmosphere of exclusivity surrounding this intersection and the ideology which justified it did not entirely lack a public dimension. The clandestine theatre was "private" insofar as one was a spectator only by invitation. Admission depended, not on one's ability to help pay for the representation, but on one's ability to contribute, as an attractive or significant personality, to the pleasure of the evening as a whole, including the theatrical production.[22] The "private" status of the theatre meant that, unlike the public theatre, it never entertained an audience of strangers. If pleasure and ecstasy result from particular conditions of knowledge (consciousness), then in this case, knowledge implies knowing the right people, knowing people who are "worth" knowing. Knowledge confers privilege. The question of the relation between knowledge, privilege, and privacy looms curiously here because *the public* by no means lacked knowledge of the clandestine theatre. Gossip about these *soirées* appeared in Parisian newspapers and brochures, dramatists published collections of their plays, and memoirists, such as Mercier in *Tableau de Paris* (1782) and Metra in *Correspondance secrete* (1782), published reflections on this theatre. Others commented on it in letters or diaries. I mention only printed sources of knowledge. What is important is that the rather deliberate effort to inform the public about the clandestine theatre suggests that the public played a significant role in perfecting the charm of the theatre by knowing about occasions to which it was never invited.

This situation complicates the "private" status of the theatre. "Private" does not mean secret or hermetic; it means exclusive, and of course exclusivity is sustained through the power to bestow, receive, accept, or reject invitations. The relation between an invitation and a seduction is not always clear, but in the milieu of the clandestine theatre, an invitation is only part of performance which attempts to seduce an entire society with its cultic idea of utopia.

Language in various manifestations was obviously very important in forming the identity of the clandestine performance as a matter of invitations, competing *salons,* and public knowledge. Specific attitudes toward language controlled the ecstatic, clandestine relation between knowledge, privilege, and privacy, and these attitudes are probably most "naked" in the texts written for clandestine performance. Such texts demonstrate very well that neither ecstasy nor orgy imply feelings which are somehow "beyond" the power of language, especially speech, to contain or provoke. For this reason, it is worthwhile to examine in detail the rhetorical devices, the specific uses of language, which construct this relation between feeling and its signification.

Of course, the *significance* of the texts, of what was said or sayable in the clandestine theatre, *is* "beyond" the power of their language to determine, for the significance is the product of ideological contexts (theirs and ours) which are never made entirely conscious because they cannot be exactly inscribed. The significance (value) of the text is not *in* the language of the text itself, but outside of it, "between the lines," or, to put it baldly, in the language of its commentary. In this respect, the significance of these texts, as constructions of ecstatic voices, lies partly in their relation to Silence, to what ought not be said or, more precisely, to what ought (or even can) only be said within a highly privileged environment. Only Silence can accurately indicate "what ought not be said." And only what *is* said in the clandestine theatre can indicate the distinction, which emerges as highly privileged knowledge, between "what ought not be said" and what isn't sayable at all (the limit of Language in representing erotic desire).

For the "enlightened" participants of the clandestine theatres, ecstasy is always a condition of superior rationality. But rationality in this context implies the manifestation of an imperturbable logic, an almost mechanical perfection of expression, which demonstrates the domination of disordered nature through "imagination," through an intelligence which regulates and transforms, as if performing a mathematical equation, everything in the world that is *given.* Rousseau's ideas about the normative (idealized) "example" of "nature" did not penetrate very deeply into the clandestine environment. For Rousseau, "nature" functions as virtually an absolute system of values, a moral code. But to *accept*, as Rousseau suggests, what is *given* by nature would seem to many within the aristocratic milieu as a form of *descent* into instinct rather than feeling, which is understood as something cultivated through "intelligence" (system and artifice). Thus, from our (rather Rousseauian) perspective, the clandestine unity of rationality and ecstasy seems linked to the production of highly artificial and "unnatural" scenes. The clandestine texts seem quite remote from the realist rhetoric of ecstasy, which associates ecstasy entirely with intense conditions of seeing, with the power of an image, with something "beyond" words.[23]

For the clandestine subculture, orgy is not simply an "excess" of bodies achieving ecstasy by touching each other; it is a *dialogue* between bodies, dialogue in the literal sense of the word as an exchange of speech between bodies. Orgy transforms the delicate intricacies and improvisations of *salon* conversation into the dramatic complexities of enacted dialogue. Pornographic writing is not the elaborate (novelistic) description of actions, bodies, and settings, but the inscription of *voices* concealing, disclosing, and savoring pleasures. Indeed, dramatically-arranged dialogue was a convention of pornographic (and libertine) writing ca. 1650-1790. Andrea de Nerciat (1739-1800), in his three-volume pornographic novel, *Le Diable au corps* (1788), perhaps the most famous of the century's output of pornographic novels, presents many events as theatrical "scenes," with speech inscribed as if it were intended for performance before a group of spectators. But this convention of pornographic fiction dates back at least to the publication of *L'Escholle des filles* (1655).[24] Why does this pornographic imagination associate ecstasy with the performance of dialogue?

The answer, I believe, has to do with the "enlightenment" mentality which pervaded the subculture. These people tended to suppose that ecstasy resulted from combining or merging conditions of seduction, indoctrination, and instruction. In the clandestine text, a state of ecstasy derives from this melange of conditions because the text perceives ecstasy as an ultimate condition of teaching or being taught. Ecstatic communication between bodies depends upon a particular relation between bodies in which one body is the teacher and the other is the student. And this relation achieves its most precise articulation through dialogue. The teaching of erotic pleasure is both a subject and a function of the clandestine representation. Characters in the texts teach, instruct, indoctrinate, seduce other characters who want to know about "secret" or "unspeakable" pleasures; the performance itself "teaches" the spectator the rhetorical conditions under which one may possess this privileged knowledge. Through a dialogic aesthetic, pornography not only assumes a didactic function, it becomes a bizarre commentary on didacticism itself.

Of course, teaching is not necessarily synonymous with indoctrination or seduction or even a dialogic relation between teacher and student. Nor do acts of teaching or being taught necessarily mean that what is being learned is what is being taught or that anything at all is being learned. But within the clandestine milieu, the dramatization of acts of teaching and being taught functions as a sign of an "enlightened," rational consciousness binding the representation to the spectator. The text links the signification of erotic feelings to pedagogical motives because such motives bestow a normative value upon the actions represented, no matter how perverse or *outré*. After all, teaching produces the *authority* of knowledge; it is the transmission of an *authoritative* body of knowledge. Teaching becomes indoctrination when it does not cultivate any questioning (or "dialogue" in a metaphorical sense) of the authority produced by knowledge. Within the clandestine text, however, dialogue (not monologue, lecture, pantomime, or ballet) remains the ideal medium for representing the transference, the *bestowal* of ecstasy through pedagogic authority. Dialogue establishes the existence of a teacher and one who is being taught. Both want ecstasy, but the existential difference between them suggests that they do not and cannot share the same *meaning* of ecstasy.

Moreover, even though the pedagogic rationale for the clandestine dramatic text entails a distinction in representation between teacher and student, between one who knows and one who does not, these distinctions are merely roles assumed by speakers, and as such, they have no empirical value to affirm any particular relation between teaching and learning. Indeed, one learns much without entering at all into a formal relationship with a teacher. But the clandestine milieu perceives "enlightenment" primarily as a condition of being taught. Teaching is understood as a theatricalized power or authority to describe a correct attitude toward a body of knowledge contained within the teacher. Learning for the clandestine milieu destabilizes perception; it constitutes a form of violence against a stable, "given" Known. What interests the clandestine spectator is the relation between teaching and ecstasy — a relation in which ecstasy emerges as a response to the authority of a privileged, "secret" knowledge. Teaching formalizes relations between speakers. It determines the conditions of "dialogue" which authorize and theatricalize orgiastic ecstasy. The chief thing taught by the clandestine representation is a specific, voiced command of language, a rhetoric which links ecstasy to a system for knowing "what to say" when the liberation of one's desire for another, no matter how perverse or "excessive," must nevertheless function as a superior sign of rationality.

Chapter Three
Orgy Calculus

The Awakening Power of Taboo Words

CLANDESTINE, DIALOGIC RELATIONS between teaching, knowledge, and ecstasy suggest that states of "enlightenment" or "awakening" are virtually synonymous with states of arousal. And within the theatrical milieu itself, the phenomenon of arousal never loses a powerful erotic significance. Acts of teaching and "awakening" involve a pornographic effect. Perhaps the most rudimentary level at which speech has the power to arouse the listener or spectator is when words possess a forbidden or taboo status outside the representation. So-called four-letter words arouse either the speaker or the listener because they name something that shouldn't be named or at least name it in way which the social context regards (by the exclusion of the words from its vocabulary) as excessively "vulgar," "familiar," or indicative of an "uneducated" sensibility.

But it is exactly because such words, when used in a *literal* sense, signify a mood of familiarity between speaker and listener, unconstrained by differences of education or class, that they are able to arouse those who speak or hear them. For at the same time that this process of naming what should not be named signifies a mood of familiarity, its *purpose* is to intensify familiarity into intimacy, a heightened sense of trust. This enhanced sense of trust in turn amplifies the vulnerability of the identity emanating from the taboo nomenclature, if not necessarily from the object for which a taboo name has been affixed. Ecstasy implies a supreme state of vulnerability, fearlessness. Enunciation of the taboo word in the literal sense signifies the immanent possibility of an ecstatic relation between speaker and listener. Conversely, the non-literal, metaphoric enunciation of the taboo word, especially the four-letter word, signifies a hostile or negative attitude toward the *identity* which "is" the taboo object, for the taboo word, because it is a stigmatized phenomenon, *reduces* an identity to something which shouldn't be named at all. As a metaphor or metonym, then, the taboo word signifies a severe estrangement from conditions of ecstasy. Consider two statements containing a taboo word:

> [A] Say now, "My cunt feels so beautiful!"

> [B] I told that cunt to call me tomorrow.

[A] presents a literal use of the taboo word, which names a specific component of the listener's anatomy. The word helps produce a pornographic effect insofar as it signifies an absence of class or educational distinctions between speaker and listener and thus suggests a mood of familiarity and trust, in which at least the speaker is free of social constraints, free to name what otherwise should not be named.

[B] however, presents a metonymical use of the taboo word: the speaker reduces the subject, not to a specific component of her anatomy, but to a specific component of female anatomy whose unpleasant existence needs to be contained or neutralized, especially if it has the capacity to "call" the speaker. The speaker creates a harsh distinction between himself and the taboo object by obliterating distinctions between the object named and the identity named. At any rate, these primitive distinctions in the use of taboo words already reveal the surprising implication that metaphor does not assume major significance in the construction of an ecstatic rhetoric.

BRIGDORE
I am young, it is true,
Hardly twenty years old; but to c[unts] well-born,
Valor relies not on the number of years.

ARGENIE
You would assail me who has rendered you so vain,
You to whom one's [prick]] never stiffens when touched?

BRIGDORE
Until now, I have never deceived any women,
And your c[unt], if you wish, will know that news.

BRIGDORE
Je suis jeune, il est vrai,
A peine ai-je vingt ans; mais aux c....[cons] es bien nees,
La valeur n'attend pas le nombre des annees.

ARGENIE
De t'attaquer a moi qui t'a rendu si vain,
Toi qu'on ne vit jamais le v.. [vit] raide a la main?

BRIGDORE
Je n'ai, jusqu'a present, jamais trompé de belles,
Et ton c.., si tu veux, en saura des nouvelles.[1]

These lines are from *La Comtesse d'Olonne* (1770?), a play with variants dating back to the 1680s and an authorship attributed variously to Nicolas Racot de Grandval, Corneille Blessebois, or Bussy-Rabutin. The lines are interesting because they show that the taboo word is not necessarily of the "four-letter" variety. "Cunt" and "prick" have equal status here and throughout the text as taboo words. Obviously it is the object named rather than the name itself which is the source of anxiety within the social context. But the mere act of naming the taboo object somehow makes the object accessible. Naming becomes a process of making naked; degrees of nakedness in turn function as an index for measuring the level of intimacy between speakers. But in his first speech, Brigdore uses the taboo word in a quasi-metaphorical manner: not only Argenie, but an entire of class of women are reduced to "well-born cunts," indicating a measure of anxiety on his part toward the woman who uses the word literally. As it turns out in this scene, which the author subtitles a "parody of *Le Cid*," Brigdore reveals his impotence, thus confirming our observation that a metaphorical use of the taboo word indicates an estrangement of the speaker from ecstatic drive. Actually, taboo words, as they appear in this text, as things which cannot even be printed out, only initialed, are quite rare in texts for the clandestine theatre. In fact, this version of the play was never performed, though it was definitely intended to be acted. Grandval in particular seems to have been obsessed with producing plays containing a scatological deployment of taboo words which allowed the obscene and the pornographic to coincide. Indeed, it is possible that the obscene becomes synonymous with the pornographic as a source of ecstasy only to the extent that taboo words, rather than the objects named, are responsible for defining a state of self-abandonment.

As an element of ecstatic rhetoric, the taboo word "awakens" the listener to a "nakedness" of expression which is meant to produce nakedness of being. But taboo words are not necessarily obscene or "vulgar." Since it is really the object named rather than the name itself which produces anxiety within the social context, the act of naming has the power to "awaken." In a sung *Dialogue* written for Sophie Arnould and the Count de Grammont, Delisle de Sales creates a pornographic effect by having both speakers name parts of their bodies in an intensifying manner similar to a striptease. The text unfolds within a rigid mechanical structure. Each speaker speaks only two lines at a time. Each strophe contains four lines or one exchange of lines between speakers. The text contains twelve strophes, a total of forty-eight lines. Within each strophe, the first and third lines rhyme and the second and fourth lines rhyme. Within each pair of lines allocated to a speaker, a response is given to a further disclosure of nudity on the part of Arnould. Each strophe entails an unveiling of Arnould's "beauty." The final strophe represents an orgasmic state of nudity for her. The entire dialogue appears in Appendix II.

The significant thing about this dialogue is that the utterances are not obscene or even taboo in themselves; they are "innocent" responses to something seen which should not be seen, or which at any rate should only be seen in such a way that language has no power to make anyone see more. What is seen are unveiled portions of Arnould's flesh. But the speakers do not describe what they see; they describe what they feel as a result of the unveilings. A pornographic state of nakedness occurs, not because speech describes and confirms something seen in order to create a mutual order of perception, but because speech describes something which really isn't seen at all, namely the emotional trajectories of the speakers. The taboo or repressed object within the social context is a particular emotion (ecstasy), not the words used to describe the emotion. But of course in assuming that the emotion can only be known or "revealed" through particular words which are not taboo, the text implies the existence of a taboo that applies not just to certain words, but to *any word.* The charm of the dialogue is that it invests seemingly "innocent" words with pornographic energy.

Consider, for example, the first line of every exchange allotted to

Arnould. Every line initiated by her begins with a single word repeated once consecutively. None of these repeated words can be said to hold the taboo or constrained status of, say, "cunt" or "prick":

Arnould Strophes (I-XII): First Lines

I   : Non... Non... D'intelligence/Not... Not... from intelligence,
II   : Non ... Non ... Vois mes alarmes/No ... No ... Observe my alarm;
III   : Quoy ... Quoy ... Tu n'es que tendre/What ... What ... You are only tender,
IV   : Prends ... Prends ... Même autre chose/Take ... Take ... something more;
V   : Ouy ... Ouy ... Quand j'idolâtre/Yes ... Yes ... When I idolize,
VI   : Vas ... Vas ... Poursuis encore/Go ... Go ... Pursue further;
VII   : Dis ... Dis ... Sois sans alarmes!/Speak ... Speak ... Be not alarmed!
VIII : Ouy ... Ouy ... Je te suis chére/Yes ... Yes ... I am dear to you;
IX   : Dieu!... Dieu!... Quelle caresse!/God!... God!... Such a caress!
X   : Non!... Non!... Toi que j'adore/No!... No!... You that I adore,
XI   : Ah! ... Ah! ... Baisse la vue!/Ah! ... Ah! ... Lower the gaze!
XII   : Dieu!!! Dieu!!! Que vas-tu faire?/God!!! God!!! What are you doing?

The repeated word is a simple, monosyllabic utterance, chosen, partly, to conform with the melodic structure of the music ("l'air de Myrza"). Further simplication results from using three of the words (*non, ouy,* and *dieu*) more than once. Exclamation points signal the release of ecstatic energy through the utterance of the word. In the final strophe, the word *dieu*, which refers to the greatest power in the universe, becomes synonymous with the naming of orgasmic feeling. The speaker names this unseeable power rather than her lover. But the word has a further significance in that the name for the great power can be compressed into an utterance which fits into the very simple, almost banal rhythmic structure that begins all the other strophes of this speaker. The *voice*, under the pressure of an emotion, transforms the simplest and most mystical utterances from an "innocent" to a taboo status; it can imbue any word which describes or discloses it with pornographic energy. And when properties of the voice becomes signifiers of ecstatic feeling, when ecstatic feeling establishes its signifiers in the voice, *all* language becomes inflamed, *all* words become like various matches, loaded with semantic energy, which ecstatic vibrations in the body can ignite. All words have the potential for producing a pornographic effect and signifying ecstasy.

Such is the ideology pervading this charming little text. But conditions of performance often modify the ideology that the author has attempted to inscribe. The *Dialogue* implies that the ideological organization of the language functions to awaken ecstasy in Arnould, the woman, who, from strophes IX to XII, apparently experiences an intensifying orgasmic rapture, which, however, never becomes so wild that it violates the metrical constraints imposed upon her speech by the author and the music. The author ends the scene at that point when the woman is "on fire" and can feel nothing greater than what compels her to cry out, "Dieu!!!" From the author's perspective, whatever follows from that point is either beyond the powers of language and theatre to describe or, more likely, a mere repetition of values already introduced within the first twelve strophes.

But in his preface to the playlet, Delisle de Sales remarks that at its first performance, at two o'clock in the morning, in the ballroom of the Paris Opera, where an invited audience had gathered for a party to celebrate an operatic triumph by Arnould, the Count de Grammont became so excited that he was unable to continue past the sixth strophe. Arnould was thus unable to represent her own orgasm, which, according to the author, was to be accompanied by a "voluptuous pantomime" featuring the nudity of various actors. In other words, the voice and language which were meant to dramatize the process by which the woman attains orgasm had the inadvertent effect of awakening ecstasy in the male addressee of her words. *His* orgasm was never inscribed into the text because, apparently, it is something which was meant to occur *after* the woman's and thus *outside* of the constraints defining the representation of orgasm within the text. Male orgasm here is a condition which occurs when the male speaker cannot or, as the author suggests, "dares not" objectify his emotion through language, let alone song. But the extent to which the failure on the part of Grammont to conform to the demands of the text resulted from his having to perform before an audience remains unclear. About an hour after the first incomplete performance, Grammont joined Arnould in her apartment, and together they repeated the scene, "without omitting a single gesture."[2] Arnould seems not to have been perturbed by the audience, which apparently was "left cold" by the spectacle of her passion.[3] At any rate, conditions of performance had the effect of undermining the ideology we have ascribed to the text. Delisle de Sales created a dialogue in which the most "innocent" utterances, in which any word in the language has a pornographic effect... *for the speakers,* but not for the spectators. The peculiar fate of this text in performance suggests that for the spectator, for the person who observes the spectacle without feeling the passion of the speakers, only taboo *sectors* of language, not just any word spoken by an excited body, can have an ecstatic effect. What pornographically unites the feeling of the spectator with that of the speaker is not the power of voice and text to signify a particular magnitude of ecstatic feeling in the speaker, but the power of voice and text to produce a *meaning* which has an ecstatic effect that does not depend on the spectator's passion for the speaker, whose mere being may inflame all language for his or her lover but not "other" bodies. Anything Arnould said would probably excite Grammont, but to excite an audience and move the performance toward orgy, configurations of language should be detachable from the bodies that actually speak it. Language is genuinely pornographic when *other* bodies can speak it with ecstatic results.

The Awakening Power of Taboo Speech Situations

For the clandestine audience, language must transgress a taboo (not a norm, for a taboo is itself a norm) in order to drive speakers or listeners toward ecstasy. But the texts considered so far indicate that a "successful" transgression entails more than the deployment of a particular sector of language, such as a taboo vocabulary, or more even than the power of the voice to transform a sector from an "innocent" to a taboo status. A relation between speech and ecstasy focused on words (names), taboo or "innocent," remains attached to an "animal cry" theory of ecstatic speech: at the moment of ecstasy, language evaporates within the ecstatic being, who, at most, can speak only a few isolated words or "animal" sounds, which usually are repeated with minimal variation. The voice of the ecstatic person is nothing more than a moaning, groaning, panting, gasping, a repetitive crying out of a word, name, or phrase.

But the concern here is with a mode of ecstasy which discloses the potential, rather than the limit, of language in signifying the emotion. Consequently, we need to consider the idea of taboo speech situations. These refer 1) to complex combinations of words which ought not be said, even if the words in themselves do not derive from a taboo sector of language, including taboo vocal transformations, *and* 2) a peculiar relation between speaker and listener which controls specific relations between words. An example of a speech situation is that in which parents and children express their love for each other. Both parents and children may signify their love through speech. The signification of this love may entail configurations of language (relations between words) that "ought to be said" (if they are to preserve assumed distinctions between parents and children) or "ought not be said." If the latter is the case, then a taboo speech situation has emerged. A taboo speech situation constructs a relation between the *identity* of a speaker/listener and relations between words which "ought not be said."

Pornographic movement toward orgy within the clandestine theatre involves the representation of taboo speech situations. However, my purpose is not to provide a comprehensive inventory of taboo or pornographic speech situations operating in the clandestine theatre or even to suggest that the clandestine drama contains such an inventory. A comprehensive inventory of taboo speech situations generally or even only in the clandestine theatre is a huge, and perhaps futile, enterprise. Others have attempted general inventories with only very modest success.[4] Rather, my purpose is to apply the definition of a taboo speech situation to the exposure of the attitudes toward language which construct a rhetoric of orgiastic dialogue. The main thing is to show how, in the clandestine theatre, orgiastic ecstasy evolves from a specific magnitude of rhetorical (dialogic) complexity. I want to show a relation between orgiastic ecstasy and an "excess" of system in speech communication. But I do not think this connection becomes sufficiently clear unless commentary on a particular text and its rhetoric achieves its own manifestation of excess. For this reason, I will focus on a single, "typical" text which discloses the complexity of discourse containing or critiquing what "ought not be said."

The anonymous *Les Plaisirs du cloître* (ca. 1778) is a brief (if not exactly modest) work in three acts requiring eight actors, six women and two men. The central character is Marton, a young "pensionnaire" in a convent. All the action occurs in Marton's room at the convent. The comic energy of the text issues from the irony of treating a convent as the site of erotic ecstasies. The simple plot depicts the "lessons" which teach Marton how to transform the ascetic environment of the convent into a "temple of pleasures."[5] Marton moves from an initial state of masturbatory solitude to an orgiastic state of intimacy with two men and another woman. The "lessons" consist of scenes in which Marton "learns" to develop the courage necessary to satisfy her voluptuous desires within a severely repressive atmosphere.

On the one hand, the play pursues in an ironic vein the dominant ideology of "enlightenment" as the value system best able to move the self from oppression to happiness. On the other hand, the play projects, in a less extreme way, the attitude toward life that pervades the (non-dramatic) pornographic writings of Alphonse Donatien de Sade, which are an interminable inventory of fantasies arising out of the assumption that the happiness of any human being depends on the suffering of another. The effort to resolve this conflict between the process of achieving ecstatic enlightenment and a very unequal assertion of power in human relations governs the construction of speech situations within the play.

In an archetypal situation, when one speaker asserts greater power or authority than another, we encounter two distinct rhetorics. The speaker asserting power relies on a rhetoric of domination, control, constraint, possession, and judgment, the materialization of which usually takes the form of commands, aphorisms, questions about the listener, narrative descriptions of the listener's or a third person's experiences, conditional statements, statements implicating the listener (e.g., sentences beginning with "So you . . ." or "Therefore you . . ."), or imperatives (sentences modalized by *must* rather than *should* or *want*).

The speaker lacking power relies on a rhetoric of submission, humiliation, offering, petition, justification, and concession, the materialization of which usually takes the form of repetitions of statements made by the speaker of power, clichés, answers to questions about himself, narrative descriptions of himself (confessions), passive voice, sentences which focus on adjectives (states) rather than verbs (actions), a preference for superlatives when speaking of some Other, statements of desire (statements modalized by *want* rather than *must*), or questions about the nature of his own actions.

Obviously no speaker operates entirely within either category of rhetoric; indeed, one can oscillate between dominant and submissive moods within the same speech. The speech situations in *Les Plaisirs* observe to a degree these theoretical distinctions in power relations between speakers, but ecstatic speech itself tends to entail, as we shall see, a peculiar juxtaposition of the two rhetorics. The text introduces a special character, Soeur Agathe, who functions, not as a seductive intermediary between the two categories of voice, but as a kind of "enlightened" voice of power in tension with the repressive voice of power embodied by the convent authorities. She enunciates an emancipatory (rather than repressive) notion of power which relies on a "teacherly" obscuring of the two rhetorics. Moreover, the ambiguity of Soeur Agathe's character serves, from Marton's perspective, to obscure the distinction between friend and lover: what she "teaches" through her rhetoric is that the courage to gratify one's desires within a repressive environment depends on one's ability to ignore taboo-driven distinctions between love and friendship.

These perceptions of power relations between speakers motivate the formation of at least three types of speech situation: *sacrificial, didactic,* and *utopian.* But the text is not completely conscious of these distinctions, and therefore the rhetorical "system" within which they are categories produces occasional distortions and fuzzy zones of signification. Indeed, I doubt whether any classification of speech situations can operate with "perfect" systematism, for language itself, as an "arbitrary" system, always prevents power from ever becoming too easily ordered.

The Sacrificial Speech Situation

A sacrificial speech situation occurs when the happiness of one person depends on the suffering of another, and the common source of happiness and suffering is language spoken by either the "victor" or the "victim." In making a decision, one must also make some sort of sacrifice. No sacrifice occurs without suffering. However, the play displays little interest in the processes by which people make decisions. The text focuses on the consequences of decisions that the characters, lacking any sort of complex consciousness or conscience, had little trouble making. The sacrificial speech situation serves, then, to dramatize the magnitude of sacrifice and suffering produced by a particular rhetoric of desire.

In the opening scene, we find Marton sitting alone on her bed, with a pornographic novel in her hands. She does not read aloud from the book; instead she delivers a 32-line soliloquy in which she describes the feelings the book has provoked in her and divulges her excited involvement with the amorous adventures of the imaginary characters. Indeed, she seems to speak *to* these creatures of fantasy:

What quick expertise! From your caressing hand
You restore ten times his dormant vigor.

Quel rapides travaux! De ta main caressante,
Tu ranimes dix fois sa vigueur languissante. (166)

Here, as throughout the text, the rhyme scheme of the verse is quite complex and will receive attention later. What is immediately peculiar about the scene is that the speaker excites herself, not by reading the text, but by speaking a commentary on herself in relation to the text — or rather, in relation to a fantasy to which the text merely refers. The book is actually a source of "suffering" (in the sense that frustration is suffering) in that it awakens desires which cannot achieve ecstatic fulfillment as long as the fantasy generated by the printed language remains only fantasy. Therefore Marton creates a commentary on her feelings, since her own words and voice establish the reality of her being, which becomes simultaneously the source and object of her desires. She employs the rhetoric of a person lacking power insofar as her speech is confessional. She uses metaphors which reveal the tormenting quality of her desires, for example:

What trouble! Ah! it's too much; stop, charming book;

Quel trouble! Ah! c'en est trop; cesse, livre charmante; (165)

A voluptuous flame
Embraces my amorous mood.

Une voluptueuse flamme
Embrasse mes sens amoureux. (165)

. . . a burning arrow
Penetrates my ardent breast

. . . un trait brulant
Pénétrer dans mon sein ardent (166)

For the speaker, language achieves ecstatic energy, not when it describes erotic actions, but when it analyzes and enunciates erotic feelings. At the conclusion of the soliloquy, the speaker discards the book altogether and begins masturbating in earnest. We might say that in this case, in which the reading of a pornographic book clearly appears as something one does in secret, that the speaker cultivates her desires by "sacrificing" any contact with a living Other. But this "sacrifice" appears obscure in relation to the imaginary Other constructed by the book, for that Other exists only as a fantasy which may *excite* the speaker's body but can never *objectify* it as a "real" (unimaginable), fleshly Other may do. In the absence of the unimaginable Other, the speaker speaks, not to enact her fantasy, but to construct herself as the object of her own desire. This narcissism, this objectification of her desire and fetishizing of her own body, puts the speaker in the mood of believing that her intensifying pleasure does not depend on her loneliness, her isolation from the unimaginable Other. It depends, rather, on *speaking*, on being conscious of herself as the "real" signifier of desire rather than something silently absorbed or subjugated by an *inscribed* language of fantasy.

In another sense, however, the soliloquy represents the speaker as a "victim." From the standpoint of a *spectator* of the play, the *speaker* appears as one who hungers for ecstatic union with another person but has no way to satisfy that hunger except by making a *spectacle* of her masturbatory mood. It is the spectacle of an isolated woman declaring her hunger for penetration by a virtually anonymous Other, by "une flamme liquide" (166) which is the greatest source of pleasure for the spectator. But of what is the speaker a victim? Here is a case in which the submissive identity does all the talking and the dominant identity remains silent. The spectator watches silently, anonymously, as the speaker describes her responses to a pornographic book. The book itself constitutes a subversion of silence, insofar as it exists as something which not only ought not be said, but ought not be thought. The speaker is a "victim" of a great silence concerning that which drives her toward ecstasy. But this silence is merely the manifestation of an ideology governing public life. The ideology produces a utopian or idealized "public," for whom language is not an aphrodisiac, but a medium for disclosing the worth of an individual to give and receive love, to establish claims upon an Other. The moral pressure exerted by the concept of worth means that what ought not be said (or thought) are desires for which no Other with any public identity exists as the object. The "public" produced by this ideology severely stigmatizes any *spectacle* of masturbation, of Otherless ecstasy. Like suicide, masturbation functions as a critique of a public silence in relation to a signification of desire.

Thus, when masturbation assumes the qualities of a spectacle, as something performed for an audience, the speaking masturbator appears also as a "victim" of her own desires, of "nature." It is really not she who sacrifices the Other, but the silent (spectatorial) Other who sacrifices her by transforming her desires into an object of aesthetic contemplation worthy of an appropriate and insurmountable "distance." "Je meurs/I die," she says at the point of orgasm, and this phrase, uttered within a theatrical context, dramatizes very efficiently the sacrificial mood of her masturbatory action.

A much less complicated example of the sacrificial speech situation occurs in the second scene of Act II. In the previous act, the Mother Superior had "caught" Marton in the process of hiding the pornographic book. II, ii dramatizes Marton's punishment for having soiled her purity. Marton appears with La Maitresse des Pensionnaires, Soeur Angelique, Soeur Justine, and Soeur Therese; more characters appear in this scene than in any other, but only Marton and La Maitresse do any speaking. La Maitresse initiates the dialogue with statements which describe the impurity of Marton's flesh, announce the need to appear penitent before God, and command Soeur Angelique and Soeur Justine each to deliver twenty blows to Marton's kneeling, half-naked body (173-174). Marton responds by begging pardon for having just once "abandoned" herself to temptation. But La Maitresse is "inexorable," and commands Marton to "arrange" herself on the bed to receive blows from Soeur Angelique. The rest of the scene consists of a complete, relentless fulfillment of the punishment announced by La Maitresse in her opening speech. But the fulfillment contains two parts. In the first part, La Maitresse issues commands to both Marton and Angelique and *counts the blows* inflicted upon the victim. For example:

[3.1]

LA MAITRESSE

Bon, demain vous serez guérie.
Dix-huit.

MARTON

Ah! Ah!

LA MAITRESSE

Dix-neuf.

MARTON

Ah! ah!
                        Vingt. C'est assez.
Vous, soeur Justine, commencez. (176)

In the second half, La Maitresse stops counting blows; instead, she expands the expressiveness of her commands to include commentary on the *quality of the blows* inflicted now by Justine:

[3.2]

MARTON

Ah! ah!

LA MAITRESSE

Paix.

MARTON

Ah! Seigneur!

LA MAITRESSE

(a Justine, qui fouette faiblement.)
Un peu plus fort, ma mie,

Vous vous ralentissez.

(Justine frappe plus fort.)

MARTON

(se regimbant.)
Ah! ah!

LA MAITRESSE

(a Marton)
Quelle folie!

Tenez vos jambes, s'il vous plait.

MARTON

Ah! ciel!

LA MAITRESSE

(a Justine.)

Sanglez-la bien.

MARTON

Ah! ah!   (177)

La Maitresse shifts from a quantitative to a qualitative assessment of the punishment, not because of any change in either the nature of the victim's responses or in the method of punishment, but because of the attitude of the person inflicting the blows, Justine, who, in speaking the only lines spoken by a third person in the scene, has disclosed a lack of conviction regarding the necessity of the commands:

Oh! Mother, Marton is well enough punished.
The poor child is all on fire.

Eh! ma mère, Marton est bien assez punie.
La pauvre enfant est toute en feu. (176)

In other words, the satisfaction La Maitresse derives from the victim's suffering depends, not only on the condition of the victim, but on eradicating any doubt as to the necessity of the punishment. La Maitresse intensifies her satisfaction by making a "victim" out of Justine, out of the person who actually inflicts the blows.

The idea that Justine is a victim becomes clearer in the scene immediately following this one, in which, alone with Marton, she begs forgiveness for "the necessity of my excessive cruelty/"Pardonnez donc, ma chère, à la necessité/Mon excessive cruauté" (178):

If I had struck gently,
She'd've inflicted on me the same punishment.

Si j'avais frappé mollement,
On m'aurait infligé le même châtiment.

Thus, in the flagellation scene, the business of counting the blows in [3.1] is somewhat obscure because it is not clear to whom La Maitresse is speaking. Counting merely intensifies focus upon a single action (the striking of Marton) with mechanical inevitability. In [3.2], however, the commands by which La Maitresse asserts control over the quality of the blows constitutes a dialogue between herself and Justine (rather than the victim). Justine "speaks" through the blows she inflicts — i.e., the cries of the victim speak for her. Though the stage is fairly crowded, no third voice emerges. Silence is all that is spoken "between" the voices of the master and the victim, which subsume all other voices. The sacrificial speech situation reduces to a primal number the range of voices necessary to establish relations between persons. It polarizes identities to the point that no one has any identity except by making choices that involve one in suffering and sacrifice. Identify with the voice of either the master or the victim: speech permits no alternative voice.

But stranger still is that throughout this scene the text maintains, as elsewhere, a very complicated rhyme scheme. The author favors couplet constructions, but occasionally introduces three and four repetitions of the same line-ending sound, as well as alternating rhymes. The rhythm shifts arbitrarily from eleven or twelve syllables per line to seven, thus indicating some power within the speakers to control language rather than the other way around. A peculiar feature of [3.1] and [3.2] is the fragmentation of lines into separate voices, so that master and victim share the same rhythm. Nowhere else in the play do we find dialogue of this nature, in which voices alternate every few syllables. Nowhere else do we find anything approaching stichomythic or even dichomythic construction. Dialogue otherwise consists of alternating blocks of speech possessing variable dimensions. [3.1] and [3.2] thus imply that alternation of voices is most frequent in the sacrificial speech situation. They also suggest that this frequency of alternation is possible because the polarized *feelings* of master and victim arise from a shared rhythmic basis, from the same organization of time. The voices of master and victim subsume each other, just as in Marton's soliloquy the body of the speaker subsumes that of the absent Other. The sacrificial speech situation always works to reduce the range of voices defining human relations. But in this case, conditions of pleasure and suffering provoked by the act of flagellation intensify according to the power of the master and the victim to *feel what the other feels*. This power to feel or at least subsume the pleasure or suffering of the Other achieves dramatic reality through the fragmentation of lines into separate voices.

Of course, one may observe that for the victim this "power" manifests itself chiefly through utterances ("Ah! ah! ah!") of such predictable simplicity that, in spite of the contrapuntal complexity producing the relation between master and victim, one discerns here a variation or inversion of the "animal cry" signification of orgasmic pleasure. But that is a peculiar insight revealed by [3.1] and [3.2]: the reductive nature of the "animal cry" rhetoric of ecstasy does indeed fit our model of the sacrificial speech situation. Subsumption entails victimization, the violation of a body, most intensely signified by the reduction of language to a "cry" and sub-categories of the "cry" (moans, sighs, panting, shrieks, and repeated "ahs," "ohs," "mmms," "oooos," and "yeses").

But it is clear that the "satisfaction" La Maitresse derives from the punishment never reaches ecstatic intensity. No one in the scene experiences any ecstasy. The "satisfaction" La Maitresse feels is nothing more than a kind of titillation. The scene implies that it is *because* she represents the values of a norm in relation to the user of pornographic representations that she is "satisfied" merely through the pleasure of titillation. The constraints she imposes upon the Other have the effect of requiring her to constrain her own capacity for pleasure. She concludes the flagellation and the scene by remarking perfunctorily and commandingly:

> Good. The business is over.
> Cover yourself, Marton, weep for your sin,
> And never do it again in your life.

> Bon. L'affaire est finie.
> Recouvrez-vous, Marton, pleurez votre péché,
> Et n'y revenez de la vie. (178)

The mood of constraint produced by the use of commands, fragmentation of lines, subsumed voices, and the "silence" of a third person (Justine) between the master and the victim suggests that the assertion of power on behalf of a norm has little to do with the experience of ecstasy. Even from the spectator's standpoint, the scene produces nothing more than titillation because the extreme polarization of identities inhibits any urge toward self-abandonment. The self is subsumed rather than abandoned by the conventions of the sacrificial speech situation. It would seem, therefore, that the scene can be understood as a devaluation of the Sadian notion that happiness (rather than mere "satisfaction") depends on the sufferings and sacrifices of others. But we have to look at the scene in relation to the text as a whole. In order for Marton to experience ecstasies greater than those provided by the masturbatory fantasies of the opening scene, she must "learn" not to fear norms, she must cultivate a courage to pursue her desires regardless of the punishment associated with the pursuit. As Soeur Agathe explains in II, iv:

> Consider, Marton, that these vigorous blows
> Render you more sensitive to amorous pleasures.

> Apprends, jeune Marton, que les coups vigoreux
> Te rendent plus sensible aux plaisirs amoureux. (179)

These pleasures are such that "one easily forgets a moment of suffering!/Q'on oublie aisement un instant de souffrance!" The flagellation, then, appears as a kind of "ordeal" by which Marton tests the strength of her will to ecstasy. But if the scene is a "test," a "lesson," then it is also an ambiguous affirmation (rather than devaluation) of the Sadian ideology.

A Contemporary Analogy

Moreover, in a different context, qualities of the sacrificial speech situation may assume a form which effectively disguises all the violence contained within the situation. Here an analogy drawn from contemporary pornography may prove useful in clarifying the ecstatic interest of the sacrificial speech situation. On 14 August 1986, a cable television station in New York City broadcast an anonymous documentary which functioned to promote viewer interest in the work of a young woman who starred in pornographic movies. The taped scene showed her being directed in the performance of a scene from one of her movies. On the television screen, one saw only the young woman and her director. The director was a woman, around forty years old, clearly upper class in her manners and language, and very elegantly dressed, while the young woman was completely naked and assumed the deferential manner (obedient nodding, smiling, bodily pliancy) of one who is conscious of her lesser status in relation to a wealthier, more mature person whom she regards as a kind of mother or teacher. As with *Les Plaisirs,* a "silent" third person inhabits the scene in the form of unseen camera operators, technicians, etc., whose identities are subsumed by the relation between director and actress. The scene for the movie requires the actress to perform masturbation, to revel ecstatically in offering her body up to the scrutiny of the camera. The director works to perfect this performance. The movie camera focuses exclusively on the nude body of the actress, who sits in an armchair of a well-furnished apartment; the video camera shuttles back and forth between the actress and the director, who sits in an elegant, Empire-style armchair facing the actress. The director perfects the performance chiefly by issuing commands in a calm, measured voice. The commands consist of two types. The first type constitute technical *instructions* regarding the physical representation of ecstasy:

> Open your legs wider ... Throw your head back ... Pant, pant
> ... That's it, show your tongue ... Now, rub it harder, harder
> ... Now, slowly ... Squeeze your breast ... Get wetter, let
> the sweat flow ... Breathe deeply ... Don't look at me, look
> at the camera ... Now slide down to your knees ... That's it,
> use both hands ... Yes, bend over ... Now, arch back ... Keep
> smiling, keep smiling ... Close your eyes ... Come, come,
> come.

The second type of commands are vaguer and allow the actress wider opportunities for *interpretation*:

Be proud, be proud . . . Shine for me, shine . . . Throb . . . More, more . . . Let everybody see: you love it, you love it . . . Make me starved for you, make me think there's nothing else . . . Give it all to the camera: that's the cock that's mad for you . . . That's it: pull me *into* you, *into* you . . . Get stronger, stronger . . .

Though this rhetoric seems to operate within a simple strategy, the relation between speaker and listener is quite complex. Presumably the movie which will contain the masturbation scene is constructed above all for the pleasure of a male spectator. The director "speaks for" this hypothetical male spectator, but her voice in no sense impersonates him. Indeed, it is because she uses a calm, detached, coaxing (rather than impassioned) voice to differentiate the conditions of *speaking for* from *imitation* that the director is able to inspire the trust of the actress and create an atmosphere in which the consequences of her extreme vulnerability do not cause the actress any anxiety. In a sense, the director "owns" language to an even greater extent than La Maitresse. The actress "speaks" in the dialogue only with her body and with wordless sounds of arousal. Yet in the movie, the director's voice is completely absent. Instead, the spectator hears an entirely dubbed soundtrack of banal disco music and heavy breathing. The film represses all the signs of a sacrificial speech situation in order to produce the illusion of an ecstatic event "beyond words."

Now it may seem that the documentary video records a rhetorical context in which a sacrificial speech situation can achieve a genuine ecstatic consequence. But it is not at all clear from either the documentary or the movie whether the actress actually attains orgasm while performing before the camera. The director displays no signs of being excited by her contributions to the scene; she constantly maintains an elegant, poised manner. Thus, if we assume that the actress does experience orgasm during the scene, then perhaps we are dealing with an unusual sacrificial speech situation in which ecstasy flowers within the "silent" victim, the one who lacks words, rather than within the speaking master, the one who articulates feelings. The implication of this assumption is that ecstasy results from an act of listening rather than speaking. However, we should approach this assumption with great caution. For one thing, the elegant pose cultivated by the director may serve as a mask to disguise her urge to feel the emotion the actress is representing. After all, the authority of the director's language results from the completely unspoken belief shared by everyone, including the viewer of the documentary, that she *knows* what it feels like to be an ecstatic male spectator watching a *convincing* display of female ecstasy.

But more importantly, all the activity documented by the video tape works to *represent* a state of ecstasy. The documentary does not record the conditions under which the young woman or even the hypothetical male spectator achieves ecstasy; it records the process by which a young woman represents ecstasy for a specific consumer of the representation. Thus, if anything, we can at best associate the sacrifical speech situation with producing the *illusion* of ecstatic experience, an illusion which functions to disguise an inequitable distribution of language between a speaking "master" and a silent "victim." The illusion in turn serves to perpetuate the pervasive belief that ecstasy is somehow "beyond" the power of words to induce. The illusion sustains the notion that ecstasy is easy to achieve; it is simply a matter of constructing and consuming the "right" image. The image equates ecstasy with a set of freedoms: freedom from language, freedom from consciousness, freedom from intelligence, freedom indeed from any concern with analyzing and objectifying the complex relation between self and Other.

Ultimately, then, the reductive operations of the sacrificial speech situation impose all sorts of constraints upon knowledge as a source of ecstasy. La Maitresse punishes Marton for knowing what ought not be known and thinking what ought not be thought. The director of the pornographic movie does not punish her actress; that is not necessary, for the director knows all that needs to be known in order to protect a conventional ideology of ecstasy. She not only speaks for the hypothetical spectator, she thinks for the actress. Ecstasy appears as a reward for being silent, wordless, unknowing, and "innocent."

Three examples of a sacrificial speech situation have appeared here: Marton's soliloquy, the flagellation scene, and the videotaped dialogue. Each example links an aspect of masturbation with particular rhetorical functions of language. In the soliloquy, the solitary speaker strives toward ecstasy by describing erotic feelings rather than erotic acts. In the flagellation scene, the punishment of masturbation and knowledge that leads to masturbation is dramatized by a dialogic fragmentation of lines shared by the punisher and the punished, in order to disclose the interwoven nature of the rhythms defining "satisfaction" and suffering. In the documentary videotape, a glorified representation of masturbation depends on a highly polarized relationship between a "hidden," commanding source of language and a "silent," displayed body. All of these examples have a titillating rather than ecstatic effect upon the spectator. The reductive rhetoric of the sacrificial speech situation well represents the theme of masturbation because both phenomena, masturbation and the sacrificial speech situation, entail a heightened sense of exclusion: the masturbator excludes the Other (or acknowledges exclusion from the Other) in order to establish his/her worthiness to experience ecstasy, while the anti-masturbator, through a rhetoric of subsumption, works to exclude the ambiguous presence of any third identity "between" the self and the Other. We should not conclude, however, that ecstasy constitutes a supreme disclosure (or nakedness) of identity which does not depend on sacrifice, on an exclusion of either the self or the Other. On the contrary, the soliloquy and the flagellation scene function within *Les Plaisirs* to dramatize the perception that one's capacity for ecstasy depends upon one's willingness to pass particular ordeals or tests contained within a sacrificial speech situation. Through solitude and suffering, one "learns" the true conditions of ecstasy, as embodied by the utopian speech situation. In this sense, *Les Plaisirs* offers a *salon* version of the ecstatic ideology of sacrifice which de Sade monumentalized in the clandestine writings that consumed his energies in prison cells.

The Didactic Speech Situation

La Maitresse attempts to "teach" Marton to resist the temptations embedded in pornographic fantasy, but that is not what Marton learns from the punishment. Both she and the spectator "learn" instead that experiences of victimization and punishment strengthen one's determination to know that level of happiness which lies "outside the norm." But the play also makes clear that because ecstasy results from a particular state of consciousness (i.e., a particular use of language which embodies a particular knowledge), it is an experience that one must *learn* to achieve. One learns to achieve ecstasy through conditions of the didactic speech situation, as exemplified by the relationship between Marton and Soeur Agathe. We may say that a *sacrifice* operates to clarify identity through mechanisms of differentiation and subsumption which create a highly polarized relationship between those who command and those who comply.[6]

A *lesson,* on the other hand, implies a transmission of knowledge from one who knows (the teacher) to one who does not (the student). The didactic speech situation resembles the sacrificial speech situation in that both situations entail an unequal distribution of language between bodies. The teacher "owns" language insofar as he or she does most of the talking. But the condition of owning language in order to transmit knowledge works at least to change the identity of the student, so that when the student knows what the teacher knows the relationship between bodies may become very ambiguous and perhaps require redefinition according to another speech situation. The purpose of the lesson is to create a unity of bodies by giving language and knowledge to the student. From this perspective, it is not difficult to suggest that learning intensifies in relation to the degree of erotic feeling exchanged between teacher and student.[7]

In *Les Plaisirs,* the roles of teacher and student are formed in I, ii, when Agathe discovers or "catches" Marton in the act of masturbation. The teacher knows what is meant to be secret, but more importantly, she does not use this knowledge to heighten the difference between herself and the masturbator. She seeks to place her own identity on an equal basis with that of one who, because of the "scandalous" quality of her behavior, is basically under her power:

> Victim, like you, of a cruel constraint,
> I suffer the same torment:

> Victime, comme toi, d'une cruelle gene,
> J'éprouve le même tourment: (167)

But this rhetoric of equality built out of "like"-ness and "same"-ness is a pretext, not for a seduction, but for a lesson, for Agathe does not disguise an ulterior motive behind an apparent one; however, she establishes her authority over Marton, not by equating her lustful motives with Marton's, but by turning their shared motive into a subject for analysis, study, and examination:

> What color! What freshness!
> What dazzling purity!
> Delicate foot, sleek leg and thigh so round;
> Let me parade my impatient gaze
> Upon these ivory globes swollen by love.

Quel coloris! Quelle fraîcheur!
Quelle blancheur éblouissante!
Pied mignon, jambe fine et cuisse faite au tour;
Laissez-moi promener ma vue impatiente
Sur ces globes d'ivoire arrondis par l'amour. (167)

But this contemplative, glamorizing description of Marton's body so excites the speaker that she leaps onto the bed and commands Marton to "embrace your lover." Marton responds with some confusion ("what are you doing? You take me outside myself/que fais-tu? Tu me mets hors de moi," etc.), then attempts a detached description of the effect of a physical action:

Your hand, passing between us both,
Carries fire to every spot.

Ta main, entre nous deux passée,
Porte en tous lieux l'embrasement. (168)

Learning, the process of revising perception, thus manifests itself through an expanding power of description. Orgasm overwhelms the women as a result of a speech by Agathe which mixes instructional commands with metaphorical descriptions of feelings:

Do like me, my dear child,
Hold me in the strong embrace of your knees;
Thrust yourself to me; pressed against my breast
We unite ourselves intimately,
And like a sweet spurt
From the grotto of Cytherea
The source of pleasure gushes abundantly.
Courage . . . Ah! I'm dying.

Fais comme moi, ma chére enfant,
Tiens-moi de tes genoux fortement embrassée;
Elance-toi vers moi; contre mon sein pressée
Unissons-nous étroitement,
Et que par un doux froissement
De la grotte de Cythérée
La source du plaisir jaillisse abondamment.
Courage . . . Ah! je me meurs. (168)

The speaker achieves her identity as the "teacher" through her complex capacity for description. Now, in a general sense, all language may be considered description insofar as it is a "translation" of raw sensations or experiences into words. But we should remember that the business of describing ecstasy or of using descriptions to provoke ecstasy is by no means simple or common in a world which pervasively regards ecstatic experience as something "beyond" the power of language to contain. Thus, the focus here is on defining the categories of description appropriate to the "learning of ecstasy" within the didactic speech situation. And we define a category of description by the formal mechanisms, the rhetorical devices, which construct the relationship between speaker and listener. In this case, perhaps the most obvious rhetorical device is the metaphor. The metaphor operates on the level of the verb, in which pleasures "gush" and the speaker "dies" of the pleasure, on the level of the simile, in which the speaker compares an abstraction (pleasure) to a highly sensuous manifestation ("a sweet spurt"), and on the level of metonym, in which the speaker assigns a mysterious configuration of names ("the grotto of Cytherea") to a problematic identity (vagina). But the metaphors operate in conjunction with a sequence of commands ("Do like me . . . Hold me . . . Thrust yourself . . . Courage . . .") and an analytical, cause-effect statement: "pressed against my breast, we unite ourselves." The ecstatic discharge of language contains only one exclamatory utterance, only one "cry" ("Ah!").

At any rate, the didactic speech situation produces an ecstatic experience when the "teacher" drifts into a kind of extravagance of language, in which, for example, an analytical statement forms the nucleus or pivotal utterance in a speech wherein a sequence of metaphorical types balances out a sequence of commands. Learning results from verbal extravagance, complicated, systematic deployment of rhetorical devices. What the addressee (i.e., Marton) "learns" from this extravagance is that she can trust completely the speaker who uses this particular configuration of rhetorical devices to describe the relationship between herself and her listener. What the spectator "learns" is that the conditions of trust which nourish ecstatic experience depend on highly systematic, mathematically precise rhetorical structures which refer to sensations ("gushes") that are peculiar not merely to the body of the speaker or that of the listener, but to a linguistically-constructed body shared by them both and designated metonymically by the phrase "the grotto of Cytherea." The extravagance of language coincides with a generosity of feeling, a voluptuous giving or offering of flesh; as the speaker advances toward a state of nudity, the more she relies on speech to construct her identity. Considering the theatrical context for this rhetoric, one may say further that the linking of verbal extravagance with an intensifying nudity of speaker and listener dramatizes a condition of ecstasy that is peculiar to an aristocratic perception of the relation between speech and ecstasy. The linking does not conform to that pervasive order of perception in which a state of increasing nudity coincides with a movement toward silence (speechlessness) for both the person becoming nude and the person(s) observing the nudity.[8]

Nudity and Silence in Contemporary Pornography

The silence-nudity link recurs in various forms in both literary and non-literary contexts. It seems that most people can find an abundance of words to describe erotic activity that they have witnessed or imagined, but only when they do not have to confront either their own or someone else's nudity. Such descriptions of erotic activity tend to lack the power to stir anyone to ecstasy. Often in a novel, for example, the author uses many words to describe an erotic act, but the characters created by the author do not use words much to construct the erotic act or even to describe their feelings, which only the author, who indeed may be one of the characters, can articulate at a moment when no one naked is present, as in this example from a pornographic novel first published in Paris in the 1960's:

> He really hadn't enough will power left to close his eyes as she slowly opened her coat and appeared naked to him in the shrine of her fur. Something happened which she hadn't foreseen: A powerful spasm contorted the boy's entire body and the sperm, no longer to be suppressed, showered forth in a high arch. The slowing orgasm lasted quite a while. The pain must have been terrible . . . perhaps the ecstasy was also terrible . . . The come ran on the squeezed penis and into his leather pocket. Finally Gerard lay unconscious.
>
> Then a sweet, somewhat shaky voice said from the platform: "What a body you have, Regine!"[9]

But the same principle applies to more clinical or "scientific" descriptions of ecstatic acts. In the following example, the speaker strives to use a "poetic" language to describe for an interviewer the experience of orgasm, yet she does not indicate that language, poetic or otherwise, has much to do with attaining or intensifying the experience:

> Orgasm: a compelling sensation of light pouring from his head and into mine. I start pouring out light to match. My vision dissolves into brilliance behind his eyes, blinding me: my body dissolves into pure light. I see nothing but light, hear nothing at all, feel nothing that can be named — but every blood cell is dancing and every pore outpouring radiance — and the spiders in the closet and the ants on the floor must be full of joy at receiving the overflow of love.[10]

And even when an author does rely on dialogue to describe an ecstatic scene, the speech entails a lack of semantic and syntactic complexity, in contrast to the language which narrates the scene for the reader or in any case describes that in the scene which no one speaks. In the following example, the author, describing a lesbian fantasy, must rely on dialogue to construct the ecstatic moment, because the moment shared by the speakers results from a telephone conversation. Yet the orgasmic speech seems but a variation of the "animal cry" theory of ecstatic rhetoric. The author tries to hide this discrepancy between speech and narrative by writing in the present tense, but this convention (for describing fantasies) merely indicates that more *can* be said during the ecstatic moment than is said:

> My clit hardens and throbs as my hips thrust it rhythmically against my cupped palm and I slide my middle finger into my slippery slit.
>
> "Oooo — feels so good," I sound like I'm raving with fever as the slurping sounds from Pennsylvania give way to a familiar beat.
>
> "Unh. Unh. Unh." It pounds, at first, slowly, but ever more insistently.
>
> "Unh, unh, unh unhunh unh unh." Is that her or me? Who cares!
>
> "Oh, baby, oh, baby!" Oh, God! Unh uhn uhn." My cunt clenches around my wet fingers as I fuck myself to

the beat. My hips rise off the bed. "Unnnh. Unnnh, I'm cumming!"

The beat goes into diminuendo. "Unnh. Unh. Aaah." Long silence. Who can talk anyway? Who wants to?[11]

Previous to this scene, dialogue of slightly greater complexity occurs, as the speakers use words to construct images of each other over the phone, e.g.,:

"... Gee, my nipples get so hard when I'm cold; they're like diamonds. Ooh, they tingle so."

She whispers, "Aah, let me feel them. Oh, yes, they are very hard. I bet they'd like to be sucked, wouldn't they?"

"Well, um, I think so," I hesitate demurely . . .[12]

These texts, then, which are rather typical for a pornographic rhetoric of ecstasy, link movements toward ecstasy with a decline in the dialogic output of ecstatic bodies. By contrast, ecstatic moments built out of didactic speech situations, as in Agathe's speech to Marton, link the ecstatic moment with the revelation, through speech, of a superior level of consciousness which the speakers dramatize through complex semantic, syntactic, and metrical configurations of language. It is this interest in representing a superior (rather than "simple") identity which marks the *aristocratic* rhetoric of ecstasy. In this case, however, the aristocratic sensibility works to produce a congruence, with speech as the signifier of congruence, of "enlightenment" and ecstasy, so that the orgasmic rapture resulting from a congruence of *bodies* involves the production of a "lesson," as Agathe herself remarks, *as* (not after) Marton sinks into orgasm: "Comment trouves-tu ma premier lecon?/How do you like my first lesson?" (168)

The Lesson as Pornographic Performance

The ecstatic "lesson" generated by the didactic speech situation requires the "teacher" to do most of the talking. The "student's" ecstasy results from listening intently. Agathe's lessons take the form of speechblocks usually running 16 or 17 lines long, but reaching up to 30 (169) or even 48 (183-184) lines in length. Marton, however, never has a speech-block greater than six lines (179) in any of her lessons with Agathe. We have already discussed rhetorical devices used in one lesson, but Agathe relies on other devices to perfect her instruction, and these include two types of narrative. In the first type, the speaker instructs and excites her listener by constructing a description of a hypothetical erotic encounter. She describes, in present tense, the actions and feelings of a hypothetical pair of lovers in a clinical manner, as if giving a lecture on some natural phenomenon rather than on what for almost any classroom is a taboo subject for discourse. This type of narrative is closer to theoretical explication than to the sort of fantasy described in Hite and Stonewall above and suggests that theoretical language has a greater aphrodisiac or pornographic effect upon the listener than the language of erotic fantasy:

> His finger, guided by desire,
> Descends lower and insinuates itself
> Into the secret cave of pleasure.
> In the same instant, the aroused girl
> Throbs with a sweet shudder.
> She defends herself lamely:
> The gallant changes posture,
> And aiming his conquering shaft,
> He forces the narrow opening [. . .]

> Son doigt, guidé par le désir,
> Descend plus bas et s'insinue
> Dans l'antre secret du plaisir.
> Au même instant la fille emue
> Eprouve un doux frémissement.
> Elle se défend mollement:
> Le galant change de posture,
> Et dirigeant son trait vainquer,
> Il force l'étroite ouverture [. . .] (169)

The pornographic charm of this type of narrative derives from descriptions of happy activities that do not refer directly either to the speaker or the listener or anyone in particular, real or imaginary. Instead, we have the abstract theoretical categories of the "jeune homme vigoreux" and "la belle," and these function, as products of the didactic language, to establish the anonymous universality of those actions which lead to erotic ecstasy. By contrast, erotic *fantasies* attempt to describe actions which are peculiar to particular persons and which, by their imaginary status, purport to be actions which no one has yet performed. They present themselves as new actions, free of any claim to universality. But that is the problem with fantasies: one cannot repeat them without undermining their power to excite. Fantasies are disposable; theoretical statements, appearing in lectures, may be spoken and heard repeatedly because of the assumption governing the speech situation that the description of new actions is less interesting than the *learning,* the revision of perception, that invariably occurs whenever a speaker ascribes a universal status to an action. It is not the strangeness of the actions described by Agathe that excites the listener, but the strangeness of the description itself, in which she does not merely translate new sensations into words, as the fantasist does — she "instructs" the listener to perceive ecstasy as the result of actions that occur again and again, everywhere, anonymously, rather than for the first time.

Yet the effectiveness of the theoretical narrative remains questionable, for Agathe relies on it only once, in her first scene with Marton. In II, vi, she teaches chiefly through the use of what we might call a historical narrative. This narrative is much longer than the theoretical narrative, but though she breaks it up into different speeches or "scenes," she only needs a single such narrative to "instruct" her student effectively. She describes, in past tense, an erotic experience in her life and elaborates on those feelings which, presumably, she can repeat through her liaison with Marton, her listener. Again, ecstasy does not result from describing something imagined, but from events preserved in memory. The narrative is new insofar as no one has spoken or heard it, but what it describes belongs to the realm of recurrent experience.

The speaker describes an erotic adventure which happened to her when she was fifteen. At the urging of her pious mother, a priest attempted to "punish" Agathe's "impure flesh" in the "secret chapel" of a monastery, using a sadomasochistic flagellation technique similar to that employed by the La Maitresse on Marton in scene ii of the same act. But then the priest changed the nature of "pious operation/la pieuse operation" by urging Agathe to "suffer with devotion/souffir avec devotion" as he proceeded to copulate with her. Yet in spite of her eagerness to obey him completely, the priest disclosed that his "vigor" was unable to respond to his desires (185) (indicating, again, the failure of sadomasochistic practices to induce ecstasy in those who select them as mechanisms for asserting power). He therefore invited "three vigorous young monks/trois jeune moins vigoreux" to consummate the "punishment." An orgy ensued, in which Agathe offered herself equally to the four men. However, the priest, jealous of his rights, abducted her, and afterwards she enjoyed a daily interlude exclusively with him ("Je passait avec lui deux heures chaque jour," 188). Unfortunately, this adventure came to an end when her brother persuaded her mother to have her placed in a convent, which she regards as simply another link in a "cruel chaîn/chaine cruelle" (189).

Though it may strike the reader as a projection of a male fantasy rather than a convincing example of an adolescent girl's initiation into heterosexual eroticism, this story nevertheless appears as a set of historical statements which derive their interest from the conditions the *author* associates with the recounting rather than the imagining of erotic ecstasies. For one thing, the speaker never links the historical narrative with any very precise description of physical actions. She concentrates on an analysis of feelings in response to generalized actions, and the analysis may even achieve a kind of symmetrical rhetorical balance:

> He inundated, he penetrated, he consumed my soul [. . .]
> I flamed, I shuddered, I sank . . . I swooned.

> Il inonde, il pénétre, il embrase mon âme [. . .]
> Je brûle, je frémis, je tombe . . . je me pâme. (186)

But the *image* of erotic ecstasy never becomes more detailed than these phrases in which the description of actions is synonymous with the description of emotional states. The speaker does not prepare her listener for the erotic encounters they plan by giving detailed instructions concerning the most effective movements between bodies. Consequently, neither the listener nor the spectator receives a clear view of what we might call the physics of ecstatic erotic activity. The description of the speaker's flagellation, for example, requires only four lines:

> My body nude down to the waist,
> I prostrated myself at his knees:
> In an instant I felt the storm fall on my back;
> I endured it with courage.

> Le corps nu jusqu'à la ceinture,
> Je me prosterne à ses genoux:
> Sur mon dos à l'instant je sens tomber l'orage;
> Je le support avec courage. (184)

The nakedness of bodies is never the subject of serious analysis. Genitals are "warm and steamy/chaud et fumant" (185), but so, too, is the temperament of the speaker (183). At one point, Father Andre "arranged her as he pleased" ("il m'arrange à sa guise," 187), but we have no idea what this pleasurable arrangement was. A little earlier, Agathe had "kissed devotedly/baise dévotement" (186) the priest's penis, which presented itself to her view as "a rope of great knots" ("D'une corde à gros noeuds qu'il présente à ma vue"). But this act of devotion is worthy of mention because it caused the priest to smile, not because it differentiated the object of devotion from others presented to the speaker's view. Thus, the emotions described in the narrative do not arise from the speaker's consciousness of specific differences between the bodies and "views" linked to ecstatic experience; they arise from an *aggregate* of bodies and actions which are presumably interchangeable. The narrative indicates that no one man can satisfy the speaker's capacity for ecstasy. Orgiastic emotions ensue from actions that are not peculiar to any particular identity; rather, it is the amplification through repetition of very generalized erotic actions which produces orgiastic ecstasy. And for this reason, the historical narrative, though it purports to describe actual actions performed by the speaker, does not differ much from the theoretical narrative in representing the relation between action and ecstatic feeling.

The description of the speaker's emotions relies heavily on metaphorical rhetoric. It is, however, the use of metaphors which obfuscates the image or physics of erotic activity. The metaphor objectifies the speaker's attitude toward an object or identity, but it does not constitute an analysis of the object. Rather than clarifying the relation between motive, action, and emotion, the metaphor merely internalizes action as emotion. Indeed, we may even say that metaphor functions as a kind of euphemism which neutralizes, not only the disillusioning impact of a more clinical or obscene vocabulary, but the failure of the (erotic) phenomena observed and generalized by the speaker to manifest pronounced aesthetic differences.

Thus, Agathe describes semen as "l'amoureuse liqueur" or "l'amoureux nectar" (187). She refers to the phallus as "sainte corde" — which vaguely links that organ with a condition of bondage — and speaks elsewhere of "torrents de flamme" and "brulante soupirs" ("burning sighs") (185). At the moment of defloration, she felt "pierced by a great dowel" ("Je me sentis percée/D'une grosse cheville [. . .] (186), but quickly enjoyed an "amorous drunkenness/amoureuse ivresse" (186). Men "conquered" her body and "marched easily" down the "road" to pleasure ("Dans sa conquête il rentre en conquêrant/Et parcourt d'une marche aisée/Des plaisirs la route embrassée.") (187).

However, when she describes emotional responses to general situations rather than specific actions, her language becomes more direct and less metaphorical:

My young heart palpitated, and my ardent soul [. . .]
Mon jeune coeur palpite, et mon âme embrassée [. . .] (183)

The laws he prescribed for me I obeyed without murmur.
Aux lois qu'il me prescrit j'obéis sans murmur; (184)

As I felt myself pressed between their nervous arms.
Que je me sens pressée entre leurs bras nerveux. (185)

At the same time, the pain ceased;
Au même instant la douleur cesse; (186)

I avidly seized [his penis]
Je me saisis avidement [. . .] (186)

Under him I throbbed voluptuously,
Je m'agite sous lui voluptueusement, (187)

Why this oddball had just what I needed!
Que ce drôle était bien mon fait! (187)

In the context of a situation which the euphemistic properties of metaphorical language have helped to designate as perverse, utterances such as these amplify the pornographic impact of the narrative as a whole by disclosing the speaker's fearlessness of her own vulnerability, so that ecstatic nakedness appears to have less to do with the image of bodily nudity than with the nakedness of identity produced by the language which describes feelings in response to nudity.

Of course, this pornographic rhetoric of fearlessness intensifies the listener's trust in the speaker, for the speaker would not disclose these perverse feelings if she herself did not place a great deal of trust in her listener, in whom she *confides,* so to speak, the secret of achieving an ecstatic state of fearlessness. That the narrative is pornographic at least to the addressee is evident from little commentaries with which Marton punctuates Agathe's speeches:

Stop, Agathe, spare me;
At this moment I am as weak as you.

Arrête, Agathe, épargne-moi;
Je suis en ce moment aussi faible que toi. (186)

Heavens! what transports! what delights!
Just the story alone inflames me and sets me beside myself.

Ciel! quels transports! quelles délices!
Le seul récit m'enflamme et me met hors de moi. (188)

The pornographic effect of the narrative depends on the speaking of the rhetorical devices, not on the writing or reading of them. (To grasp this point further, try speaking the lines aloud; the lines will not *look* so banal!) Indeed, the speaker herself discloses the aphrodisiac effect of speech by embellishing her narrative with quotations of speech. The aphrodisiac effect results, not because the speaker and those she quotes voice taboo statements, but because the quotes, when voiced, render naked those emotions, in herself or in others, which excite her and her addressee:

"I'm going, he said, into the monastery
To find some friends; it is in their arms, my dear,
That you will have a taste of solid pleasures."

"Je vais, dit-il, au monastère
Chercher quelques amis; c'est dans leurs bras, ma chère,
Que vous allez goûter de solides plaisirs." (185)

— Ah! I said, at this moment, Father,
I feel more than ever that it is necessary.
it = "an application of saint cordon [chastity belt]"

— Ah! dis-je, en ce moment, mon père,
Je sens plus que jamais qu'elle m'est nécessaire. (187)
elle = "une application du saint cordon"

But neither of these examples of quoted speech, in themselves, constitute ecstatic speech. The quoted speech represents other states, such as consent or avidity, connected with the multiplication or magnification of the phallus as the "solid pleasures" of several men or as a "necessity" for the female speaker. Yet the narrative which contains these quotations is ecstatic because what excites the speaker is her power to describe conditions in which people are free to speak their perverse desires with an almost banal casualness. And it is this casualness and freedom to reveal (through speech) emotional states that the text associates with conditions of ecstatic experience. The teacher-student relationship between Agathe and Marton contrasts dramatically with the mother-daughter relationships alluded to in the narrative and symbolized in the flagellation scene between La Maitresse and Marton. The instructional narrative given by Agathe supplants the commanding instructions given by mother figures (La Maitresse, Agathe's mother in the historical narrative). Put more theoretically, the didactic speech situation appears as a travesty of the sacrifical speech situation insofar as the oppressive sacrifices and "punishments" inflicted by religious authority result from the anti-ecstatic instructions and sentiments issuing from mother figures. The ecstatic historical narrative, given by the "teacher" figure, functions as a kind of pornographic parody of ritual actions such as confession, offering, and worship of "mysterious" emblems (the phallus). In this sense, "enlightenment" means a parodying, indeed a pornographication, of the sacred.

The Utopian Speech Situation

The purpose of the sacrificial speech situation is to establish the power or identity of a speaker at the expense of another speaker. As embodied by La Maitresse, power not only means an organization of language to deny access to ecstatic experience; it is the assertion of identity in the absence of any belief in the possibility of ecstasy. The rhetoric of the sacrificial speech situation involves a complex use of commands, rhythmic (quantitatively valued) interweaving of dominant and submissive voices, and the presence of a silent third person, whose feelings are divided between the dominant and submissive figures but who has no "voice," no power to intervene in the polarized dialogue. The didactic speech situation seeks to teach the possibility of what the sacrificial speech situation denies. The distribution of language is also unequal, but the "teacher" employs a rhetoric which amplifies the trust of the "student." This trust allows the identity of the student to become dynamic: the student "learns," and the unity of consciousness shared by teacher and student enables the didactic speech situation to evolve into an ecstatic or utopian speech situation. The rhetoric of teaching consists primarily of descriptions of feelings and actions (not bodies or motives), which assume their most complete form as theoretical or historical (not fictitious or fantasy) narratives.

The third act of *Les Plaisirs du cloître* presents a utopian speech situation. The fifteen-page act introduces two men, Le Jesuite and Clitandre, who secretly appear in Marton's room in response to Agathe's intrigues. Nearly the entire act dramatizes the orgy enjoyed by Marton and Agathe, who switch partners and thus understand better each other's capacity for pleasure. Theatrical performance of the text requires rather explicit representation of several erotic actions, yet verse dialogue is continuous. Indeed, the text here is a rare example of an attempt to represent a sex orgy through an abundance of talk, an elaborate interplay of voices. The norm for representing orgiastic speech, if in fact a norm exists for representing this phenomenon, is perhaps a sort of choral hysteria, such as those described at the end of Chapter One. In *Les Plaisirs du cloître,* however, the abundant dialogue constructs the perception that erotic orgy indicates, not the end of a decadent society, but the beginning of an "enlightened" and extravagantly polite civilization. The play ends with Agathe and Marton preparing for early morning prayers as their lovers depart: in other words, orgy functions as the complement rather than antithesis of a life governed by religious pressures.

Orgy as a Mathematical Abstraction of Speakers

As constituted in the third act, the utopian speech situation entails a nearly equal, almost symmetrical, distribution of language between the speakers. Language, as a source of power, feeling, or consciousness is not concentrated in or "owned" by a dominant speaker. The text dramatizes the state of fearlessness attached to ecstatic experience by allowing speakers to say what they feel about the "scene" with a regularity of exchange which avoids positioning their statements within a hierarchy of speakers. But this economy of discourse does not mean that the *rhetoric* of the utopian speech situation lacks commands, questions, analytical descriptions, and other rhetorical devices associated with sacrificial and didactic speech situations. It is the case, rather, that rhetorical devices do not "belong" to any particular speaker, with the result that no particular speaker functions as the dominant source of power, feeling, learning, or consciousness.

This vaguely promiscuous distribution of rhetoric undermines the production of "characters," highly individuated speakers. The difference, as a textual construction, between Le Jesuite and Clitandre is not great, and after Agathe and Marton have enjoyed erotic interludes with these men, the difference between the two women, rather pronounced in the first two acts, appears very minor as far as the language that constructs them. In one sense, the utopian speech situation produces an anonymity or abstraction of identity; in another sense, this abstraction implies a repetition of identity, which generates a set of equations:

$$\text{ecstasy} = \text{orgy}$$

$$\text{orgy} = \text{abstraction of identity}$$

$$\text{abstraction of identity} = 2F + 2M = \frac{A+M}{2} + \frac{J+C}{2}$$

$$or: 2F + 2M = \frac{R}{4}$$

where F = female speaker; M = male speaker; A = Agathe; Ma = Marton; J = Le Jesuite; C = Clitandre; and R = the set of all rhetorical devices employed by A, Ma, J, and C. Language is the equalizer. And here the anonymity of the author is significant insofar as the language of the text apparently does not need an "author" — i.e., someone for whom the text is a signifier of the self. The three inter-related speech situations constructed by the text are the product, not of an "author," but of a consciousness permeating language itself, implying that ecstasy derives from language mechanisms shared by speakers and listeners rather than from mechanisms which differentiate speakers and listeners. But these statements apply only to the language of the text. In theatrical performance, of course, acute differentiation of the speakers develops through variations in voice production, gesture, physique, costume, complexion, and comportment. It is therefore these "performed," rather than inscribed, differences that awaken desire for the orgiastic unity provided by language.

Though the utopian speech situation avoids constructing a hierarchy of values or speakers, it nevertheless involves, as the set of equations indicates, a quantification of relations between speakers. The sacrificial and didactic speech situations quantify relations between speakers in terms of *more or less* amounts of speech distributed between them: the "mistress" or the "teacher" has "more" language than the "victim" or "student." Their words are "greater" in that they compel the listener to listen rather than speak. The utopian speech situation quantifies relations between speakers by creating *new combinations* of speakers. Thus, in the third act, dialogues form according to the following combinations or sets of speakers:

$$D = A, M, J, C \quad (191\text{-}195; \ 197\text{-}200; \ 201\text{-}204)$$

$$D = A, M \quad (190\text{-}191)$$

$D = M, J$ (196-197)

$D = A, J, C$ (200-201)

$D = M, C$ (191-192)

$D = J, C$ (200-201)

$D = A, C$ (197-198)

$D = A, J$ (192-193)

where D = a set of dialogue speakers/listeners and M = Marton. The text embeds some sets in others to complicate the combinatory process; this embedding occurs when a speaker directs words to a particular listener but feels excitement because someone else is listening as well. However, the scene excludes the set $D = M, J, C$, perhaps to indicate that the difference between Marton and Agathe remains one of "more or less." Although the women switch partners, the scene never presents Marton alone with the two men. She *alternates* between men, whereas, in scene v, the possibility emerges that Agathe's capacity for erotic rapture is such that she can enjoy a *simultaneity* of men. No one man is capable of satisfying the erotic appetite of either woman, but the A, J, C set of dialogic relations presents Agathe, the "teacher" figure and chief negotiator or ambassador for the orgiastic situation, as the woman who intervenes between men, yet binds them more closely to each other.

A, J, C is a curious triangle of speakers. The dialogue set begins with a homosexual connection between the men, as Le Jesuite "attacks Clitandre from the rear/attaquant Clitandre par derriere" (200). *During* the act, Le Jesuite speaks of his inability to "defend himself" against an "Italian taste/goût italien," which the sight of Clitandre's "joli postérieur" awakens in him. *After* the act, Clitandre, with rather debonair courtesy, quaintly "excuses" Le Jesuite for his "Jesuitical habit/l'habit jésuitical," and asks how it is that when the opposite sex is available to satisfy all wishes, he enjoys the "disgraceful business/commerce honteux" of pederasty. Le Jesuit then delivers a brief speech in which he refers to famous homosexual pairs in myth and history (Hylas and Hercules, Alcibiades and Phaedo, Jupiter and Ganymede, Caesar and Nicomedes, etc.) to assert that his pederastic "taste is not at all ridiculous/ce goût n'est point si ridicule." All of this activity takes place in the presence of Agathe, to whom neither man speaks during the dialogue set and who remains silent until the end of Le Jesuit's speech on the transnational, transhistorical nature of homosexuality, at which point she inserts herself between the men with a little speech of her own condemning "this impious sect/cette secte impie," which only "excites" her wrath ("Ne peut qu'exciter mon courroux"), for to "outrage nature/outrager la nature" is in her eyes "the greatest of crimes/le plus grand des forfaits." The subset J, C of A, J, C seems to entail one of two functions:

[1] the identity of A in the utopian speech situation is such that J and C may pursue without fear a notion of ecstasy which excludes A — i.e., the homosexual rapture depends on *displaying to* A an indifference toward her, so that A appears as a superfluous identity, in which case, we actually no longer have a utopian speech situation: J and C together constitute "more" or "greater" identity than A, who becomes the silent third figure in a parody of the flagellation scene. Agathe's speech, however, undermines this function of the dialogue set.

[2] for J and C, the display of homosexual ecstasy is a strategy for exciting A, who is witness to the fact that her power to give ecstasy does not reside exclusively in either her body or her sex; it resides in both sexes simultaneously. The female body is not necessarily the signifier of this power to make the phallus a signifier of ecstasy; the phallus responds to that which magnifies or multiplies it, including actions which reveal the homosexual power of the phallus to transform maleness into femaleness. The spectacle of homosexuality exerts pressure on the female witness to be "more" open to the phallus than her previous encounters with it have allowed. The spectacle urges her to intervene between the men and become the source of simultaneous ecstasies in both of them. It is this simultaneity of ecstasy in different bodies with regard to the body of the ("excluded") Other which determines the orgiastic condition of ecstasy. Agathe does intervene, but the spectacle excites her "wrath" rather than her senses. Yet this "outrage" on her part does not necessarily mean that the strategy has failed. Marton then conveniently reenters to form a different dialogue set with a different theme.

[1] contradicts [2]; thus, A, J, C does not operate to synthesize the ecstatic drives or functions defining J + C and A. Rather, the subset J, C functions (as J + C) to reveal an incomplete set of ecstatic speakers, in relation to which A is simultaneously present yet excluded from appearing as an operand. More precisely, A intervenes, even when she remains

silent, between J and C to function as an operator; she is, in effect, the +
in J + C = orgy = JAC, which is in contrast to the *linear sequence* of speakers
(dialogue turns) as unfolded by the text (i.e., J, C, J, A). The main
implication of all this logic is that the utopian speech situation operates
entirely upon a heterosexual field of relations. Completely homosexual or
phallic ecstasy is virtually a mathematical impossibility within a system of
language distribution which seeks to prevent any subset of speakers from
achieving "more" or "greater" speech than another subset within a
dialogue set. In scene iv of Act II (180-182), Marton and Agathe engage
in homosexual actions, and the language they use to construct their
ecstasy is fairly evenly distributed between them, a fundamental condition for the utopian speech situation. But the ecstasy pursued by M, A is
as incomplete as that pursued by J, C, for the homosexuality of M + A is
understood by the operands as merely a preparation or rehearsal for the
orgy AJMC. In this case, the operator (J or C) is absent from the scene,
but not from language. Moreover, the gratuitous, pornographic representation of M + A suggests the existence of another operator who is also
absent from the scene but who in a sense stands in for J or C and without
whom the theatricalized ecstasy of M + A is impossible, namely the (male)
spectator (S). The (silent) spectator intervenes between M, A insofar as
the ecstasy of M + A depends on a theatrical context. We then have M +
A = MSA, although of course this equation expands the concept of
dialogue set to include identities outside of the representation.

At any rate, the text seems troubled by the logic which governs it. If
ecstasy depends on a larger set of identities than the couple and on
continuously shifting combinations of identities within the larger set,
then homosexuality will eventually constitute a new combination. But
this new combination threatens to produce a sacrificial speech situation,
in which subsets dominate dialogue sets. The text therefore attempts to
transform excluded operands into intervening operators. The fact that
Marton reenters so abruptly and conveniently indicates that the JAC orgy
combination is not a satisfying resolution of the problem created by
homosexual subsets. The only way out of the anti-utopian pressure
exerted by the (phallic) subset is to place constraints on the number of new
combinations of identities. But the only constraint perceived by the text
is to expand the number of identities in the dialogue set: Marton simply
reappears to announce that the bell-clock has struck and all ecstasies must
come to an end. Time itself functions as a quantitative constraint on the
number of new combinations that make for orgiastic ecstasy.

The process by which orgiastic ecstasy results from new combinations of identity extends also to the mathematical organization of the language itself. The speakers employ complicated rhymed verse forms which shift patterns within and between speakers. In the field of rhyme schemes, the text presents a highly unstable trajectory of shifts from one pattern of line-endings to another. These patterns include: aabb; abab; aaaa; aabab; abba; ababcbcacac. Clitandre concludes the play with a speech which contains the following rhyme scheme: ababcbcbcbddbebeb. The b sound (té) predominates to produce a kind of tonal center for the speech, but the significance of this dominance is obscure. Perhaps it merely dramatizes a state of exhaustion, "excess," (or just plain dullness), a condition of overdependence on a sound which one can append to a very large number of words (e.g., cupidité, liberté, fausseté, volupté, etc.) and thus perpetuate, albeit rather facilely, the ideology of new combinations. But the important thing about the rhyme schemes is that they persistently avoid the symmetry of the alexandrine (aabb), and this lack of symmetry is peculiar in a speech situation which strives to create symmetry in the distribution of language between speakers. In other words, the distribution of tonal values *within the language* does not reinforce the distribution of language *between speakers*. An axiom for orgiastic dialogue results: the symmetrical distribution of language between speakers does not inhibit the production of complex, asymmetrical tonal structures within the language. Yet the language always remains rhymed verse, suggesting that ecstatic speech is inescapably a mode of poetic language, an intricate, highly self-conscious musical structure which no one will mistake for a burst of "spontaneity."

A similar condition of asymmetry prevails in relation to line lengths. Between and within speeches, line lengths shift to construct variable rhythmic combinations which operate in conjunction with the variable tonal schemes. Line lengths may contain six, seven, eight, eleven, or twelve syllables, but eight and twelve beat lines predominate, probably because these lengths allow for a sufficiently diverse vocabulary while at the same time they assure the musicality of the language. But the shift from one length to another seems rather arbitrary: an eight beat line may rhyme with a twelve beat line and vice versa. A speaker may continue the meter adopted by the previous speaker or shift to another meter. The speakers shift meters capriciously within speeches. For example:

SOEUR AGATHE *apercevant Marton a cheval sur le Pere*
Ah! Ah! la drôle invention!
En courant de la sorte, aimable postillon
On arrive bientôt au gîte.

LE JESUITE
Ma nonne, il vous sied bien de parler sur ce ton.
Je me venge de votre fuite.

MARTON
Je te fais, cher Clitandre, une infidélité;
Faillait-il me laisser seule avec un Jesuite?
Va, va, tu l'as bien mérité.

CLITANDRE
Oublions chacun notre injure,
Et pour réveiller nos désirs,
Par une nouvelle posture
Diversifions nos plaisirs.
[. . .]   (197)

Shifts in line length do not depend on peculiar semantic objectives attached to the relationship between words and sentiments. Rather, the shifts dramatize the impulse of the speaker to accept or modify the rhythm of the previous speaker. Shifts within speeches have the effect of representing a state of erotic excitement as an internal dialogue between a rhythm and a counter-rhythm which dramatizes an ambivalent attitude toward time, insofar as the rhythm and the counter-rhythm constitute a protracting or contracting of that time which is constructed in a vertical sense by tonal patterns. Orgiastic ecstasy is a horizontal and vertical convolution of time, a complex configuration of rhythms circulating within and between speakers, and only speech of a distinctly artificial character can signify this convolution and configuration.

Further complication of the horizontal and vertical rhythms results from variations in syllabic stress appointed to lines. Speakers shift from iambic:

Du trésor qu'on livre à mes feux (196)

to anapestic:

Dans la bouche de sa maîtresse (169)

to trochaic:

> Rendez-vous aux désirs de l'amant le plus tendre. (191)

with iambic meter heavily favored by all speakers. Moreover, spondaic and pyrrhic shifts within these meters add to the difficulty of constructing any set of "correspondences" between rhythmic structures and highly specific formations of meaning.

Ralph Gordon remarks that "the meter is the perfect pattern, the rhythm the poet's variation upon it."[13] In other words, the meaning of the language is embedded in variation rather than unity of rhythm; and the variation in speech rhythms of the play "corresponds" to the deviation, on the part of speakers, from norms of erotic activity as well as from norms of "natural" speech. But the variations are so convoluted that speech deviates from *poetic* norms which produce a more pronounced connection between words and music. The text is clearly poetic in its determination to produce an intricately structured web of voices, yet the language is not distinctly *lyrical.* The voices generated by the text simply have no interest as highly subjectified externalizations of the "world" of the speaker's self. This language of orgiastic ecstasy is neither a choral fusion of a mass voice nor a collection of exquisite, hyper-lyrical, metaphor-laden voices blooming together like gorgeous hot flowers. The poetry of orgiastic language is too abstract, too depersonalized, and at the same time, too convoluted (perhaps too theoretical) to assume a lyric mode.

All the observations concerning the verse of the utopian speech situation apply also to the verse of the sacrificial and didactic speech situations. The utopian speech situation does not entail any new verse forms, any new rhythmic patterns developed exclusively by orgiastic speakers. But the lack of poetic invention within the orgiastic context does not lessen the significance of the rhythmic attributes ascribed to the language. What is new in the utopian speech situation is the (symmetrical) combinations of speakers, the distribution of language, not combinations of words. The utopian speech situation cannot exist independently of the sacrificial and didactic speech situations, for the text perceives orgy as a phenomenon "outside the norms" represented by those other speech situations; orgy is not the formation of a norm which supersedes the sacrificial and didactic norms; orgy is the "learned" result of what those norms "teach." Verse patterns are what bind the three speech situations together. Because orgy entails enhanced abstraction of speaker identity, not enhanced particularization, the representation of this abstraction can emerge through the use of verse patterns common to all speech situations, but not common to "nature" (i.e., common to the speech of "real" persons). Orgy is not possible without a language which facilitates free exchange of bodies and identities, a language containing values (rhythms) symmetrically shared by all participants.

Of course, the implication of this mode of abstraction is that ecstasy resides *in language*, not in the self, not in the speaker, not in some "translation" into words of an intensely unique perception of the Other. As a result, orgiastic speech appears less lyrical, less cryptic, less "mysterious" than we might suppose (or wish), and yet it also appears more complex, more deceptive, and more "difficult" than either lyrical or theoretical language can claim to be, for it is rare indeed that one encounters language like this text which awakens in the spectator such a powerfully ambivalent and uncertain attitude toward the *mechanisms* by which people can experience ecstasy. Nearly everyone fears the abstraction of his or her own identity, and yet the formal pressures on the language of the text indicate, tacitly, that it is this fear of abstraction, not the fear of censure or the "norm," which is the dominant obstacle to ecstasy.

Abstraction of identity also results from the failure of the utopian speech situation to produce any new rhetorical devices, either. Indeed, what is perhaps most remarkable about this speech situation is the paucity of rhetorical devices needed to sustain it. Hypothetical and historical narratives are completely absent, and so is the stichomythic interweaving of voices. Commands crop up fairly often:

Yield to your desires for your most tender lover
Rendez-vous aux désirs de l'amant le plus tendre (190)

Come, dear girl, unveil without scruple
Venez, aimable enfant, dévoilez sans scruple (197)

Let's punish this faithless couple
Punissons ce couple infidèle (196)

Banish these odious suspicions
Bannis ces soupçons odieux (194)

Soothe my torment
Soulage mon tourment (194)

Let's put this project into practice
Mettons ce projet en pratique (198)

But these are "weak" commands insofar as they signify a sense of urgency or heightened invitation on the part of the speaker rather than a compulsion to act exerted upon the listener. In a context of symmetrically distributed language, commands such as these assume an ironic quality, as pressures to actions which the listener wishes to perform but for which he/she does not want to take full responsibility. The command abstracts an action without naming the desire that motivates it, and thus, "ironically," frees both speaker and listener from fearing each other's desires.

Similarly, speakers make only subdued use of metaphor. Some metaphors are banal to the point of being cliches: "temple of pleasures/temple de plaisirs" (194), "I taste the supreme happiness/Je goûte le bonheur suprême"(199), "love's labyrinth/le labyrinthe amoureux" (196), "love's nectar/le nectar amoureux" (199). Speakers frequently compare kisses and hearts to flames and fire. At one point, a pair of lovers eats and drinks while another pair makes love, which dramatizes a parallel between sex and hunger drives but does not mean that one activity is a metaphor for the other. In any case, it is extremely rare for a speaker to produce a metaphor of any distinction:

> Ah! what abundance of dew
> Inundates my secret charms [vagina].

> Ah! quelle abondante rosée
> Inonde mes secret appas. (198)

But even here, the metaphor seems diluted by idiomatic expression and a not especially exaggerated descriptive function of the language. Why is metaphor so weak in the orgiastic context? Metaphor reveals a *hidden relation* between one identity and another. However, the orgiast regards orgy as a condition devoid of any hidden relation, a state of supreme nakedness and trust between *like-minded* participants. Under these circumstances, metaphor can only reveal banal, clichéd relations between otherwise discrete identities. Orgy is not a metaphor for utopia; it *is* utopia. Metaphor is appropriate for an environment in which the "real" meaning of relations between identities remains hidden, sublimated, repressed. In a sense, then, utopia is where one has no need to speak with metaphors.

The chief rhetorical device of the utopian speech situation is the description of speaker feelings and moods. Since for the most part the speakers talk about what they are feeling at the moment, the language remains steadily in present tense. Except for Le Jesuite's speech on mythic and historical homosexual pairs, no one refers to the past or slips into past tense. What interests the orgiast is the *immediate* connection between words, actions, and emotions. Speech is the mediator between actions and emotions. Speech does not describe (erotic) actions, it provokes them. But it provokes action by describing the object of action, which is an emotional state (ecstasy). Orgiastic dialogue consists of the fragmentation of a communal ecstatic feeling into a convoluted set of variable rhythms, shifting tonal patterns, and words which signify a cluster of emotions subsidiary to the dominant emotion of ecstasy. The representation of subsidiary emotions often involves a convolution of rhetorical devices:

Apprehension (question combined with metaphor and imploration):
> In what abyss, Agathe, o heaven! have you conducted me?
> Dans quel abîme, Agathe, ô ciel! m'as-tu conduit? (191)

Courtly admiration (command linked to naming of listener qualities):
> Let me contemplate the whiteness, the elasticity,
> the freshness of your body.
> Laisse-moi de ton corps contempler la blancheur,
> L'élasticité, la fraîcheur. (192)

Exhilaration ("softness" in tension with "penetration"):
> I feel a soft warmth,
> Which penetrates me to the heart.
> Je sens une douce chaleur,
> Qui me pénètre jusqu'au coeur. (193)

Intimation   (naming the listener's perception of the speaker):
> Beautiful Agathe, you know your power over me;
> Belle Agathe, sur moi tu connais ton pouvoir; (195)

Tenderness (progression of prepositional states — "on," "with," "to"):
> Mounted on this bed with me,
> I abandon myself entirely to you.
> Monté sur ce lit avec moi,
> Je m'abandonne toute à toi. (194)

Of course, we could extend this list considerably to include every line in the text and thus chart the categories and patterns of emotion which precede and produce the utopian speech situation. Such a chart is beyond the scope of this analysis, since it requires a theory of relations between rhetorical devices and emotional states which no one, certainly not myself, is yet able to provide. Moreover, the emotional texture of the language is complicated by the phenomenon of irony, when a speaker intends a meaning besides the one grasped by the addressee, or when the listener reads a meaning in a statement to which the speaker remains "blind." Irony derives completely from the context of a statement, but defining the context of an ironic statement is often an exasperating task. Mildly ironic statements occur in the text when Marton professes, early in the scene, to feel disgust at the debauchery she obviously enjoys in front of the others or when she produces a false sense of regret for the loss of her innocence:

> Farewell virtue, wisdom, honor,
> One instant has sullied my glory and my modesty.

> Adieu vertu, sagesse, honneur,
> Un instant a souillé ma gloire et ma pudeur. (194)

What is ironic, if anything, about this statement is that it has no power to elicit sympathy for the speaker's sense of loss; on the contrary, it makes her seem more available to lust than ever. I say a statement such as this one is "mildly ironic" because one should never assume that irony implies a false or insincere statement. Good actors can give an ironic tone to almost any statement; thus, the whole of the last act might be played ironically if the actors conveyed, through their voices, that they do not enjoy themselves as the text obviously intends the characters to do. In general, though, the speakers do not rely much at all on ironic statements to sustain their enjoyment.

Ironic statement is as subdued as metaphor in the utopian speech situation, for, like metaphor, irony thrives in an atmosphere of constraint and repression, where one cannot say exactly or entirely what one means or where, in any case, the ambiguity of a statement prevents the speaker and the addressee from treating the statement as a mutually shared piece of consciousness. And yet the context for the orgiastic dialogue *is* ironic, hugely ironic: an orgy in a convent, pornographic abstraction of identity as the manifestation of "nature," feelings of power that do not depend on any significant act of sacrifice, such as choosing one sex partner over another — these are all ironic *conditions* for orgiastic speech. The text itself discloses the ironic foundation of the utopian speech situation when

Clitandre concludes the play by saying (without irony) that only through a cloistered life can one know the reality of carnal ecstasy:

> In the world, love is a dull slavery.
> Feelings and language
> All breathe fraud and infidelity.
> The modesty of woman is a hypocritical mask;
> In her sweetest transports reigns a falseness.
> It is in the cloister alone that there lives
> The true voluptuousness.

> Dans le monde, l'amour est un rude esclavage,
> Les sentiments et le langage,
> Tout respire la fraude et l'infidélité.
> La pudeur d'une femme est une masque hypocrite;
> Dans ses plus doux transports regne la fausseté.
> C'est dans le cloître seul qu'habite
> La véritable volupté. (204)

We have, then, a paradox: utopia is a condition of trust and nakedness in which no one has any strong motive for speaking with irony. Yet utopia is the result of a set of ironic conditions. But because the ecstatic motive for the text, which merely intends to amuse a worldly society, is larger and more complex than it consciously acknowledges, the text fails to exploit satisfactorily the rhetorical connection between irony and orgiastic ecstasy.

The text, one might say, is "blind" to its own paradoxicality. For example, suppose we assume, as the text does, that orgiastic ecstasy depends on abstraction of identity, which undermines the exclusivity felt by or toward a particular identity and facilitates the (alternating or simultaneous) exchange of ecstatic partners. But suppose, too, that we assume, as the text does, that the context for orgy depends upon an ironic set of relations, not between statements, but between conditions for utterance. Then a rhetorical device appropriate for orgiastic speech would be the aphorism. The aphorism is a highly compressed abstraction of a reality that is peculiar, not to the speaker, but to people generally; it thus abstracts the identity not only of the speaker but of "life" itself. Yet the aphorism is *insightful* to the degree that it is ironic, for it is irony which separates the aphoristic generalization ("learning is the alias for disillusionment") about life from banal commonplace assumptions about people ("one learns by doing"). However, the text does not rely much at all on aphorisms, and those aphorisms that do appear are not especially distinctive:

> One attacks, one subjugates, one forgets a beautiful woman.
> On attaque, on subjugue, on oublie une belle. (194)

> > The less easy is our course
> > The greater our pleasure.
> > Moins la route sera facile
> > Et plus nous aurons de plaisir. (196)

> The modesty of woman is a hypocritical mask.
> La pudeur d'une femme est une masque hypocrite. (204)

The subdued status of aphorism in the text indicates a significant problem in the production of orgiastic speech. For in this theatrical context, orgiastic speech entails an abstraction of speaker and listener identities through a pornographic description of immediate erotic feelings (not actions). Aphorism, however, is perhaps the most acute rhetoric of abstraction because it exposes the speaker's consciousness of abstraction. The text *implies* a connection between abstraction and ecstasy by formal choices it makes in representing ecstasy; but the text does not *expose* this connection, and for this reason, the text *assumes* that the most one can learn — and it is not a trivial thing to learn — from ecstatic experience is something about the immediate condition of others' feelings toward oneself. This knowledge is simultaneously, paradoxically the source and object of ecstasy, insofar as the speech which constructs it is the work of speakers, who, according to the definition of ecstasy, have no fear of the immediate consequences of their words, which of course are the most apparent signifiers of knowledge.

The pornographic rhetoric of ecstasy is possibly the most intense disclosure of the immediate power of speech to move people to action. Speech which arouses either the speaker or the listener in an erotic sense is that speech which at once urges one to act in conformity with the desire of a theatricalized, lascivious Other, who, in the sense that ecstasy is a release from the self, is simultaneously in both the speaker and the listener because it is *in language*. But the knowledge the text ascribes to ecstatic experience is *nothing more* than this knowledge of other people's feelings at a moment when no one fears his feelings. It is not knowledge of "life," not language (i.e., aphorism) which produces significant actions or consequences "outside the cloister," so to speak. A more satisfying representation of orgiastic speech would link ecstasy with a higher state of consciousness, with a rhetoric whose consequences extend beyond the immediate set of relations and which gives orgiastic speech a more overt political significance. Such a representation entails the aphorism, or rather, the pornographication of the aphorism. However, to construct an aphorism which produces a pornographic effect is extremely difficult, and indeed, I am unable to to locate a text which seems conscious of this rhetorical potential. On the subject of orgiastic speech, theory advances far ahead of practice.

The rhetorical choices defining the text indicate that an orgiastic rhetoric of ecstasy is *reductive*. The orgiasts do not cultivate any new rhetorical devices unique to the orgy context; on the contrary, orgiastic speech entails the elimination of rhetorical devices appropriate to other (sacrificial, didactic) speech situations. The orgiasts focus almost exclusively on moment-to-moment descriptions of those immediate, subsidiary feelings or moods which are, so to speak, the components of the ecstatic experience. These present-tense descriptions accommodate variations which include commands and questions, but generally the utopian speech situation relies upon language which is free of metaphor and a sense of irony. The orgiasts describe feelings, but not the (erotic) actions which provoke the feelings. These actions include kissing, masturbation, intercourse, cunnilingus, fellatio, which the text designates through either stage directions or interpretive choices on the part of the actor. In the orgiastic context, such actions apparently do not need to be "learned" or "taught" as long as none of the orgiasts is afraid to learn the immediate feelings of the others. Only *in language and speech* can this absence of fear, which is so essential to ecstatic experience, signify itself to other, immanently ecstatic bodies. Description, however, only *represents* this fearlessness. The (utopian) conditions under which such representations are possible result, not from rhetorical devices employed by speakers, but from the equal distribution of speech among speakers, which has the effect of abstracting the identities of speakers and facilitating the orgiastic exchange of ecstatic partners. But these conditions of the utopian speech situation function only in relation to pressures exerted by the sacrificial and didactic speech situations: orgy is what is "learned" from the "teaching" of these earlier speech situations.

It may seem that a text such as *Les Plaisirs du cloître* is too trivial or "marginal" to justify the protracted analysis that has occurred here. Nevertheless, to dismiss the text as "trivial" is to assume that literary or theatrical imagination is capable of producing a more complex or "mysterious" representation of orgiastic ecstasy. Perhaps it is, but the evidence for it in dramatic literature, outside of the texts produced for the clandestine theatres, is virtually non-existent. A text such as *Les Plaisirs* indicates emphatically that it is not poetic imagination but ideology, the *abstract* values attached to representations by classes of spectators, which determines above all what may be spoken or represented on stage. "Mysterious" language that is heavily dependent upon metaphor to achieve "poetic" effect is appropriate to a repressive rather than utopian speech situation. But even if the rhetoric of orgiastic ecstasy is "reductive" in its focus on description, it is, as detailed analysis indicates, by no means lacking in considerable complexity. *Les Plaisirs* is worth bothering about because it is an extremely rare example of orgiastic speech constructed in dialogue form, as an intricate interplay of discrete voices, bodies, feelings, and actions rather than the fused, trance-like delirium of a mass or choral voice. Even in pornographic novels, the description of orgies rarely entails much in the way of dialogue. The language which constructs the novelized orgy belongs almost entirely to a narrator who describes actions and feelings which are *imagined* (by author and reader) but not "performed" with the seriousness of meaning which theatre gives that word. The rhetorical devices in *Les Plaisirs* exploit the performance value of utterances, whereas the rhetorical devices in pornographic fiction exploit the power of language to make the reader "see" what is "forbidden"; but this power operates independently of any performance value or any "real" relation between voice and language which is pornographic in itself. By emerging as dialogue, orgiastic speech manifests itself through new combinations of speakers. And these new combinations issue from "nature" as mathematically organized distributions of words, bodies, feelings, and actions, a point effectively dramatized by the verse forms, which involve complex rhythmic and tonal patterns. But this is to say that orgiastic speech arises out of rationality, out of the values of the "enlightenment." In contrast to the "sentimental" disclosure of feeling advocated by Diderot and Mercier, the orgiastic disclosure of feeling depends on highly artificial forms of speech. With its inclination to abstract the identities of speaker and listener, orgiastic speech seems closer to theoretical than to poetic forms of discourse.

Chapter Four
Orgy Politics

Orgy and Revolution

IT IS OBVIOUS AND EVEN "natural" to suppose that the great Revolution of 1789 put an end to the clandestine theatres, although evidence (or an obscurity of evidence) suggests that, due to very complicated social rivalries and deepening financial pressures, the cult faded considerably a half-dozen years before the revolution. But the impact of the Revolution upon attitudes toward orgy is perhaps not so obvious. The aesthetic tension between sentimental and orgiastic modes of feelings monumentalizes an irreconcilable tension between revolutionaries and aristocrats in the perception of utopia. The clandestine theatre links the performance of the orgiastic mode to an aristocratic milieu, wherein even the most intimate connections between human beings are perceived as highly theatrical gestures. The elaborate artificiality of this aesthetic, its devotion to complicated "rules" of speech signification, ensures that this mode of orgy, this construction of utopia, rests firmly upon conditions of "clandestine" exclusivity and privilege. Not just anyone has access to the theatre of orgy; only one who has sufficient "competence," only one who has "learned" the performance code, can hope to enjoy the orgiastic happiness produced by the cult. Of course, these attitudes were anathema to revolutionaries, who sought to link ecstatic freedom to conditions of Equality and Fraternity. But more importantly, the Revolution itself, with all its excesses, exhilarations, and spectacular gestures, gradually constituted a deeper, darker definition of orgy than any subculture might propose.

When the Revolution erupted in 1789, the aristocracy, suddenly in the unprecedented position of having to defend even its right to exist, could not pretend, nor afford to pretend, that their private theatres could go on providing the sort of entertainments that had prevailed in them up to that point. The clandestine theatres vanished completely. For aristocrats and royalists, the concept of "action" operated almost entirely outside the theatre, in the realm of political, military, and diplomatic ventures. The private theatres could not even muster the resources to stage anything interesting in the way of counter-revolutionary satires, tragedies, or propagandistic spectacles.

The Revolution, however, pursued grandiose plans for the theatre. As one might expect, the initial phase of the Revolution produced considerable confusion about what sort of theatre should embody the revolutionary spirit. Indeed, it took a couple of years to reach with confidence the conclusion that theatre itself was not inherently an instrument of aristocracy or despotism. Even as late as 1794, Joseph Le Bon, the venomous proconsul of Arras, contended that all plays produced under the *ancien régime* were insignificant when they were not obscene.[1] With such sentiments pervading the various revolutionary committees, assemblies, and conventions, one could well expect a radically new kind of theatre to appear. But as it turned out, agreement about the old theatre did entail agreement about the identity of a new theatre. On 13 January 1791, the National Assembly voted to grant theatres "complete" freedom, meaning that it was abolishing official censorship of theatrical performances and leaving questions of taste, propriety, and public security in the hands of dramatists and theatre personnel. The moderate Girondists firmly supported this position. But the Convention of 2 August 1793, which coincided with the fall of the Girondists, produced a decree that retracted the 1791 law.[2] The Convention acted under pressure from the Commune of Paris, which perceived the theatre as a hotbed of counter-revolutionary (Girondist) activity. During the September massacres of the following year, the theatres remained closed.

But apart from that moment, the Revolution inaugurated and sustained a prodigious amount of theatrical activity. It was the conviction of leading revolutionaries, of whom Marie-Joseph Chenier was perhaps the most prominent, that the theatre had a significant revolutionary function as an "educator of the people." But the methods and forms for realizing this function were a constant source of controversy and violent factionalism. Unlike the Académie Français under the monarchy, the Revolution never laid down specific "laws" for the production of "good" drama and performance. Consequently, while drama successfully and continually showed the evils of monarchy and despotism, it was never able to construct convincing or resonant representations of utopia; indeed, drama had a treacherous time representing any aspect of reality that occurred *after* the Revolution. Occasionally the government sponsored spectacular ceremonial pageants, such as *L'Inauguration de la Republique française* (1793), which glorified the Revolution and its emblems in an allegorical style in which the performance of all five acts required five separate public sites in Paris.[3] But ambitious revolutionaries could denounce even these performances as vestiges of royalist ceremonialism.

The extreme puritanism of so many revolutionaries resulted from an intense awareness of the frailty of human defenses against illusion and of the terrible vulnerability of people to seductive deceptions, misrepresentations, and secrets. It was therefore necessary to maintain constant, rigorous vigilance over all forms of representation. Police surveillance of theatrical activities on and off stage was never more efficient nor exhaustive. The revival of an "old" play required an exasperating effort at lobbying and negotiating; "new" plays could not represent aristocrats or kings, or they could only represent such persons at a time before the Revolution, or they could not represent revolutionary citizens as being uncertain in their feelings toward "enemies" of the Revolution, or they could only represent these "enemies" as people who said things which no one should say anyway, even in the context of a play. No one in the theatre, as a performer or a spectator, was free of suspicion. Power over theatre was *arbitrary,* and where power is arbitrary, the dominant emotion circulating within a society can never be ecstasy, but *terror,* or, as Paul d'Estrée calls it, a "theatre of fear."[4] A coherent, alluring program or theory of revolutionary theatre never emerged; instead, it was by a monumental conglomeration of arrests, denunciations, prosecutions, prohibitions, ominous intrigues, riots, and self-congratulatory propaganda that the public "learned" the identity of revolutionary theatre. It is therefore touching to observe the vast amount of theatrical activity inspired by the Revolution, in spite of the many dangers the theatre presented to both its artists and its audiences.

In one of his posthumous essays on "Institutions Republicaines," Saint-Just, who composed specific programs for many aspects of the Revolution but not the theatre, remarks: "Terror may release us from monarchy and aristocracy, but what will deliver us from corruption? . . .

Institutions." He then contends that "an institution composed of many members and an institution composed of a very unique membership are both despotic. A particular will triumphs in the one and in the other, and it is less the law than something arbitrary which is in control." He therefore suggests that the revolutionary society should contain many institutions composed of few people, for "it is best to diminish the number of constituted authorities."[5] This thinking is not altogether remote from the anonymous intelligence which produced *Les Plaisirs du cloître*. Like the clandestine author, Saint-Just believes that the greatest happiness results from the abstraction of human identity, and for him institutions of a particular type are what provide this abstraction. But whereas the clandestine theatre typifies an institution defined by a "unique (aristocratic) membership," the revolutionary institution contains a membership which is not "unique" but "constituted" through laws bestowed by other institutions; the laws or codes governing an institution are never created by its own membership. It is rare to encounter language about people that is more abstract or less "human" than Saint-Just's, and one could treat his language, his oratorical *addresses,* his consistently (unrelievedly!) aphoristic style, as a model for a revolutionary ecstatic discourse. But the interpretation of the relation between institutions and utopia by the theatre, the government, and the public was far less abstract than Saint-Just anticipated.

With the Revolution, the monopoly of the Opera and the Comédie Française over theatrical activity collapsed. Large new public theatres appeared on the boulevards to gratify an insatiable public appetite for theatrical gesture and dramatic action. The Revolution introduced and perfected a distinctive kind of performance for these unintimate "theatres of the people": melodrama. This genre probably functioned according to many more "rules" of construction than classical drama of the most severe order ever did, but these rules eluded consciousness or objective codification, and thus melodrama sustained the illusion of being a "freer" genre than the "aristocratic" dramatic forms. Indeed, to identify all the conventions defining melodrama would consume a huge amount of space.[6] I merely point out that, in addition to spectacular scenic effects, stirring changes of mood, and an ever-present musical "soundtrack," melodrama depended for its success on a drastic devaluation of dialogue as a source of dramatic interest and emotional energy. Intricate verse forms gave way to prosaic sloganeering, clichéd functionalism, and bathetic outbursts which had some chance of being heard in large halls filled with restless and not always "well-mannered" spectators.

The melodramatic attitude toward speech is perhaps most naked in *Coelina* (1800), by Guilbert Pixérècourt, the mastermind of this genre, who, believing himself to be an aristocrat, was in fact ever-regretful of the Revolution. In this stupendously popular play, Virtue and Innocence, in the guises of the father, Francisque, and his daughter, Coelina, are in a sense aligned to Silence. The evil baron Trugelin is a slick, suave talker, who has more lines than anyone else in the play. Francisque can't speak at all because the aristocrat has ripped out his tongue, and Coelina is one of those archetypal innocent maidens whose slightest utterance unwittingly provokes danger, misunderstanding, or fantastic malevolence. Thus, one "understands" goodness primarily through non-linguistic signs, the musicalized "call of the blood," birthmarks, mysterious heirlooms, distinctive gestures, peculiarities of costume.

The writings of Saint-Just imply that ecstatic abstraction of human identity results from the operation of a super-theoretical "voice." But in the melodramatic theatre of the Revolution, movement toward ecstatic abstraction depends on significations that are "beyond" the power of language altogether. In both cases, abstraction entails a severe depression of the speaking voice as a signifier or pleasure center of the body. The revolutionary spirit regards speech (but not literacy) with such deep suspicion because speech, as dialogue, is a profound marker of *power differences* between bodies. The orgiastic happiness pursued by the aristocracy depends on conditions of exclusivity and privilege which manifest themselves through highly sophisticated and "difficult" modes of dialogue. But that's not all. Any happiness or utopia based on the gratification of erotic desires *invariably* entails the privileging of particular bodies. The incredibly complex sexual life of the pre-Revolutionary aristocracy indicates that desires and bodies are so intricate, so mysterious that any notion of social happiness linked to a revolutionary eroticism yet encompassing more than a clandestine cult requires far "more" in the way of "enlightenment," economic resources, linguistic competencies, and "institutions" than either theorists or partisans of revolution ever accommodate.

We can perceive the Revolution as the release of a colossal anxiety toward the body, which in an unprecedented fashion appeared as the dominant source and ultimate, untranscendable, even arbitrary *limit* of human happiness. Revolution awakens an intense materialism in its enthusiasts, but this materialism hesitates to accommodate the sexual appetities of bodies. Revolutionary ideology accommodates well a utopia based on some notion of healthy bodies, but not of "beautiful" or *desired* bodies, for erotic desire always introduces the phenomenon of difference which subverts the great unifying ambition of revolution. Thus, in spite of its materialism, revolutionary anxiety toward the body encourages the pursuit of a grand, social idea of ecstatic abstraction whereby utopia is that society which somehow transcends the body or at least those (erotic) codes and desires that make the body a signifier of difference, *distinction*. The revolutionary anxiety toward the body achieves an orgiastic social dimension when it evolves into an ideology of Terror, which reaches its "final" manifestation through mass death, through the construction of a monumental state apparatus of doom. With the Revolution, the concept of orgy, of "excessive" mass or communal action, assumes a non-erotic or anti-erotic identity. But to neutralize the erotic significance of orgy is to invite a pervasively metaphorical use of the word. And when the meaning of orgy operates primarily as a metaphor, it becomes embedded in fantasy rather than in any "real" or theatrically realized interaction between bodies.

The Revolution weakened its anxiety toward the erotic body by depressing the differentiating value of the voice and by favoring those modes of communication (oratory, melodrama, Saint-Justian theoretical inscription) in which the voice became "free" of the body or the body was "free" of the voice. This observation is significant in relation to the subsequent history of pornographic theatre. After the Congress of Vienna (1815), when the French aristocracy recovered many of its rights and privileges and the dream-world of romantic subjectivism began to formulate a new, anti-mechanical, anti-institutional ideology of "nature," erotic theatre reappeared in Paris in a bizarre form which flourished (if that is the word) intermittently and somewhat timidly in the otherwise extravagant, pompous decades leading up to the Third Republic (1871). This was the pornographic theatre of marionettes.

Orgy and Bourgeoisie

Before the Revolution, the marionette theatre belonged to "the people" as a "popular" art aligned with the pantomimes and vaudevilles offered by the police-harrassed fairground theatres (*théâtre de la foire*). In the nineteenth century, however, the vigorous and perfectly legitimate

presentation of melodramas in the boulevard theatres completely under-
mined the appeal of a theatrical practice (marionettes) which evaded or
confounded litigation launched against it by the state and the official
theatres (Opera, Comédie Française). Marionette theatre then ceased to
be "popular"; it dwindled into an entertainment of interest primarily for
children. The erotic marionette theatre was much more obscure. Its
occasional performances were not on the boulevards, but on side streets
and in small cellars or undesignated studio-garrets. Moreover, both
marioneteers and spectators seemed to have been exclusively male. The
tiny audience for this theatre constituted more of a connoisseur's club
than an orgiastic cult, a club which very discreetly and erratically
commissioned texts and performances in an atmosphere that was much
less clandestine than utterly marginal. The spectator did not revel in the
erotic marionette theatre; he *sneaked* into it, for any "public" disclosure
of his interest in this theatre would be a source of embarrassment, not
pride, for the gentlemanly spectator during the "bourgeois century."

In 1979, Gil Sigaux published several texts of the erotic marionette
theatre.[7] These plays may have some interest as pornography, but they do
not disclose any interest at all in representing or constructing conditions
for orgy. Technical limitations on marionette production may account in
part for the absence of orgiastic action. The pornographic effect arises
chiefly from dialogue (banter) between a couple of marionettes. It is a
couple-centered world of erotic action. The language is entirely devoid of
the complexity and systematic intricacy that governs the clandestine
texts. No one speaks in verse, except occasionally when a character
introduces a risqué song. Characters saturate their speech with innuen-
dos, "naughty" puns, and bawdy jokes. One of the more successful of
these plays is Henri Monnier's *Les Deux gougnottes dialogues infâmes.
Scènes réelles de la vie de nos mondaines* (1866), first performed by the most
documented of the erotic marionette theatres, Le Théâtre erotique de la
rue Santè (Erotikon theatron), for which Monnier was a founding club
member.[8] In 1868, a national court proscribed the sale of the book in
which Monnier had published the play. Fifty-two out of its 55 pages of
text consist of a dialogue between two "worldly women," married
aristocrats, Louise de Laveneur and Henriette de Fremicourt. Once their
scene begins, the text does not provide a single stage direction. The
performance by marionettes of actions indicated only by the dialogue is
therefore profoundly titillating (if it is possible for titillation to be
profound). In leisurely fashion, the dialogue itself exposes the motives

and communicative aesthetic by which Louise and Henriette cultivate a passion for each other. After much teasing interrogation of each other, Louise finally takes off her dress and stands nude before Henriette. From this point on, the two women devote themselves entirely to the performance of various erotic actions, kissing, masturbation, breast-sucking, cunnilingus, pseudo-intercourse, all of which the text strives to represent entirely through speech. The women alternate having orgasm, then finally they have a grand orgasm simultaneously. But the play does not end with this final "discharge," as they call it: Louise and Henriette go on for several pages to question each other about how the experience compared to homosexual encounters with other women. The curtain falls when Louise and Henriette agree to recommence their pleasures "tomorrow."

The language of this text strives for much greater simplicity and "realism" than the clandestine theatre appreciated. The author tries to maintain a stichomythic symmetry in the distribution of speech between the speakers. Here Louise has a few more words than Henriette, but at other moments, Henriette will slightly exceed Louise in the number of words assigned her on a given page. The passage is interesting because of its metalinguistic aspect:

LOUISE
It's my little cunt, my sweet pussy, my little cunt. —
Say my cunt, treasure, my little cunt! . . .

HENRIETTE
Your little cunt.

LOUISE
Give it your mouth as a present, your dear little mouth! — Say it again, that word, so pretty in your mouth: my cunt . . . say: my cunt.

HENRIETTE
Your cunt, my angel, your fine little cunt!

LOUISE
Would you like to slip into it, my little man?

HENRIETTE
Yes, yes, I want to slip into it!

LOUISE
What would you put into my cunt, in filling it?

HENRIETTE
My you-know-what.

LOUISE
What you-know-what? or rather, what machine?
Its name, please, the name of the you-know-what [machine]? —
If I say it to you, will you repeat it?

HENRIETTE
Immediately.

LOUISE
My cock.

HENRIETTE
Your cock.

LOUISE
It is a cock, love; with your cock, your cock in my cunt,
your swollen cock!

HENRIETTE
Your beautiful cock, your swollen cock in my cunt . . .

LOUISE
Would you like to suck my cock?

HENRIETTE
I want to suck it, I want to put the whole thing in my mouth,
as I put my tongue in your cunt . . . Now spread your legs
as I put it there again.

LOUISE
Yours, yours, yours! . . .

HENRIETTE
Thanks! Thanks! how I suck it, your pretty cunt! . . . [8]

* * * *

LOUISE
C'est mon petit con, ma minette chérie, mon petit con. —
Dis mon con, trésor, mon petit con! . . .

HENRIETTE
Ton petit con.

LOUISE
Donne ton bec pour te remercier, ton cher petit bec! — Dis-le encore,
ce mot, si jolie dans ta bouche: mon con . . . dis: mon con.

HENRIETTE
Ton con, mon ange, ton bon petite con!

LOUISE
Voudrais-tu m'enfiler, mon petit homme?

HENRIETTE
Oui, oui, je t'enfilerais!

LOUISE
Que mettrais-tu dans mon con, en m'enfilant?

HENRIETTE
Mon machin.

LOUISE
Quel machin? or plutôt quelle machine? son nom t'en prie, son nom,
à la machine? — Si je te le dis, le répéteras-tu?

HENRIETTE
Tout de suite.

LOUISE
Ma pine.

HENRIETTE
Ta pine.

LOUISE
C'est une pine, mamie; avec ta pine, ta pine dans mon con,
ta grosse pine!

HENRIETTE
Tu me la sucerais ma pine?

HENRIETTE
Je te la sucerais, je la mettrais tout entiére dans ma bouche,
comme je mets ma langue dans ton con . . . Ecarte les jambes,
que je l'y mette encore . . .

LOUISE

Tiens, tiens, tiens! . . .

HENRIETTE

Merci! Merci! comme je le suce, ton jolie con! . . .

The text assumes that a pornographic effect results in large part from the naming, by female speakers, of taboo words and actions, and the process of naming entails the employment of a particular set of rhetorical devices. Louise names organs and actions that give her pleasure. She then *commands* ("say: my cunt") Henriette to repeat what she has named; then she *asks* her listener to name organs that have not been named and actions she would "like" to perform in relation to organs that have been named. These questions are no more coercive than the commands because they do not arise from any genuine sense of doubt about their answers. Louise asks them as a way of signifying that she already "knows" that it excites her listener to speak the answer both of them want to hear. Henriette repeats names using little signifiers ("Yes, yes"; "immediately" instead of only "yes"; "your beautiful cock" instead of merely "your cock") which disclose her desire to obey commands and answer questions. An equilibrium of desire signifies itself through the simple, bantering symmetry or economy of the dialogue. Louise's pleasure derives from speaking what her listener desires to speak, and Henriette's pleasure derives from speaking what Louise desires her to speak. Each speaker does not desire quite the same thing, and each speaker does not experience quite the same pleasure, but the pleasure of each depends on the pleasure of the other, and that dependence operates through the mechanism of symmetry — symmetry between a commanding and an obeying speaker, which is also a symmetry between a questioning and an answering speaker. In this instance, the speakers sustain the mechanism through the metalinguistic devices of naming (Louise) and repeating what is named (Henriette) in such a way that the naming of taboo organs and actions is itself the source of an intensifying, teasing source of pleasure that can go on indefinitely. The passage bears qualities similar to the didactic speech situation employed in *Les Plaisirs du cloître*. Louise seems to be "teaching" Henriette how to speak their pleasure, and Henriette apparently "learns" to speak with the authority of the teacher when she herself appropriates a device associated with the teacher, the command: "Now spread your legs . . ." Elsewhere in the text, however, the speakers reverse these power relations many times, indicating that the capacity of the speakers to go on having orgasm after orgasm depends on constant fluctuation between them of the power to name something that both want to hear spoken. The pornographic effect of the piece does not depend on the performance of sexual acts (interesting as these may be) but on the *speaking* of desires and actions. The sex acts performed by the marionettes are probably no more enchanting than the wonderful (especially for marionettes!) business of lighting the candle which precedes all the sex talk. But the pornographic speech of the characters infuses more "life" into the wooden bodies than any technical effort to satisfy a voyeur's desire to see the "real" performance of such sex acts.

But of course, the most peculiar thing about this dialogue is that it is performed in a marionette theatre. The performance ascribes voices to the ecstatic bodies on stage which actually belong to another, invisible body, that of the (male) marionetteer. The performance detaches the ecstatic voice from the ecstatic body. In the nineteenth century, no one could witness language of such erotic explicitness spoken by the living bodies which claimed to feel the desires signified through the language, except perhaps in a brothel. Only in the marionette theatre, with its technical inability to introduce orgiastic scenes, could one hear such pornographic voices of ecstasy. Western social reality in this post-Revolutionary century seems to believe that the *desire* to say and hear such things is not *in* the body at all, but in something external to it, something invisible or "bodiless," a sort of god of ideology, which "speaks for" the bodies that merely denote, rather than contain or motivate, such strange desires. The Revolutionary anxiety toward the body perhaps reaches its most bizarre consequence in this form of theatre, which thrives only secretly in an atmosphere of severe repression directed against even the reading, let alone the speaking, of pornographic desires. Indeed, desire of any kind must now "transcend" the body, transcend the materialism of the industrial revolution, if one is to speak it at all.

It is possible to suggest that this example of the erotic marionette theatre embodies the effort of the male sex to "speak for" female bodies, to appropriate woman's voice, and in doing so, reduce her and her insatiable, "infinite" capacity for erotic pleasure to the mechanical functions of a puppet, whose real source of "life" is male fantasy and desire. The male author and the male marionetteer control the strings that animate the female body because it is a male who controls the language and voice ascribed to the "performing" body. However, I have tried to show that the pornographic effect of the scene depends, not on the referents of the language, but on the *rhetorical devices* employed by the characters, and these devices are not gender-specific. This point becomes evident by reversing the sexual context of performance. If it is possible to suggest that erotic marionette theatre signifies a male effort to appropriate the female voice and body, it is also possible to suggest that a pornographic effect will result if a female author and a female marionetteer dramatize an ecstatic encounter between two male homosexuals using the same rhetorical devices employed by the two lesbians. (Of course, most of these marionette plays focus on heterosexual couples.) In other words, the speaking of desire through this bizarre aesthetic is not peculiar to a "dominant" male sensibility, nor even to the marionette theatre. It is peculiar to a post-Revolutionary ideology of sexual difference which does not contemplate the possibility of either an "authentic" female porno-graphic discourse or a wholly female marionette theatre. The aristocratic clandestine theatre, where pornographic performance puts the voice of rapture in the living body, is complete antithesis of this gender-troubled ideology.

Orgy and Democracy

Obscure though it is, the erotic marionette theatre functions as a powerful sign of the success of post-Revolutionary forms of discourse in detaching the voice of desire from the desired and desiring body. Michel Foucault has described this process of detachment in terms of a "medicalization" of the erotic controlled by a "new" intellectual category: "sexuality." Through sexual discourses, social reality attempts to mediate and regulate its great anxiety toward the body and the mysterious pressures of the erotic by making the erotic the subject of scientific inquiry and surveillance. The erotic body is something one talks *about,* in a medicalized (therapeutic) context, but does not talk into being. One does not speak desire by applying a complex, class-distinct aesthetic; one speaks *of* desire, not to fulfill desire, but to "cure" oneself of it. Sexual discourse detaches desire from the body by formulating a "scientific" language that detaches its user from any particular body or desire.[9] The erotic marionette theatre is yet more bizarre because it seeks to subvert this process of detaching voice and body by making the detachment a source of pornographic pleasure. However, the marionette mode of performance also suggests that even if it succeeds in being pornographic, the ideology

ideology of detachment is utterly inimical to the manifestation of orgy. Post-Revolutionary ideologies of sexual difference and detachment seem pervasively locked into an obsession with the Couple.

The return of live bodies to pornographic theatrical performance is an obvious phenomenon of twentieth-century history. Occasionally, spectacular, and often shocking, "sex shows" have moved toward the performance of orgy. Nightclubs in Weimar Berlin and pre-Revolutionary Havana apparently staged some really monumental orgies. Frank Caprio mentions elaborate brothel theatres in Havana in which dozens of men and women performed all sorts of sexual acts together, simultaneously.[10] In Germany, orgy theatres cultivated the theme of audience participation. One female performer described how she was suspended, nude, in the air, by having her hands and feet handcuffed and chained to the floor and the ceiling. In this position she experienced orgasm over and over again while as many as fifty men took turns licking her vagina [or anus] and reaching orgasm themselves.[11] Yet in all these manifestations of orgy, the Revolutionary theme of detaching the voice from the erotic body prevails. Dialogue is scarcely a significant element in the construction of orgiastic action. Indeed, actions "speak for themselves" — or rather, ecstasy never depends on anything that cannot be seen or touched, such as words, the voice, the extraordinarily *strange*, differentiating, powerful, exclusive, and incomparably exquisite feelings which only speech can signify and provoke. Performance remains bound to the perception that ecstasy is a condition "beyond words," for it is assumed that in its excitement, the ecstatic body "naturally" reduces the voice to a wordless "animal cry," a loud breathing. Even in a play such as *Oh! Calcutta!* (1969), which tries to create a "literate" sex theatre, the language seems infantile and tediously impoverished compared to *Les Plaisirs* or even *Les deux gougnottes*.

A Postmodern Example of Orgy

Perhaps the strongest way I can demonstrate this argument is to describe in some detail my own experience of an orgy in a democratic society, which, in diligently striving to make even the most ardently and secretly desired pleasures "accessible" to the public, makes those "secret" desires more public than the public itself ever cares to acknowledge. I do not say that this experience is definitive of orgy in democratic society, but it does seem to me to *typify* orgiastic performance in post-Revolutionary and, indeed, postmodern culture. The "accessibility" of the performance depended on special, anti-dialogic distributions of language between bodies in performance; it depended on carefully structured constraints on speech in performance. And for this reason, the orgy became a sign, not of a cult operating "clandestinely" within democratic society, but of a culture striving to find a way to "appropriate" orgy from cultic exclusivity and inaccessibility.

In January 1976 I visited Hamburg. While browsing in a sex shop, an advertisement for an "orgy club" attracted my attention. Eventually (several days later) my curiosity triumphed over my nervousness, and I went to the theatre for a performance scheduled to begin at 10:00 PM. The theatre was in the basement of the sex shop. Before descending the stairs, one encountered an affable, elderly gentleman, who insisted that I read a sign over the door before buying my ticket. The sign inscribed "Instructions for Patrons," and these included the statement that the theatre was not a house of prostitution, that customers could not receive refunds, and that customers must obey all rules of conduct for the theatre. The sign listed these rules of conduct: "1) always follow the instructions of the goddess and her attendants; 2) do not attempt sexual actions with other patrons or persons not specified by the goddess; 3) place all money or valuables in the designated black bag; 4) no smoking or eating; 5) no photography." Having assured me that I had nothing to fear from my orgiastic desire to "worship the goddess," the old man sold me a ticket for about $20.00.

The little theatre downstairs was very warm and bathed in a torrid orange light. The place looked cheap but clean. It offered almost nothing in the way of decorative embellishments, except for a mural on the wall to the rear of the audience which depicted, in something of an expressionist (Beckmannesque) style, a throng of nude men and women masturbating or posturing voluptuously on a nocturnal city street. The audience sat on individual folding metal chairs. One wall was panelled with mirrors. The other wall was just bare cement; however, I soon discovered that it made an excellent surface for casting shadows. Behind the audience was a very small bar, and before the audience was a somber black curtain. A huge black rubber mat covered the floor. The theatre probably had enough chairs for about forty spectators, but for this performance only about twenty persons, all male, attended. These men varied in age from their mid-twenties to mid-fifties (I myself was 27). I was not the only foreigner; a couple of men in their thirties conversed quietly in some sort of

Yugoslavian dialect. But except for another pair who conversed in indecipherable German, all the other spectators were lone individuals who waited silently and somewhat sullenly for the orgy to begin. Behind the little bar stood a tall, shadowy man who never left his position and never said anything yet apparently assumed a mysterious function in relation to the performance which gradually unfolded. A pretty and cheerful barmaid, wearing heels, tight jeans, and black blouse, approached me and asked if I wanted something to drink. Using a black felt marker, she noted down my request for a glass of mineral water (I don't think she sold anything else), then asked me to put my money and valuables in a black plastic bag. When I had done so, she inscribed the number of the bag on the back of my right hand, thanked me, and pushed her little cart toward another customer. Before buying the ticket, my anxiety had been enormous, but now I was resigned to the fact that I was the victim of a strange desire or curiosity which no one, including myself, could understand. I did not know what to expect anymore. My determination to enter an utterly unique realm of pleasure had, apparently, made me a fool who deserved anyway to be swindled and disappointed. I therefore looked upon myself as I did the other spectators, with an amiable indifference. I was not so much nervous as just rather weary of myself.

A little after 10:00, the performance began with the recorded sound of an ominous organ preludium. Then the black curtain parted. But all one could see was the face of a woman gazing at the audience through a window frame. As the organ faded away, the woman spoke to the audience in a warm, oracular voice:

> I am the goddess Sylvia! Always obey me and you will be happy. I know you want to worship me — and you shall! For I tremble with anticipation of the pleasure you will give me. I sweat with excitement at the orgy my body will make. I am naked. I see you and I masturbate. But you can't see me masturbate. You can't see my beautiful body, my sweaty breasts, my slimy cunt. You can't see what you want to worship. You can't see me on fire [*entzuendet*]. Because you are not ready! Obey me and we will be so happy. First you must show me yourselves. Show the goddess how excited you are. I want to see your penis. Show me how strong and beautiful your cock [*Schwanz*] is. Show me, show me. I must see it. Take off your clothes, take off your clothes.[12]

Sylvia exhorted the audience in this fashion for a couple of minutes. I can't say that the language aroused me, though the speaker herself was quite attractive. She was about thirty, blond, with very red lips. But she did say one thing that continues to this day to echo in my mind, even at the most unexpected moments: "Nothing inflames me like the sight of *your* cock throbbing before me as wildly as your heart/Nichts entzuendet mich wie der Anblick von *deinem* Schwanz, der vor mir schlägt, wild wie deinem Herz." I had never heard a woman speak so boldly of her desire for a male body, and the memory of those words and the voice that spoke them still has the power to stir me, even though, at the moment, they were too strange to have an immediate pornographic effect. Indeed, my inclination then was not to believe anything she was saying. In any case, the purpose of her speech and the "hypnotic" style of its delivery, I later realized, was to *disarm* the spectator and make him feel that his pursuit of orgiastic pleasure was not something that anyone had to take very seriously. Then the possibility of not being aroused by this utterly unsubtle effort to excite me suffused me with embarrassment, so I took off my clothes in a rather leisurely manner, thinking that even if I didn't become excited I would at least learn something profoundly decisive about my capacity for erotic pleasure.

It was at this point that a couple of spectators left the scene, apparently overwhelmed with anxiety. But as I was sliding down my pants, a warm rush of pleasure spread through my body. It was instantly a delicious feeling to appear naked before so many people whose names I did not know but who shared my intense sense of freedom in regard to the display of phallic strength, motivated by the completely spoken "lust" of a pretty woman. But of course, my excitement did not entirely depend on the provocation of the woman; *it* also depended on the perception that the completely unspoken disclosure of *my* lust was something other men wanted to see and I wanted them to see. This disclosure, this group *performance* of masturbation, established the credibility of the woman's "lust" and released the spectator from concern about the differences in desirability between himself and other men. Because the woman treated all men as "equal" by reducing them to their erections, the spectator perceived that no one phallus was "enough" to satisfy her; he could bask in a situation in which his own nakedness was important precisely because it contributed to an "excess" of phallus. Under these circumstances, group masturbation was now as "normal" as talking about a mutually desirable woman at a luncheon. In fact, exquisitely tense with excitement, I imitated a couple of other spectators by standing up so that Sylvia would have a perfect view of my "readiness" to worship her. The goddess, however, instructed the spectators to stay in their places until she told them to do otherwise:

> Stay where you are. I will call you. And you will show me how excited I make you. I want you to show everyone. I'm growing hotter and hotter. Millions of orgasms are inside me. I want you to see me completely insane with pleasure. Obey me and you shall.

As we spectators became more comfortable with the situation, we glanced at each other and exchanged grins. But none of us spoke. All eyes and bodies remained focused on Sylvia, and everyone seemed proud of the excitement he felt. As the goddess herself said: "Be proud you lust for me. Show me how proud you are." She then began to "call" spectators by the numbers inscribed on their hands. Some spectators were called in pairs or trios, others were called individually. When called, the spectator moved to an open space before the stage. The goddess then commanded the spectator to perform actions which signified their great eagerness to worship her. For example, she told two men to masturbate facing each other. A group of three men was told to kneel in front of the mirrors and masturbate. She commanded me to perform a "solo" which did not differ much from the other solos she commanded:

> Number 12, come forward! Kneel down. Make your cock as hard as possible. Let it drip. [I remember blushing and smiling at her, and she smiled back with such warmth that I felt *saturated* with a lurid sweetness. Her smile made me feel luscious.] Ja, ja, beautiful. Now masturbate. Harder. Harder. Now turn around. Show everybody how happy you are to worship me. Show them! Show them! Now go back until it's time for you to show us more.

But this part of the performance seemed only partially successful. Though I was intensely excited while performing the actions, I believe my pleasure would have been even greater if I could have spoken to Sylvia, if I could have said myself what she said I was feeling. But she did not permit anyone to speak, and I suppose no one dared to speak for fear of making his emotions seem grotesque rather than pornographic. The introduction of dialogue between Sylvia and the spectators would have protracted the performance considerably, and each of us was conscious that his pleasure was not going to continue indefinitely. As it was, a couple of spectators, so overwhelmed with excitement, ejaculated helplessly, with all of us gasping, in the midst of performing their "solos." They slipped out of the orgy and out of the theatre. "Oh, beautiful, beautiful," said the goddess. "I love to see your cock spurt. I want to see it spurting everywhere, always, all over." It never occurred to me that Sylvia actually believed or felt what she was saying — it was just an "act" designed to make money off of the male's delicate capacity to become inflamed with sexual excitement.

But this act "worked" because it inverted a unique relation in a man's life. The spectators obeyed Sylvia as if she were their mother. She spoke with the authority of a mother. Yet a masturbating boy always fears "discovery" by his mother. The performance estranges the spectator from this norm. Here the mother does not "catch" the spectator in the secret act of reveling in his sexuality. On the contrary, she expects him to masturbate, she treats masturbation as a glorious sign of her own capacity to inspire "worship," she makes masturbation seem as "natural" to herself and men as a mother commanding her son to show her his muscles or his smile. It's an exhilarating sensation. Thus, even though Sylvia probably did not really feel anything she said, she still constructed a powerful relation between language and feeling — a feeling in the spectator which did not depend on any greater proof of the speaker's sincerity than her speaking, not of things a man has heard many women say many times, but of things he has not heard any woman say. The speech situation, rather than the speaker's motive for speaking, controlled the emotive interest of the language. You can enjoy this kind of performance only if you believe that the signification of any erotic feeling is inherently theatrical. However, it's difficult to imagine any woman being in this business if she didn't derive some pleasure in it.

When all of us had demonstrated our eagerness to worship her, Sylvia announced that she herself was now "ready" for the next phase of the performance:

> Oh, my body screams [*schreit*] for more and more. I'm dripping with lust. Watch me pulsate with the strangest pleasures. Worship my insatiable body. Drench me with sperm [*Saat*].

She pushed the sill of the window which framed her face and a door holding the window and the curtain below it opened to reveal her sitting on a bar stool, nude, bathed in orange light, her legs spread, and masturbating rapturously — a spectacularly voluptuous image. But almost as soon as she initiated this action, the woman who had marked our hands with numbers appeared from out of the audience; she closed the door on Sylvia and drew a curtain over the window. "Please wait," the nameless woman said, "She will come back, she will come back." The organ music returned, the orange lights went out, and a white light came up on the audience. Now an especially interesting moment of the performance occurred. The nameless woman, who remained fully clothed, spoke to the audience in a cheerful, quite casual manner: "Don't mind me. I have to set up for the next part. I know you're terribly excited, so go on and masturbate. It doesn't bother me at all." She then moved briskly about the space, tidying up, fixing the curtain, returning empty bottles to the bar. Meanwhile, 15 or 16 naked men continued to masturbate without receiving from her the slightest sign that she was going to do anything other than she said she was going to do. It was a peculiar thrill to masturbate before her, because she did not embarrass me by the ease with which she excited me, I felt no pressure to make my excitement "mean" something special to her. She treated mass masturbation as a "natural" response to her most banal actions. No one even spoke to her, yet upon reflection, I wish I had said to her what I have written here. But at the time, I understood intuitively that to speak such sentiments would complicate the performance considerably.

This little interlude lasted a few minutes, then the lights grew dim and the nameless woman disappeared behind the curtain. In the dark, the audience seemed poised like a great phalanx of phallic power, ready to *plunge* at whatever beckoned it. The curtain opened and there, in a hot white light, was Sylvia, suspended nude above the floor in a stunning pose. Her hands were bound over her head by a nylon rope attached to the ceiling. Her legs were spread very wide, with her feet inserted into stirrups also suspended from the ceiling by nylon ropes. The stirrups allowed her to balance the weight of her body so that she could appear *stretched*, in a shockingly provocative manner, without feeling much strain on her arms or shoulders. But although the ropes bound, suspended, and stretched her, they *also* allowed her to sway, to signify a convulsive, turbulent aspect to her desire to appear naked. Bondage gave her nudity a seething quality; it suffused her body with a wildness or voracity which might go "out of control" were she not bound. Her lust seemed tremendously strong. Her flesh, her muscles glistened; her ribs dilated exquisitely with her breathing. She was not totally nude insofar as she now wore a necklace and a tiara which glittered, and these functioned, I suppose, to remind the audience of her status as a "goddess." She was breathtakingly raw and glamorous at the same time. Standing beside her on a small stool was the nameless woman, who had removed her blouse to display her small breasts. But now she wore long black gloves which extended above her elbows. The skin of both women looked extremely white in the glaring light; a great heat seemed to emanate from them, yet the nameless woman performed actions with an almost clinical composure. In her right hand, she held a black hose with a chrome nozzle, and with this somewhat sinister-looking device she sprayed warm water onto Sylvia's genitals and into her anus. With her left hand, she massaged Sylvia's labia and masturbated her.

When the organ music stopped, the nameless woman said, "Are you ready, my dear [*Liebchen*]?" "Ja, ja," Sylvia replied, "Ja!" From this point on, the nameless woman discarded her informal way of talking and assumed the regal, imperative voice which Sylvia had previously used. Sylvia herself no longer spoke to the audience, but she was by no means silent. "The goddess awaits you," said the nameless woman:

> She wants your sperm [*Saat*] to flow . . . all over. She wants orgasm to shatter her. She wants waves of male orgasm [*Maenner-Orgasmus*] to fill the room. That is her dream: choral orgasm [*Chor-Orgasmus*]. World orgasm! Every man coming before her. Everything dripping with sperm.

She signaled for the audience to move forward and kneel in two rows before Sylvia, who then *loomed* over us and yet seemed such a great *offering* to us. I knelt in the second row, as designated by my number. The rhythm of the performance accelerated considerably. In a prodding, "hypnotic" tone, the nameless woman explained the method by which each man should "worship" the goddess, and she called by number a man in the first row to demonstrate this "routine." It was apparent that he was familiar to the women from previous performances, because he performed with the assurance of one who knew exactly what would happen to him, whereas I was quite conscious of acting (blushingly) as if everything I did was part of a strange experiment. Of course, even well before the performance began, I surmised that, in this public milieu, "worship" of a woman meant acts of cunnilingus rather than "normal" intercourse, but I was not at all sure how such acts were central to the creation of an orgy.

One can imagine, and, indeed, "manage" intercourse with (penetration of) almost any woman, but cunnilingus signifies a measure of enthusiasm reserved for only some women, including both Sylvia and the nameless woman, who would have interested me if I had merely seen them walking down the street. Cunnilingus discloses *the power of the man* to give the woman pleasure, because, I suppose, her pleasure results from a sense of being swallowed up rather than filled. This situation reverses the conventional feeling of intercourse and makes it seem like the man is *not afraid* of the woman's power to fill *him*. The pleasure of the man remains grounded in an assertion of power (rather than submission), and this pleasure reaches orgiastic intensity through the disclosure of the power to other men and women. Woman is "worshipped" by turning the act of cunnilingus into an orgasm-inducing public spectacle.

The summoned man stood up, strode forth, and sort of bowed his head between Sylvia's legs. If he had knelt before her, his lips would not have reached her genitals, but if he stood fully upright he would have kissed her navel. It was an awkward position, which, based on my own experience of cunnilingus, required amendation. With her left hand on the back of his head, the nameless woman pressed the man's face tightly against Sylvia's vagina, while Sylvia herself writhed violently and gasped convulsively. The nameless woman said something like, "More, more! She's coming, she's coming!" Then she pulled his head back and exhorted him: "Now from behind, from behind!" He pivoted, so that he now "faced" the audience, but of course, in attempting analingus, Sylvia's "behind" eclipsed his face. He pressed his left hand against her buttock to steady her and open her up, while with his right hand he continued to masturbate vigorously, in a wildly thrusting movement. Sylvia squealed and twisted, but it was only a matter of seconds before he ejaculated. He collapsed against her leg, panting and pumping himself until he was completely spent. Then the nameless woman sprayed Sylvia's genitals with the nozzle and called another number. The man slipped off into the shadow behind the audience; he vanished.

This scene, repeated again and again, with each number called, was tremendously exciting to watch, and, indeed, I greatly feared I would become so overwhelmed with pleasure that I would reach orgasm before I had actually "worshipped" the goddess. Such was the fate of a couple of men, who, unable to hold back any longer, simply lunged forward and came helplessly on the floor in front of everyone without ever touching anyone. With this type of orgy, the power embodied by one's penis felt enormously amplified by the sight of so many other erections, as if every penis mirrored one's own — or rather, as if one's penis embodied the phallic energy of all men. My whole body felt exquisitely taut with an intense pressure to exceed an unprecedented threshold of pleasure, but proof of my strength seemed to depend on sustaining this tautness for as long as possible. It was a matter of *self-control.* I therefore had to move and touch myself with extreme delicacy to avoid "triggering" orgasm before I was "ready." One man was not "ready," even though he had taken more time to "worship" the goddess than anyone, so the nameless woman issued a command: "Number seven, help him." Another man came forth, masturbated him, and very quickly set off the "trigger" in him, while the nameless woman exclaimed: "Go ahead, spill it, shoot it, let it flow!" This, too, was a terribly exciting scene. The nameless woman did not call on me to "help" anybody, although I was quite willing, partly because of the sense of power over another man that I might feel. The homosexuality of the action seemed unproblematic when viewed as no more perverse than the nameless woman's masturbation of the goddess.

All this "worship" occurred at exhilarating speed, in a real orgiastic frenzy, with Sylvia convulsively crying out, "More, more!" Because numbers were not called in sequence, I constantly expected to be "next," and yet the cumulative effect of witnessing so many orgasms before me was to suppose that my own orgasm should depend on doing something wilder than anyone else had done. But the wildest thing I could think of was to *speak* my passion. It was, however, obviously against the "rules" for anyone to speak but the nameless woman. So I grew very hot with a concealed, unaccommodated sense of being "abnormal." I was about the tenth man called: my heart trembled violently as I rose toward Sylvia and firmly planted my mouth on her vagina. It was a wonderful sensation, like a great flame leaping within me, to taste the salty nectar of those lurid-pink petals of flesh, but she twisted so savagely that she immediately knocked my head back. The nameless woman was not much help by placing her hand on the back of my neck rather than the back of my head. I tried to steady Sylvia by placing both my hands on her thighs, but the strength of her excitement was astonishing, and the kiss I offered her wound up being smeared across her genitals, labia, and pubic hair. Then the nameless woman pulled my head back with the command: "Now from behind, from behind!" I crouched under and behind Sylvia, masturbating wildly for a few seconds to show everyone how flush with anticipation I was over the opportunity to perform such a "dark" action.

A whirlpool of sensations flooded me: the floor was slippery with semen; the air was heavy with a luscious fragrance of sweat, perfume, and sperm; the nameless woman smiled at me; her eyes were soft blue; the remaining half-dozen men masturbated at the sight of my hunger; Sylvia's buttocks were a beautiful mosaic of visual minutiae: tiny, gossamer blond hairs, beads of perspiration, mysterious freckles, delicate creases, goosepimples, milkwhite glow, reddish impressions left by the hands that had previously touched her. I desperately wanted to speak, to say anything that entered my mind, regardless of whether it achieved a pornographic effect: "You make me so happy!" "I love you!" "I wish I could do this every day!" "You are the most beautiful woman in the world!" But I was afraid to say anything; speech would have exposed zones of feeling which would have been "embarrassing," indeed *excessive*. Instead, I used both hands to spread Sylvia's buttocks and silenced myself by plunging my tongue straight into her crevasse. Instantly, a great, delirious rush of heat overpowered me. I started coming helplessly, sank to the floor, my mouth pressed against Sylvia's right foot, my eyes closed, squeezing all the seed out of me in voluptuous spasms. As usual, the nameless woman paused to make sure I was completely spent, then spray from the nozzle splattered off of Sylvia onto me, urging me to leave the scene.

I returned to my clothes in something of a daze, but I was in no hurry to dress. I felt like a cloud, supremely relaxed, and sat contentedly naked watching the rest of the performance with the detachment of a "normal" theatre spectator. Unlike the rest of the audience, I wanted to know how the whole thing would end. Sweat and semen felt cold against my flesh, yet a languid warmth suffused me.

And though my body had experienced a very great shock, I would have welcomed a chance to kiss Sylvia some more, and the nameless woman, too. They were enchanting women. I enjoyed watching them bring off the rest of the men in pretty much the same way they had brought off everyone else; it was like watching myself come again and again. Sylvia never seemed to tire of discharging signs of orgasm, and the nameless woman never ceased to maintain her brisk aplomb. The last man, however, was a special case, because he had no audience whom he could excite through the intensity of his own excitement. To compensate for this "problem," the nameless woman employed an entirely different rhetoric. "Arouse me," she commanded. "Make me pull off my pants. I want an orgasm. I love watching you kiss her, watching you masturbate [onanieren]! Show me, show me!" All along, the detached "coolness" of this woman had functioned, subconsciously, to incite the men to perform actions which would "melt" her. Her sudden unmasking of this strategy perhaps drove him wilder than I had been driven, and even Sylvia seemed to want to close out the performance with an especially reverberant outpouring of orgasmic cries, although of course her audience, which from her field of vision could hardly include me, consisted only of the man and the nameless woman. But the nameless woman did not pull off her pants. Instead, once the man had spent himself, she performed her usual action of spraying Sylvia with the nozzle. The man crept away, the hot light went out, the organ music returned, and the nameless woman drew the curtain over the scene.

I then dressed quickly, along with two or three other men, who were now shadowy phantoms in the subdued, orange light. I went to the bar to retrieve from the mysterious man there the bag containing my wallet. The sound of the spray gun washing down the rubber floor emanated from behind the curtain. As I was slipping on my gloves, the nameless woman, wearing her blouse again, emerged from behind the curtain and moved toward the bar. In her informal, cheerful voice, she thanked me for visiting "our club," looked forward to seeing me again, and wished me a good evening. In clumsy, foreigner's German, I said, "It is already a happy evening." She smiled and briskly slipped away into a whispery conversation with the man at the bar.

Outside, it was snowing, and I walked in the cold air and the empty city for nearly an hour before returning to my hotel room and a deep, sweet sleep. Images of the orgy entered my mind only intermittently, yet I felt profoundly changed by the experience, perhaps "revolutionized." I had discovered in myself an ominously complex capacity or appetite for pleasure which exceeded the power of fantasy alone to accommodate. This appetite caused me no guilt nor even embarrassment, but it did make me feel quite estranged from the world, pressured by an urge for communal pleasure which made me alone in any "normal" sense of community. That is the "tragic" irony of orgy, this desire for "more than enough" bodies: its *realization* depends on conditions so complex that only persons who are distinctively alone, capable of intense contemplation, can figure them out. So, happy though I was, I was also rather mystified by myself, by my desire, by my fate. Much as I liked Sylvia, the nameless woman, and even my anonymous "comrades," I knew I would never return to that club, because I also knew that I wanted "more" out of orgy than they would ever offer. Being reduced to a number did not bother me at all; but being reduced to silence constrained my pleasure in complexity of performance. Only the pleasure of speaking could make my nakedness more powerful. In the club milieu, woman recovers her maenadic identity by appropriating all speech and by making all men equal through silence. Maenadic woman "democratizes" orgy through a symmetrical tension between speech and silence, not a symmetrical distribution of speech; she wants to democratize orgiastic performance without losing control over it. But I want her to know — and desire — through speech, feelings which she provokes in me and can't control. Orgy, then, will become "more" democratic, not by effacing differences between bodies, but by effacing our fear of speech and its consequences in bodies which we desire precisely because they *are* "different." One must feel free to say things which even the orgy calculus of the Parisian aristocracy would not accommodate.

Orgy and Pornocracy

That the repression of speech in the construction of pornographic discourse and orgiastic performance derives from the Revolutionary ideology of "sexuality" and democratic suspicion of privileged or exclusive modes of feeling is perhaps most evident in the attitudes which inspired the invention of the term "pornocracy." The first person to offer a crude theory of pornocracy was Pierre-Joseph Proudhon (1809-1865), a radical activist who sought to move the Revolution to its final phase of utopian Anarchy. He is famous for observing that "property is theft." In 1858, Proudhon published *La Justice,* which was the subject of an unenthusiastic critique by a pair of pseudonymous feminist writers. In response to this critique, Proudhon worked on another pamphlet, *La Pornocratie ou les femmes dans les temps modernes,* which he never completed. The fragment was not published until 1875.

For Proudhon, pornocracy is a concept as demonic as the Antichrist. "Pornocracy is today the second world power, for it is second only to money. It is a secret power . . . which issues from women." Moreover, "Pornocracy and Malthusianism go hand in hand . . . Malthusianism preaches that no more children be conceived; pornocracy teaches how no more will be conceived."[13] What is pornocracy? It is the merger of sensuality and idealism;[14] that is, it is the perception that utopia has reality only through erotic pleasure. But Proudhon asserts that the pursuit and expansion of erotic pleasure entails *tyranny*, for one can enjoy such pleasure only at the expense of those who must work without pleasure. The expansion of erotic pleasure entails a point when the happiness of the pornocratic pleasure-seeker requires "more than enough" bodies and it is necessary to acquire these bodies through their sale to the pleasure-seeker, which means that the acquired bodies are working to produce pleasure without consuming it. Thus, Tyranny operates through Prostitution, which "in its deepest sense is exactly that which [feminists] call the liberation of woman or free love."[15] Feminism is a mask that conceals the "secret power" of pornocracy because "the liberation of woman" implies the release of a vast, insatiable desire for ecstasy which no man can ever satisfy, for, indeed, it is the animal nature of woman "to lust after kisses like goats after salt."[16] Pornocracy inflates the value of the erotic body and depresses the value of the "working" body, and this inflation will lead inevitably to an economy based on prostitution, in which only money (ownership of bodies) controls all relations between bodies. One of Proudhon's ambitions is to reunite pleasure and labor, and this utopian aspiration depends on undermining the power of money to dominate relations between bodies. For Proudhon, it is not language (dialogue), but money which defines power relations between people; to overthrow the tyranny of money, society must move toward an anarchistic economy, in which labor is always pleasure. A society which is happily free of all government, all despotic power relations, all class conflict, and all forms of money is a society in which Marriage satisfies all desires and all needs. The anarchist strives to create a world that has no need of any economic unit larger than marriage; in which man and woman sustain each other by doing gender-specific work for each other.

Pornocracy is obviously anathema to anarchy. Orgy and anarchy do not co-exist. Anarchy is a world which has transcended all difference except that between male and female. Pornocracy is a world which thrives on difference, distinction, exclusivity, and for that reason, it is not possible to detach the manifestation of pornocracy from the idea of aristocracy. But aristocracy objectifies itself above all through forms of theatre, through the notion of life itself as an aesthetic "performance" which is possible only through the perfection of complicated, difference-intensifying "rules" of communication, an intricate "calculus" of signification. Utopia from an aristocratic perspective is a matter of privileged cults, not pervasive cultures. Orgy is but one form of "calculus" (or theatre) sustaining the concept of aristocracy. Yet this calculus builds upon the assumption that it is always language (dialogue) which controls all relations between bodies. Orgiastic ecstasy depends on allowing the rapturous body to *speak* "for itself" in such a way that either the speaker or the listener feels that his or her unique body has become in some sense the Body, an abstraction, an intimation of infinity, which harbors the "excessive," self-abandoning feeling that one can never have or enjoy "enough" bodies. In relation to these assertions, it is worth observing that the rhetorical device which Proudhon relies on most in his attack on pornocracy is the aphorism, the statement of conditions that apply to reality as a whole, not just this or that identity. We noted in the analysis of *Les Plaisirs* that aphorism was not a device of any significance or interest in the orgiastic speech of the text. The difficulty of composing a pornographic aphorism is astonishing. I do not say it is impossible; but I do say that the theatricalizing *voice* which speaks the aphorism, which turns any language into an aesthetic performance, can function as a powerful signifier of a unique body *in tension* with the difference-effacing energy of language released through aphorism, and in this tension between a body and the Body, between voice and language, is an intimation of pleasure sufficient to initiate a "calculus" for orgiastic ecstasy.

Of course, in recent years, the frightening phenomenon of AIDS reinforces the Revolutionary anxiety toward the body and sustains the perception of orgy as an utterly inaccessible mode of performance. This mysterious epidemic probably has the effect of pushing orgy ever more deeply into the realm of metaphor. Erotic orgies of the magnitude pursued by the clandestine theatre perhaps now exist only as unspoken fantasies in the minds of secluded, masturbating individuals. But one should not suppose that these fantasies are insignificant because people feel powerless to bring them to "life" or even to disclose them. Rather, these fantasies signify a kind of limit to a capacity for happiness which is controlled by relations between words and actions. But of course, fear of the epidemic controls the performance of this relation. "Real" orgy entails a theatrical "calculus," a complex, pornographic relation between word and action, the *performance* of which is the "ultimate" disclosure of the body's mysterious capacity to make its vulnerability an ecstatic source of power, a supreme locus of desire and desirability. It is power based on trust rather than fear; it is power based on dialogic interactions between bodies rather than "master teacher" indoctrinations of them. Through its abstraction of the body, orgiastic performance releases the body from the metaphorical status we tend to ascribe to it when we fear the consequences of the language which exposes the "real" condition of our desires and capacities for pleasure. The pornographic relation between word and action is perhaps the strongest test of what is possible as theatre . . . and therefore of what is the happiest possibility of collaborative action.

Notes

Chapter One: Orgy Theory

1. Marghanita Laski, *Ecstasy. A Study of some Secular and Religious Experiences* (Bloomington: Indiana University Press, 1961), 145. Eduard Fuchs, *Geschichte der erotischen Kunst,* Vol. 2 (München: Langen, 1922-1926), 286, says that orgy is the exhaustion of all possibilities of pleasure. But this definition is too metaphorical to be of practical use in grasping the significance of orgy as an ecstatic *performance.* Orgy is more likely an expansion (rather than exhaustion) of particular pleasures, but definitely not all pleasures nor even all possibilities of a pleasure.

2. Bakhtin elaborates on the theory of the carnivalesque in *Rabelais and His World,* trans. Helene Iswolsky (Bloomington: Indiana University Press, 1984). This translation first appeared in 1965, but Bakhtin had completed the project well before then. See also his *The Dialogic Imagination,* trans. Caryl Emerson and Michael Holquist (Austin: University of Texas Press, 1981).

3. On the subject of the bacchantes, see Michel Bourlet, "L'orgie sur la montagne," *Nouvelle revue d'ethnopsychiatrie,* 1 (1983) (issue devoted to "Dionysos: le même et l'autre"), 9-44; and in the same issue, Philippe Guerin, "Bacchanales et defense maniaque," 45-56. Both authors treat the cult as a social problem or pathology which the Greek patriarchy could not resolve merely by spreading myths about the cult; the problem required a change in the institutional organization of Greek society. See also Louis Sèchan, *La Danse grecque antique* (Paris: Boccard, 1930), 151-182.

4. Agriculture did not cease to be of central importance to the Greeks, but the Persian War made them realize that agriculture could prosper only through international trade and that the resources of the land were not sufficient in themselves to support either their material aspirations or their sense of security

in the Aegean region. Moses I. Finley, *Ancient Slavery and Modern Ideology* (New York: Viking, 1980), 139: "Markets in antiquity were regularly 'expanded' only by conquest and the incorporation of new territories, and that opportunity was to all intents and purposes closed with Augustus, except for the internal settlement of the new acquisitions which rapidly followed." Maenadic Dionysos-worship, with its rural rather than maritime focus of spiritual energy, presents a serious obstacle to the pursuit of world markets and power. Froma Zeitlin, "Playing the Other: Theater, Theatricality, and the Feminine in Greek Drama," *Representations* 11 (Summer 1985), 63-94, puts the matter somewhat differently when she asserts that a "sacred vocation" of the *polis* and Greek political institutions was "to instruct men as to how they might transcend feminine influence" (88). But what is most significant to me is that, beginning with the Greeks, the concept of orgy seems deeply embedded in perceptions of a powerful release of "feminine influence," and this influence puts tremendous pressure on men to strive toward some heroic or even god-like identity.

5. George E. Mylonas, *Eleusis and the Eleusinian Mysteries* (Princeton: Princeton University Press, 1961), 229-237.

6. Mylonas, 224-225.

7. Joseph Fontenrose, *The Delphic Oracle* (Berkeley: University of California Press, 1978), 204-212.

8. Otto Kern, *Die Religion der Griechen*, Vol. 2 (Berlin: Weidman, 1963, reprint of 1935 edition), 147.

9. See Ramsay MacMullen, *Paganism in the Roman Empire* (New Haven and London: Yale University Press, 1981), 1-18.

10. Oliver Taplin, "Emotion and Meaning in Greek Tragedy," in Erich Segal (ed.), *Greek Tragedy* (New York, Harper, 1983), 1-12, seems to agree: "Many attempts have been made to find invariable ritual elements in Greek tragedy, but all have failed and all (so far as I can see) are bound to fail [. . .] Greek tragedy reflects and exploits the rituals of the real world, of course: but it is not itself a ritual [. . .] This break with the repetitiousness of ritual may well have been one of the great achievements of tragedy's creators" (3).

11. K.J. Dover, *Greek Homosexuality* (New York: Vintage, 1980), 124-135, explains, largely from the evidence of vase-painting and sculpture, that the Greeks idealized a diminuitive penis; the possibility then emerges that the image of an enlarged or erect penis was as comic as a large, flacid penis and therefore had no inciteful or pornographic effect on an audience. But the motive for idealizing the diminuitive penis is not clear. Are we to assume that because Greek artists were "extremely interested in the penis" (134), but not in the vagina, which they consistently concealed in their images of women, that neither the sight nor the image of the vagina excited Greek men? We should not confuse the intention to idealize or caricature with the power of an image to excite its spectator. My hunch is that the Greeks "idealized" the diminuitive penis to

signify an ambiguous attitude toward looking at the penis. This strategy obfuscates spectator expectation that an exposed penis "ought" to be erect, that the display of genitals signifies the excitement of the displayer and a desire to excite the spectator.

12. In *The Rhetorica* (II, 8: 1386a; Oxford: Clarendon Press, 1928), Aristotle observes that "what we fear for ourselves excites our pity when it happens to others." In *The Poetics,* of course, Aristotle claims that tragic *katharsis* results from stimulation of both fear and pity (pathos) in the spectator. Orgiastic performance, however, does not justify itself in relation to the stimulation of either emotion — orgiastic performance must stimulate intense *desire* in the spectator to extend the performance outside any containing framework. Orgy does not provoke compassion, but *passion,* a magnitude of trust between performers and spectators which is possible within a cult but perhaps not within a culture as a whole.

13. Helen P. Foley, *Ritual Irony* (Ithaca and London: Cornell University Press, 1985), 29-30.

14. Carl Niessen, *Handbuch der Theaterwissenschaft,* Vol. 1, Part 1 (Emsdetten: Lechte, 1953), 622-630.

15. Anne Carson, *Eros, the Bittersweet* (Princeton: Princeton University Press, 1986), 45.

16. Eric A. Havelock, "The Oral Composition of Greek Drama," in his *The Literate Revolution in Greece and Its Consequences* (Princeton: Princeton University Press, 1982), 261-313.

17. See Thomas Bertram Webster, *Greek Theatrical Production* (London: Methuen, 1970), 85-110.

18. Kathleen Schlesinger, *The Greek Aulos* (London: Methuen, 1939), 140.

19. Alois M. Nagler, *A Source Book in Theatrical History* (New York: Dover, 1959), 5, quoting an ancient biography of Aeschylus.

20. Jean-Pierre Vernant, *The Origins of Greek Thought* (Ithaca: Cornell University Press, 1982), 145.

21. Milman Parry, *The Making of Homeric Verse* (Oxford: Clarendon Press, 1971), 112-244.

22. Bernd Seidensticker, *Die Gesprächsverdichtung in den Tragödien Senecas* (Heidelberg: Winter, 1969), 15-90.

23. Formulaic refers to conventions, *habits* of signification which recur in response to a fixed, and often localized, perception of audience. System, however, refers to *modes* of signification which evolve in response to a theoretical perception of audience.

24. George Thomson, *Studies in Ancient Greek Society* (London: Lawrence and Wishart, 1978), 435-462.

25. Eric Havelock, *Preface to Plato* (Cambridge, Mass: Harvard University Press, 1982, originally published in 1963).

26. See Moses Hadas (ed.), *The Complete Plays of Aristophanes* (New York:

Bantam, 1962), 258 (translation by R.H. Webb).

27. In *The Frogs* (405 BC), a comedy of unsurpassed sophistication, the language of tragedy is the subject of an elaborate *enacted* crtique by Dionysos, Aeschylus, Euripides, Pluto, and the Chorus ("Rapt spectators of bouts between critical minds magistratic," Hadas, 396). But in situating the language of tragedy, as it evolved out of the Dionysian myth, within an extremely complex dialogic language of critique, the play implies that social reality (or at least the highly sophisticated audience) enjoys significant doubt about the value of either tragedy or the myth to embody convincing impulses toward utopia. Indeed, the strange formal organization of the play suggests that utopia *is* this comic dialogic critique of the tragic, of intensely serious language, of "expressions awe-inspiring," of "great heroic models" (387), "of a dance, of a song/To enrapture thy heart" (390), "of something heavier to depress the scale, something big and strong" (412). In the end, Dionysos chooses Aeschylus over Euripides because the language of Aeschylean tragedy projects a greater or "nobler" vision of the world; but by involving himself in the critique, the god no longer signifies a power (to ecstatify the world) which humans must control through language: rather, he *merely* represents that power as something which the language of "poetic genius" (394) has reduced to a problem of rhetoric, of persuasiveness, of something either its speakers or spectators can believe in at all. Even more interesting, however, is that the play fuses theoretical consciousness and theatrical action; it is an *enactment* or theatricalization of (tragedy) theory. Dialogic critique and theorization (symposia language) are, for Aristophanes, comic modes of dramatic conflict and impersonation. This excess of language and theatrical complexity would be orgiastic except for one thing — it all strives toward a comic effect, toward the deflation of desire for the objects of conflict and critique. Orgy is always a *serious* business insofar as it dedicates itself to the exposure, intensification, and fulfillment of a desire, not to the purgation (*katharsis*) or transcendence of the desire. But the seriousness of pleasure dominating orgy performance does not, of course, mean that orgy is a category of tragic action.

28. For an exhaustive commentary on the Hellenistic controversies concerning the relation between pleasure and virtue, see J.C.B. Gosling and C.C.W. Taylor, *The Greeks on Pleasure* (Oxford: Clarendon Press, 1983), especially 193-224.

29. John Onians, *Art and Thought in the Hellenistic Age* (London: Thames and Hudson, 1979), 42.

30. See Moses I. Finley, *Economy and Society in Ancient Greece* (New York: Pelican, 1983), 129: "It was a firm doctrine in the ancient Near East that man was created for the sole and specific purpose of serving the gods: that was the obvious extension by one further step of the heirarchical structure of society. Neither Greek nor Roman shared that idea [. . .] Institutionally the distinction may be expressed this way: whereas in the Near East government and politics

were a function of the religious organization, Greek and Roman religion was a function of the political organisation."

31. Emily Vermeule, *Aspects of Death in Early Greek Art and Poetry* (Berkeley: University of California Press, 1979), 37; see also 8, on the difficulty for the Greeks in imagining a soul. Walter Burkert, *Greek Religion*, trans. John Raffan (Cambridge, Mass: Harvard University Press, 1985) contends that this difficulty of the Greeks in imagining (and dogmatizing) the soul or an after-life urged them, "finally," to perfect an elaborate Platonic metaphysics: "And yet with the idea of the immortal soul the discovery of the individual had reached a goal which is only fulfilled in philosophy" (300-301). It is difficult to believe that impulses toward orgy can emerge out of an intense fear of death or finality, but perhaps they do emerge out of an acute sense of not having "enough" *time* to feel pleasure.

32. Friedrich Nietzsche, *Basic Writings of Nietzsche*, trans. Walter Kaufmann (New York: Modern Library, 1966), 121, 125, 130.

33. Antonin Artaud, *The Theater and Its Double*, trans. Mary Caroline Richards (New York: Grove Press, 1958), 19.

34. Artaud, 27.

35. Artaud, 71.

36. Hermann Nitsch, *Das O.M.* [Orgien-Mysterien] *Theater Lesebuch* (Wien: Freibord, 1985), 312-322, subsequent citings from this book, which is the first volume of a projected multi-volume encyclopedic documentation of the O.M. theatre, appear in parenthesis within the text. For further documentation on Nitsch, see Nitsch, *Orgies Mysteries Theater* (Darmstadt: März, 1969); issue No. 2 of *protokolle*, ed. by Otto Breicha (Wien: Jugend und Volk, 1981); Wilhelm Höck, *Kunst als Suche nach Freiheit* (Köln: DuMont, 1973), 63-77; Peter Gorsen, *Sexualästhetik: zur bürgerlichen Rezeption von Obzönität und Pornographie* (Hamburg: Rowohlt, 1972), 159-188; Gorsen, *Sexualästhetik: Grenzformen der Sinnlichkeit im 20. Jahrhundert* (Hamburg: Rowohlt, 1987), 453-471. See also Ekkehard Stärk, *Hermann Nitschs Orgien Mysterien Theater und die "Hysterie der Griechen"* (München: Fink, 1987), which connects the O.M. theatre to specifically Viennese attitudes toward and appropriations of ancient Greek mythology and culture, as found in the work of such men as Freud, Rank, Hofmannsthal, and Bahr.

37. See Gorsen (1972) and especially Ludwig Leiss, *Kunst im Konflikt* (Berlin: De Gruyter, 1971), 454-484.

38. See Jacques Lacan, *The Four Fundamental Concepts of Psychoanalysis*, trans. Alan Sheridan (New York and London: Norton, 1981), 20, 187, 278.

39. Leo Spitzer, *Eine Methode Literatur zu interpretieren* (München: Hanser, 1975), 46.

40. Richard Wagner, *Tristan and Isolde*, trans. Stewart Robb (New York: Dutton, 1965), 93, subsequent citings within parenthesis. The score for the opera was published in New York by G. Schirmer, 1906.

41. See James M. Baker, *The Music of Alexander Scriabin* (New Haven: Yale University Press, 1986).

42. Boris de Schloezer, *Scriabin: Artist and Mystic*, trans. Nicolas Slonimsky (Berkeley: University of California Press, 1987, originally published in 1924), 183-184.

43. de Schloezer, 213.

44. de Schloezer, 189-190.

45. de Schloezer, 184.

46. de Schloezer, 241; Clemens-Christoph von Gleich, *Die sinfonischen Werke von Alexander Skrjabin* (Bilthoven: Creygton, 1963), 22.

47. Gleich, 22; Alexander Skrjabin, *Prometheische Phantasien* (Stuttgart: Deutsche Verlagsanstalt, 1924), 87-89.

48. Scriabin had very little experience of writing for the voice. The chorus in the final movement of the First Symphony (1900) is unusually dull. It is perhaps this failure to find a "voice" for orgy which pushes Scriabin's project completely into a death-permeated realm of the "impossible." For more on Scriabin's ideas about the "synthesis" of instrumental tonality and color, see Leonid Sabanejew's 1912 article, "Prometheus von Skrjabin," and Charles S. Myers' 1914-1915 article, "Zwei Fälle von Synästhesie," in Alexander Skrjabin, *Briefe* (Leipzig: Reclam, 1988), 374-388.

49. These are William Arrowsmith's translations which appear in David Grene and Richard Lattimore (eds.), *The Complete Greek Tragedies*, Vol. 4 (Chicago: University of Chicago Press, 1960).

50. The language seems to reach metaphorical complexity by being a description of fantastic actions performed or provoked by Dionysos. But since the chorus really believes these actions have occurred or has actually "seen" them happen, the language is merely "objective" description. Of course, the spectator of the performance treats such non-metaphorical, orgiastic description of fantastic action as a sign of delusion or "madness."

51. Stagnelius' stunning drama, which has never been translated into English, appears in Erik Johan Stagnelius, *Samlade Skrifter*, Vol. 4 (Stockholm: Bonnier, 1915), 235-279. For a more detailed discussion of this work, see Karl Toepfer, "Orfeus and the Maenads: Two Modes of Ecstatic Discourse in Stagnelius' *Bacchanterna*," *Scandinavian Studies*, forthcoming.

Chapter Two: Orgy Salon

1. See Paul d'Estrèe and Henri d'Almeras, *Les Théâtres libertins du XVIIIe siècle* (Paris: Daragon, 1903), a very rare work. For an excellent, opulent survey of public theatre in Paris during the eighteenth century, see Max Aghion, *Le Théâtre à Paris au XVIIIe siècle* (Paris: Librairie de France, 1926), which never discusses the clandestine theatres.

2. G. Capon and R. Yve-Plessis, *Les Théâtres clandestins* (Paris: Plessis, 1905); Arthur Maria Rabenalt, *Voluptas ludens* (Emsdetten: Lechte, 1963). Rabenalt discusses some aspects of the clandestine theatres in his *Theatrum Sadicum* (Emsdetten: Lechte, 1963), but focuses primarily on the theatrical activity of the Marquis de Sade. Sade, however, seems not to have participated very actively, if at all, in the clandestine network of theatres; or rather, his theatre was "clandestine" in the sense that it is largely the work of a prisoner and strives more for some kind of therapeutic than pornographic effect. Peter Weiss, in *The Persecution and Assassination of Jean-Paul Marat as Performed by the Inmates of the Asylum of Charenton under the Direction of the Marquis de Sade*, trans. Geoffrey Skelton and Adrian Mitchell (New York: Atheneum, 1965), makes the "asylum" theatre of de Sade the subject of a drama on the theme of revolution. Weiss ingeniously employs the play-within-a-play device to show how, from the aristocrat de Sade's perspective, life and history are modes of theatrical performance. But the asylum context of the action, and the use of the "sick" Marat as the antagonist of de Sade, raise the problem of theatre's "healing," therapeutic, or cathartic function. Eventually, the performance incites the inmate-performers to a revolutionary "orgy" which completely destroys the theatrical and institutional framework for "containing" the violent ideas that the performers had merely enacted. The play "ends" in orgy, which implies that orgy is the end of theatre rather than a mode of theatre. In Sweden, the aristocracy, imitating the French, also cultivated an aesthetic of clandestine theatres, but these apparently devoted themselves exclusively to the representation of political subjects; see Bertil H. Van Boer, Jr., "Gustaf III's 'Divertissement med sång' *Fodelsedagen:* A Gustavian Political Satire," *Scandinavian Studies* 61/1 (Winter 1989), 28-40. Richard Wunderer, *Treibhaus der Erotik. Pansexualismus und Orgiasmus in erotischen Wunschträumen und sexueller Wirklichkeit* (Schmiden bei Stuttgart: Freya, 1967), 420-424, superficially discusses the French "Geheimbühne," but provides the interesting perspective of encyclopedically situating this theatre within what seems like a vast subculture of "orgyism" in Western culture.

3. Major studies of libertine literature include: Jean-Pierre Dubost, *Eros und Vernunft. Literatur der Libertinage* (Frankfurt am Main: Athenaeum, 1988); Frédéric Lachevre, *Mélanges sur le libertinage au XVIIIe siècle* (Genève: Slatkin, 1968, originally published 1909); Francais Moureau and Alain-Marc Rieu (eds.), *Eros philosophe. Discours libertin des lumieres* (Paris: Champion, 1984); Peter Nagy, *Libertinage et révolution* (Paris: Gallimard, 1975).

4. Dubost, 225.

5. See, for example, Dubost, 188-211.

6. Capon and Yve-Plessis, 44.

7. Capon and Yve-Plessis, 249.

8. Franz Blei, *Formen der Liebe* (Berlin and Wien: Trianon, 1930), 205.

9. For more about Audinot, see Emile Campardon, *Les Spectacles de la foire,*

Vol. 1 (Paris: Berger-Levrault, 1877), 29-74.

10. Capon and Yve-Plessis, 209.

11. Capon and Yve-Plessis, 207.

12. For further details about the Verrier sisters, see Adolphe Jullien, *La Comédie et la Galanterie au XVIIIe siècle* (Paris: Rouveyre, 1879), 109-154, which, however, does not discuss their clandestine theatre activities in any significant way.

13. On Raucourt's perverse career, see Jean de Reuilly, *La Raucourt et ses amis* (Paris: Daragon, 1899), especially 120-125.

14. Capon and Yve-Plessis, 7.

15. Marian Hobson, "Diderot et la maniere," in *Saggi e ricerche di letteratura francese,* XXV (Roma: Bulzoni, 1986, 99-123), 114, 119.

16. Quoted from the translations of these articles in Bernard F. Dukore (ed.), *Dramatic Theory and Criticism* (New York: Holt, Rinehart and Winston, 1974), 287, 293.

17. See Restif de la Bretonne, *La Mimographe* (Genève: Slatkin, 1980, reprint of 1770 edition).

18. Marian Hobson, *The Object of Art. The Theory of Illusion in Eighteenth Century France* (Cambridge: Cambridge University Press, 1982), 139-179.

19. Hobson, *Object,* 181.

20. All this "surveillance" of public theatre may not have achieved the intended effect of creating a more "enlightened" public. In an article published in the 10 August 1782 issue of the *Journal de Paris,* Le Vacher de Charnois complains that the theatre is teaching the public to enjoy rather than fear or despise wicked morals: "I mean here the denigrators who, out of system, ignorance, or habit, accumulate pleasantries on the austerity of morals credited to *la Foire.* They are in their element, and me, I present myself to them as a citizen to ask why, after having erected theatres for the people, we persist in amusing ourselves with the spectacle of bad manners, in laughing at vicious equivocations and licentious scenes when it is possible to turn our amusements to profit as instruction [. . .] The people of Paris resemble a huge child who has long neglected education and needs to be guided by clear-minded friends toward a career of morality and truth," cited in Felix Gaiffe, *Le Drame en France au XVIIIe siècle* (Paris: Colin, 1910), 84-85 (my translation).

21. As I understand it, "sexuality" refers to conditions of sexual difference, to biological, political, or cultural "constructions" of sexual identity. It is a "scientific" concept which entails an infintely repeatable ("socially reproduceable") meaning. The erotic refers only to the pleasure derived from a "construction" of sexual difference. It is a complex category of aesthetic experience which therefore functions to intensify the participant's sense of uniqueness. As such, the erotic "construction" of sexual difference cannot repeat or "reproduce" any pleasure without being the consequence of ideology rather than desire. As an intimation

of the ecstatic, the erotic entails the production of meanings which elude any desire for their repetition, stability, or constancy; erotic desire "recurs" or "stays with us" only to the extent that it intensifies, surpasses, exceeds, transforms, or transcends all previous "constructions" of sexual difference, which is why discourse on and manifestations of the erotic inevitably drift into the domain of "perversity." But most discourse on "sexuality" seems obsessed with exposing "normal" (unpleasurable) constructions of "difference."

22. Capon and Yve-Plessis do not present any evidence to suggest that orgiastic performance was ever a commercial enterprise. Some actors, musicians, and designers received modest fees for their contributions to clandestine productions. The ever-busy Audinot shuttled his theatrical schemes between the official, the fairground, and the clandestine theatres. And of course, orgiastic theatre parties often functioned as "presents" exchanged between courtesans and their aristocratic lovers. But in the clandestine milieu, it was probably impossible for such orgiastic performance to evolve into a *business*; no matter how great the desire or "market" was for such performance, no one could really *sell* it. You could *give* "real" orgies, but you couldn't sell them. The clandestine impulse toward orgy seemed to operate in tandem with an "excessive" signification of generosity, with a desirable indifference toward the cost of pleasure. For these reasons, *erotic* theatre implies a different "construction" of relations between audience and performance than theatre which exposes the transparent, socially reproduced values that "construct" sexuality (gender). Achievement of this latter objective depends on performance which depresses the desire of the spectator to imitate the theatrical action; but erotic performance, focused on the inflation or recovery of desire, invites some mode of imitation from the spectator. Erotic performance moves toward orgy only to the extent that it promotes difference, not between itself and the spectator, but between cult and society. A democratic society tends to evaluate pleasures on the basis of their "accessibility," but it also tends to equate accessibility with "saleability." Thus, within democratic society, orgiastic performance can become a commodity, as described in the subsection, "A Postmodern Example of Orgy," of Chapter Four. However, the commodification of orgy seems to involve relations between spectators, as well as relations between spectating and performance, which inhibit the formation of cultic identity and difference. Instead, orgy commodification tends to make orgy a kind of hyperkinetic microcosm of general social relations which does not make the spectator feel like a member of a cult (or "elite"); it makes the spectator feel like an "individual" on the "dark" periphery of society.

23. An excellent articulation of the realist ideology of ecstasy, which associates ecstasy with heightened powers of seeing (rather than speaking) and with seeing something "naked" ("without illusions"), appears in Gert Mattenklott, *Der übersinnliche Leib* (Hamburg: Rowohlt, 1982), 14-15 (my translation): "We sense that truth is something unveiled [. . .] To discover, to disclose, to undress

something of all prejudices and represent it as nothing else . . . — here as in love we prefer not to approach quietly until that unconcealed condition presses in on us, in which we have to look away. From outside we penetrate toward the center like a conqueror. But the closer we come to the core, the more language becomes occluded. Nakedness silences. We shudder in an incomprehensible perplexity — such is the assumption of theories of the sublime — that we perceive it [the ecstatic sublime] as something utterly bare, to which nothing more or nothing else can be added. For this reason, nakedness is more frequently shown than described, remains an inexhaustible theme for images, while it is immediately without literary charm, as we already know from the last two centuries of pornographic *belles lettres.*" But these statements are perhaps an oversimplification of the relation between speech and nudity, because it is not nudity itself which atrophies the speech-making powers of its witnesses, but the degree to which nudity functions as an index of proximity to ecstasy. Nudity brings one closer to ecstasy only insofar as being naked or watching nakedness entails a desired nakedness of feeling. Such *nakedness of feeling* is not always simply a matter of seeing a body naked; or rather, the pleasure of feeling naked may depend on acknowledging the voice, speech, as a part of the body which must be "unveiled."

24. See Phyllis and Eberhard Kronhausen, *Erotic Fantasies* (New York: Grove Press, 1970), 3-18, 106-126, 329-335.

Chapter Three: Orgy Calculus

1. B. de Villeneuve (ed.), *Le Théâtre d'amour au XVIIIe siècle* (Paris: Bibliotheque des Curieux, 1910), 34-35.

2. Capon and Yve-Plessis, 169, 173.

3. It is indeed strange that Arnould's pleasure depended on making a spectacle of her erotic feelings, even though the audience for the spectacle felt no pleasure at all in the spectacle. She seems to have acted as if her pleasure depended not only on the extreme exclusivity of her feelings, but on signifying that exclusivity to an audience. Her motives are intractably complex: perhaps she wished to cultivate a condition whereby her pleasure depended on making a spectacle of her erotic feelings, but not on the pleasure her pleasure had for others. That's an extraordinary condition of freedom to seek, for it entails the freedom to put one's most intimate feelings on display and freedom from any compulsion to "please" the audience for the display. She can have orgasm anytime and anywhere she wants, without needing the approval of any audience. Perhaps only a professional actor can grasp the appeal of this kind of freedom over audiences. Like most persons involved with the clandestine theatre, Arnould led a complicated social life, which is the subject of a chatty, entertaining biography, Robert B. Douglas, *Sophie Arnould. Actress and Wit* (Paris: Carrington, 1898); this book, however, is not very helpful

in explaining Arnould's personality as an aesthetic system.

4. General inventories of taboo speech situations in the realm of the erotic had a rudimentary beginning with Paul Englisch, *Irrgarten der Erotik* (Leipzig: Lykeion, 1931) and *Geschichte der erotischen Literatur* (Stuttgart: Püttmann, 1927); these are works of literary history, which treat linguistic statements as taboo only when they assume a literary form which one can publish or read only in secret. This approach, however, produces categories controlled by theme or subject matter rather than unique relations between words and feeling. Milan Chlumsky, "Estheticité, erotisme, et pornographie," *Revue d'esthetiques* 1-2 (1978), 191-213, applies Prague structuralist methods of literary analysis to construct a theory of pornographic *writing*. Chlumsky concludes that pornographic language "has a tendency to eliminate acausal description and concentrate above all on the action itself and on the augmentation of the number of actors" (207). But in the realm of pornographic *speech*, it is not the description of actions but the description of feelings which contributes most to a pornographic (ecstatic) effect.

5. This text appears in Villeneuve, 162-204. All citations from this edition appear in parenthesis.

6. Rene Girard, *Violence and the Sacred*, trans. Patrick Gregory (Baltimore: Johns Hopkins University Press, 1977, originally published in 1972) has explained at length (though perhaps not always accurately) how sacrificial violence constructs identity.

7. Michel Foucault develops this theme in *The History of Sexuality. Volume I: An Introduction*, trans. Robert Hurley (New York: Vintage 1980, originally published in 1976), in which the concept of "sexuality" appears as a mode of knowledge (discourse), for in "creating the imaginary element that is 'sex,' the deployment of sexuality established one of its most essential internal operating principles: the desire for sex — the desire to have it, to have access to it [. . .]" (156).

8. For further elaboration of this major point, see note 23 for Chapter Two.

9. *Training. Being the Fourth Tale of Male Masochism from the Garden of Delicate Torments* (Paris: Sinistre, 1984), 47.

10. Shere Hite, *The Hite Report* (New York: Dell, 1977), 201.

11. Bonnie Stonewall, "Lovelines," *On Our Backs* (Winter 1986, 9, 11), 11.

12. Stonewall, 9.

13. Ralph Gordon, *Verse and Prose Technique. A Study in Rhythm and Tone Color* (New York: City College Cooperative Store, 1938), 10.

Chapter Four: Orgy Politics

1. Paul d'Estrèe, *Le Théâtre sous la terreur (théâtre de la peur)* (Paris: Emile-Paul, 1913), 103.

2. d'Estrée, 3-5.

3. d'Estrée, 268-272.

4. d'Estrée, ix.

5. Saint-Just, *Oeuvres choisies* (Paris: Gallimard, 1968), 320-321.

6. A good, but hardly complete, effort to identify the huge mass of conventions defining melodrama is Frank Rahill, *The World of Melodrama* (University Park and London: Pennsylvania State University, 1967). See also, Peter Brooks, *The Melodramatic Imagination* (New Haven: Yale University Press, 1976) and Julia Przybos, *L'Entreprise mélodramatique* (Paris: Corti, 1987).

7. Gil Sigaux (ed.), *Le Théâtre érotique du XIXe siècle* (Paris: Les Classiques interdits, 1979).

8. *Les Deux gougnottes* appears in Sigaux, 29-85. Henri Monnier (1799-1877) spent his life chronicling the bizarre, curious, and eccentric aspects of Parisian cultural life. These chronicles assumed various forms, beginning with the *Scènes populaires* (1830): histories, novels, plays, and works which combined these genres. Monnier was also a well-known caricaturist, whose drawings appeared regularly in the popular media. Perhaps his most significant creation was the comic character of Monsieur Prudhomme, a caricature of a blithe, complaisant, and respectable bourgeois whose composure always survives his encounter with some disreputable aspect of Parisian life. This character not only appeared in stories and plays; he was also the "author" of various pseudo-philosophical "reflections" on contemporary morality. Monnier's drawings of Monsieur Prudhomme were so delightful to the public, that other artists, including Daumier, appropriated the character in their own drawings. Monnier himself acted the part of Monsieur Prudhomme on the stage, and of course, the character emerged again in several plays for the marionette theatre. Most of the marionette plays have a brothel setting or depict erotic actions between adventurers and *grisettes*, young working women who seek to improve their material circumstances by dispensing erotic favors. For more about Monnier, see Daniel Gerould, "Henri Monnier and the Erotikon Theatron: The Pornography of Realism," *The Drama Review* 25/1 (March 1981), 17-24; this article also contains a translation of Monnier's one-act *The Tart and the Student*. See also Paul-Emmanuel-August Poulet-Malassies [Alfred Delvau], *Théâtre érotique de la rue Sante, son histoire* (Paris: Pincebourse, 1871, originally published in Bruxelles, 1866). The bibliography for Max von Boehn, *Puppets and Automata*, trans. Josephine Nicoll (New York: Dover, 1972, originally published in 1929) lists two books related to the erotic marionette theatre which I have had no success in locating: D. Bonnaud, *Pierrot pornographe* (Paris, 1902) and Edouard Doyen, *Les Marionettes amoureuses* (Paris, no date).

9. See Michel Foucault, *The History of Sexuality. Volume I: An Introduction*, trans. Robert Hurley (New York: Vintage, 1980), especially 53-73.

10. Frank S. Caprio, *Female Homosexuality* (New York: Grove, 1962), 98-99.

11. John Elsom, *Erotic Theatre* (New York: Taplinger, 1974), 176. I am aware of male and female homosexual variations of this German theatre performance, which invites the audience to "worship" the genitals of the performer. But I am not familiar with any evidence of a "real" performance in which the stringing up of a man incites an audience of women to orgiastic worship of his penis. Indeed, I find it very difficult to believe that persons of either sex ever even fantasize about such a performance, although I suppose the "original" Dionysian mysteries contained some sort of orgiastic phallic worship by groups of maenads. But since the mysteries excluded men, the phallus was symbolic, rather than "real." I have no explanation for this "construction" of sexual difference. Laurence Senelick, calling my attention to Ladies Only stripper clubs, wonders if the business of female spectators "stuffing dollar bills in a jockstrap can be construed as phallic worship"? My knowledge of such clubs is extremely small, but I am not familiar with any evidence which indicates that the male performer actually displays an erection or that the female spectators achieve some kind of mass (orgiastic) orgasm, take off their clothes, make physical contact with the penis, or masturbate in response to the male performer. The women seem to "worship" the penis by bestowing a dollar value on it. Moreover, this "value" of the penis seems implied, rather than revealed, by the wearing of the jockstrap. But despite the delight some women take in such performances, I still find it difficult to believe that this theatre has a basis in the erotic desires or fantasies of any women, unless, perhaps, money itself has an aphrodisiac or fetishistic effect upon the woman. But in that case, with money as the sign of castrative control, it is not "worship" of the phallus, but power over (ownership of) it which accounts for the pleasure of performance. From my perspective, to commodify the worship of the phallus, the spectator should pay *to* worship a desired manifestation, rather than *equate* worship with payment.

12. Obviously my description of this performance relies heavily on an old, but vivid memory of it. Therefore, my transcription of the speech is often approximate rather than precise. But I have tried to maintain strict accuracy regarding the rhetorical structures employed by the speakers and the emotions provoked by their speech. At the time of the performance, I did not anticipate ever writing about it, because, back then, the study of performance simply did not encompass such performances. It has taken me a number of years to grasp the relevance of this "subjectivity," as well as the nerve to disclose it. I must suggest, however, that accurate "reconstruction" of pornographic performance depends heavily on researchers who are not "outside" of the performance, because we cannot understand this type of performance, which blurs distinctions between performer and spectator, by analyzing it with the spectatorial "detachment" applied to "standard" reconstructions of theatrical performance. I am not convinced that a more "anthropological" approach to this performance is more "scientific" than my rather literary account of it, but I am eager for guidance about how to inscribe

the subjectivity without being, so to speak, inscribed by it.

13. Pierre-Joseph Proudhon, *Von der Anarchie zur Pornocratie*, trans. L. Kundig (Zürich: Arche, 1970), 13.

14. Proudhon, 31.

15. Proudhon, 8.

16. Proudhon, 41.

APPENDICES

Appendix I

Orgy Cult and Slave Culture

The use of theatre by the Greek patriarchy to marginalize the Dionysian orgy cult and the violent "feminine" power associated with orgiastic performance was possible only because the theatre functioned in conjunction with ideological structures controlling other institutions within Greek society, such as the family and slavery. Proudhon asserts that orgy (pornocracy) is the antithesis of anarchy, a world-utopia governed by one almighty institution, marriage. Orgy, for Proudhon, is therefore the product of an overly-institutionalized, overly-regulated, excessively specialized society or "tyranny." A question then emerges: if ecstasy signifies the supreme value a person feels for him or herself, what is the relation between the pursuit of orgiastic ecstasy and the value ascribed to people through the bonding mechanisms of marriage or slavery? Is orgy the negation of slavery or is orgy only possible in a non-utopian world in which persons systematically denied ecstasy must "pay" for the ecstasy of the orgiast? Obviously this question has no definitive answer one way or the other. But theories of Greek attitudes towards their own instituions are such as to indicate why answers to the question are much less interesting to us than they were to the maenads, the Greek patriarchy, or Proudhonian post-Revolutionary consciousness.

Philip Slater, *The Glory of Hera* (Boston: Beacon Press, 1968) used psychoanalytical theory to support his contention that Greek perceptions of the heroic arose in response to profound anxieties toward the mysterious manifestation of female being (chiefly the mother) within the home.

Eva Keuls, *The Reign of the Phallus* (New York: Harper, 1985), adopting a feminist perspective, more narrowly locates the source of these anxieties in the female body or image (rather than being) and argues that what is at stake in the containment process is not the search for heroic identity, but the sheer embodiment of power. However, I might suggest that the monumentalization of Amazons in Greek art may signify an effort to objectify a feminine aspect to the *male* desire for heroic, warrior identity.

But K. J. Dover, *Greek Homosexuality* (New York: Vintage, 1980) denies that Greek homosexuality emerged as a strategy for accommodating this aspect: homosexuality is "natural" only to the extent that the man assumes the active ("masculine") role (67-68). Yet homosexuality is "natural," not because it enacts an heroic attitude, but because "social competition," which seems to lack a historical dimension (88, n. 52), determines what is "natural": in the "natural" order of sexualization "pursuit is the role prescribed for the male, flight for the female, and both are judged and valued in accordance with their success in carrying out their respective roles" (88). The value of the female and the feminine in maintaining a "*family* of whom enterprise and virility are expected" [by other families in "social competition" with each other] (88, my italics) thus derives from interpreting "flight" in terms of a "containment" of the feminine. A woman's value was proportional to her success in sequestering herself from the male desire which established her value; but this success was as much a test of the woman's competitiveness as of the man's, since, according to Dover (67), Greek men believed that women experienced sex more "intensely" than men (the Dionysian myth is the representation of this belief) — i.e., woman is "heroic" to the extent that she transcends or sacrifices her more "intense" drives in order to accommodate the desire of the male for a woman whom his desire cannot devalue by being met.

But a limitation of Dover's explanation is that by focusing on power relations within the family as the foundation of a "natural" (ahistorical) social order or construction of sexuality, we lose sight of the political significance attached to the containment of the feminine: we do not see the connection between the social construction of sexuality and the motives which mobilize people and resources to realize a particular idea of utopia, to cultivate distinctive aesthetic strategies for signifying the utopian idea, and to cultivate language in a way that is unique (drama).

Moses I. Finley repeatedly stressed the immense importance of slavery in ancient economies. This extremely complex institution endured because it was very profitable, and it was very profitable because overpopulation depressed the exchange-value of labor in societies which perceived little or no benefit in "saving" labor through technological innovation. Within a slave society, a person does not achieve a distinctive value or identity through labor. As an institution, slavery urges everyone in society to construct an identity which produces some aesthetic rather than purely economic value, and it is out of this prioritization of aesthetic over economic value that the concept of *arete* begins to circulate. But *arete* is a value determined and identified by a class of persons — warriors primarily—who are, in a sense, outside of the institutions and communities they administer: they are those *men* who are "greater" than the motives which bring men into conflict with each other. As an aesthetic mode of living, *arete* is apparent and appreciable to complete strangers, even enemies. *Arete* is the thing which can unite men into a kind of brotherhood of the elite, charged with bringing unity of meaning and identity to a world fragmented into competing factions. *Arete,* which is not a cult but a character trait, cannot be tested or "proved" unless he who possesses it turns his gaze away from the home and toward the horizon of something *foreign.* The family does not produce *arete;* on the contrary, the concept of *arete* governs the operation of family (and sexual) relations. *Arete* and slavery combine to reduce marriage to an economic value which has only incidental interest as a source of aesthetic or ecstatic experience. Marriage propertizes sexual relations in order to preserve the "authenticity" of the family: woman remains "in flight," sequestered, veiled, "contained" because, should she submit to her supposed maenadic desires, doubt would arise regarding the "authenticity" of the children to whom she gives birth, children she can never deny are "hers." "Naturally" this ideology suggests that ecstasy, as the abandonment of the self, of an "authenticated" identity, manifests itself as something which cannot be "contained" within marriage.

But *arete* and slavery also combine to depress the value of the erotic as a source of ecstasy. On the one hand, *arete* embodies an aesthetic which supposedly transcends the power of erotic phenomena over male desire. Hippolytus, in Euripides' play of that name, is perhaps an exaggerated portrayal of this determination to transcend the erotic. On the other hand, as Finley, *Ancient Slavery and Modern Ideology* (New York: Viking, 1980), 96, observes, slavery sustained the illusion that erotic or (from the slave's perspective) sexual experience was easily accessible, pervasive, unregulated: thus, if the erotic produces an ecstatic intersection of the free and enslaved classes, then neither the erotic nor the ecstatic will appear to add value or distinction to the members of either class. Ecstasy is "cheap" and "easy" when it derives from the enslavement of the Other, from the right to enslave. Slavery opens up possibilities for orgy while depressing the value of orgy. Indeed, given its historical context, the Dionysian myth embeds within its ideological function the assumption that the will to ecstasy cannot be detached from conditions of slavery.

The Nigerian author Wole Soyinka has dramatized this perception very effectively in his play, *The Bacchae of Euripides* (in *Collected Plays 1*, New York: Oxford University Press, 1973, 233-307), in which Dionysos inspires the worship, not only of maenads, but of slaves, who perceive in the ecstasy he offers the conditions of *freedom*. The play obviously links the discharge of ecstatic erotic feeling in the feminine Other (for a god) with the release of revolutionary energy in the slave class: maenads and slaves form a "mixed" (234) chorus. But the play also shows that this drive for freedom through worship of the superhuman, through myth, through orgiastic ecstasy, through the linking of the repressed desire of the feminine Other to the oppressed desire of the enslaved Other, is a terrible illusion, which has as its consequence the brutal violation rather than unity of the body and bodies. At the end of the play, the decapitated head of Pentheus spurts "red jets" which the characters at first misperceive, as they have misperceived throughout the play, as blood which Tiresias identifies as wine. As if hypnotized by this "magical" transformation, the entire community drifts into a "dream-like" (307) state: the myth has drugged the entire community, and the "final glow around the heads of Pentheus and Agave," around the king and the mother, signifies the origin (not the resolution) of crisis within the community and between the sexes in doubt about the authenticity of identities formed through sexuality: or, as Dionysos puts it at the beginning of the play, the "seed" which engendered his ecstatic being "burgeons," "bursts," "springs," "flowers," "pounds," "beats" throughout the ancient, myth-saturated world to bring "vengeance on all who deny my holy origin and call my mother — slut" (235). Orgy appears as a category of slavery, not a release from it.

Yet it is language by which the illusion of ecstatic salvation manifests itself: Soyinka's play contains many more words than the original version by Euripides, and this prolixity is the corollary of the repression and oppression the speakers seek to overcome. It is not that slavery and containment operate through language as such, but rather that language (of metaphoric prolixity) sustains the illusion of freedom through ecstasy.

As the Leader of the Bacchantes remarks at one point:

> Night, night set me free
> Sky of a million roe, highway of eyes
> Dust on mothwing, let me ride
> On ovary silences, freely
> Drawn on the rein of dreams. (291)

In this metaphor-saturated speech, language structures a poetic ideology in which 1) darkness and silence signify the utopian conditions of freedom; 2) freedom is nevertheless "drawn on the rein of dreams" — i.e., contained or enslaved within the unconscious, an *image* of a fantastic sky or a *way of seeing* as if through a "highway of eyes or the *state of suspension in space* enjoyed by a moth; 3) the "ovary silences" connects freedom to the darkness and silence of an interior, feminine space inhabited by the nameless and unnameable identities of the unborn and unconceived. Thus, ecstasy and freedom do not result from the fulfillment of an "authentic" or "born" identity that is analogous to the reality of birth and the mutations of identity(ies) which phenomenalize the Mother, but from the recovery of a state of being without identity, without name, without language, without bondage to another cell or another being. But this "nameless" (and impossible) condition of freedom strikes me as a cryptic way of saying that slavery is ultimately a matter of being "born" (into it), it is an unhappiness issued by the Feminine — an interesting perspective for a "modern" writer.

Appendix II

From Capon and Yve-Plessis, 169-173.

DIALOGUE

sur l'air de Myrza/to a tune by Myrza

Delisle de Sales

(1778?)

Personnages:
Sophie Arnould, Le Chevalier de Grammont

La scène se passe d'abord dans la salle de bains de Sophie.
Ensuite au bal de l'Opéra.

The scene takes place in Sophie's bathroom.
After the opera ball.

(Sophie Arnould était occupée dans son bain, quand son boudoir, mal fermé, peut-être à dessein, s'ouvrit de lui-même: à la vue de son amant, elle ne put que jeter avec une heureuse gaucherie sur son corps parfumé une robe de gaze qui voilait moins qu'elle ne dessinait ses charmes.)

(Sophie Arnould is preoccupied with her bath when the door to her boudoir, incompletely closed, perhaps by design, opens to him: to the view of her lover, she merely tosses over her perfumed body, with a delightful awkwardness, a gauze robe which veils less than she intends of her charms.)

I

GRAMMONT

Enfin je vous vois, Arnould, sans défense
La pudeur seule a voilé ces appas . . .

> At last I see you, Arnould, without defense
> Modesty alone veils your charms . . .

ARNOULD

Non . . . Non . . . D'Intelligence,
Mon coeur ému va voler dans tes bras. *(bis)*

> No . . . No . . . from intelligence,
> My excited heart flies into your arms. *(repeated)*

II

GRAMMONT

Ta main, Arnould, me cache mal tes charmes,
Laisse mes yeux parcourir ta beaute . . .

> Your hand, Arnould, can't hide your charms,
> Let my eyes traverse your beauty . . .

ARNOULD

Non . . . Non . . . Vois mes alarmes;
Je crains mon coeur ardent de volupté.
(Grammont fait un pas en arrière et tombe aux genoux de Sophie.)

> No . . . No . . . Observe my alarm;
> I fear my ardent and voluptuous heart.
> *(Grammont steps forth, stops, and falls to his knees before Sophie.)*

III

GRAMMONT

Charmante Arnould, je suis fait pour t'entendre,
J'étais ton maître, et je te rends tes droits . . .

> Enchanting Arnould, I was born to listen to you,
> I was your master, and I submit to your laws . . .

ARNOULD

Quoy . . . Quoy . . . Tu n'es que tendre,
Je ne crains plus de rentrer sous tes lois.
(Souris amoureux de Sophie, elle fait signe à son amant de se rapprocher.)

Why . . . Why . . . You are only tender,
I no longer fear going back to your rules.
(Smiling amorously, Sophie makes a sign for her lover to approach her.)

IV

GRAMMONT

Sur cette bouche où s'entr'ouvre la rose,
Laisse-moi prendre un baiser amoureux . . .
On this mouth which open like a rose,
Let me place an amorous kiss . . .

ARNOULD

Prends . . . Prends . . .
(Avec un sourire agacant)
Même autre chose;
Pour ta réserve on a droit d'être heureux.
Take . . . Take . . .
(with an irritated smile)
Even the other thing;
Your reserve gives one the right to feel lucky.

V

GRAMMONT

Quoy! je pourrais, de ta gorge d'albâtre,
Sans t'offenser, effleurer le satin?
Why! Would I spoil it, your alabaster throat,
To touch the satin without offending you?

ARNOULD

Ouy . . . Ouy . . . Quand j'idolâtre,
Je ne crains pas qu'on profane mon sein.
Yes . . . Yes . . . When I idolize,
I don't fear the profaning of my breast.

VI

GRAMMONT

Sein de Vénus, que ta pudeur ignore,
En palpitant tu redoubles mes feux . . .

*(Arnould passe une main autour du cou de son amant et l'invite par ses yeux
ardents à être téméraire.)*
>Breast of Venus, which your modesty ignores,
>Its throbbing intensifies my fire . . .
>*(Arnould places a hand around her lover's neck and,
>with her ardent eyes, invites him to be bold.)*

ARNOULD

Vas . . . Vas . . . Poursuis encore;
Le bonheur même amène d'autre voeux.
(Grammont est ému, il s'incline vers le dos de Sophie, à demi entr'ouvert.)
>Come . . . Come . . . Pursue further;
>Happiness itself brings other desires.
>*(Grammont, moved, presses behind Sophie to disrobe her.)*

VII

GRAMMONT

A mes transports livre, Arnould, d'autres charmes,
(Se tournant du côté de la gorge de sa maitresse.)
Mon coeur palpite et n'ose s'exprimer . . .
>Give my rapture, Arnould, your other charmes
>*(Caressing her throat [or cleavage].)*
>My heart throbs yet dares not express itself . . .

ARNOULD

Dis . . . Dis . . . Sois sans alarmes!
(Elle replace la tête de son amant dans sa première attitude.)
Offense-t on lorsqu'on sait aimer?
>Speak . . . Speak . . . Don't be afraid!
>*(She returns her lover's head to its first attitude.)*
>Does it scare you when one knows you love?

VIII

GRAMMONT

(Lui montrant le faisceau de myrthes.)
Tu vois ces fleurs, c'est ainsi qu'à Cythère
Tout doucement, Vénus punit l'Amour.
*(Sophie conduit le chevalier sur un fauteuil où elle le fait asseoir, se met à ses
genoux et se découvre avec une ingénuité feinte, mais pleine de charmes.)*

(Showing her a bundle of myrtle.)
You see these flowers, through them on Cytherea
Did Venus so sweetly punish Love.
(Sophie conducts the chevalier to an armchair, where she sets him, sits on his knees and uncovers him with little ingenuity but much charm.)

ARNOULD
Ouy . . . Ouy . . . Je te suis chère;
Souris, pardonne et frappe tour à tour.
Yes . . . Yes . . . I am delicious to you;
Smile, forgive, and strike by turns.

IX

GRAMMONT
Ce coups charmants redoublent mon yvresse
Releve encore tous ces voiles jaloux.
(Sophie se prete avec grace; le chevalier, avec un feint courroux, la parcourt avec son myrthe amoureux depuis la naissance du dos, jusqu'a l'extremite de ses deux demi-globes d'albatre.)
These charming strokes intensify my wildness
Raise again all the sails of jealousy.
(Sophie plays along gracefully; the chevalier, with feigned wrath, teases her by caressing her with the myrtle from the base of her spine to the nipples of her breasts.)
ARNOULD
Dieu!. . . Dieu!. . . Quelle caresse!
De volupté je meurs à tes genoux!
God!. . . God!. . . What a caress!
So voluptuous I could die at your knees!

X

GRAMMONT
(Il relève Sophie.)
Fille d'amour, un bijou reste encore . . .
Gaze indiscrète, écarte-toi soudain.
(Il fait de tendres efforts pour enlever ce dernier voile: Arnould résiste, mais comme désirant d'être vaincue.)

(He lifts Sophie.)
Child of love, an eternal jewel . . .
Indiscreet gauze, suddenly makes you aloof.
(He makes a tender effort to lift the last veil:
Arnould resists, but like one who desires to be defeated.)

ARNOULD

Non!. . . Non!. . .
(La résistance devient de plus en plus faible.)
Toi que j'adore,
Puisque je n'ose, ôte-la de ta main.
(Le dernier voile disparait.)
No!. . . No!. . .
(Her resistance becomes weaker and weaker.)
You whom I adore,
Since I don't dare, you take it away.
(The last veil disappears.)

XI

GRAMMONT

Céleste Arnould, tu rougis d'être nue,
Ton oeil ému se détourne de moi . . .
Celestial Arnould, you blush to be nude,
You gaze away from me . . .

ARNOULD

Ah!. . . Ah!. . . Baisse la vue!
Ou mon délire est indigne de toi.
Ah!. . . Ah!. . . Kiss what you see!
Or my frenzy is unworthy of you.

XII

GRAMMONT

Oui, tout me dit d'être plus téméraire;
Ma bouche ardente ici va se poser.
Yes, everything tells me be bolder;
My ardent mouth shall settle here.

ARNOULD

Dieu!!! Dieu!!!
Que vas-tu faire?
Je suis en feu par ce nouveau baiser . . .
  God!!! God!!!
  What are you doing?
  This new kiss sets me on fire . . .

Translated by Karl Toepfer.

Index of Names and Titles

ILLUSTRATION CREDITS

The author is grateful to the following publishers, institutions, and collections for permission to reprint illustrations in this book. Fig. 1: Bram Dykstra, *Idols of Perversity* (New York: Oxford University Press, 1986), p. 112. Fig. 2: Gene Ringold and DeWitt Bodeen, *The Films of Cecil B. DeMille* (Secaucus: Citadel Press, 1966), p. 213. Fig. 3: Erich von Stroheim and Herman G. Weinberg, *The Complete Wedding March* (Boston: Little Brown, 1974), p. 163. Fig. 4: Museum of Modern Art, New York, N.Y. Figs. 5-6: Max J. Friedlander and Jakob Rosenberg, *The Paintings of Lucas Cranach* (Ithaca: Cornell University Press, 1978), plates 204-206. Fig. 7: Arthur Maria Rabenalt, *Mimus eroticus*, Teil 2 (Hamburg: Verlag für Kulturforschung, 1963), p. 241. Fig. 8: Eva Karcher, *Otto Dix 1891-1969* (Köln: Taschen, 1988), p. 218. Fig. 9: Hermitage, Leningrad. Fig. 10: Prado Museum, Madrid. Fig. 11: Badischer Kunstverein, Karlsruhe. Fig. 12: Alec Flegon, *Eroticism in Russian Art* (London: Flegon Press, 1976), p. 178. Figs. 13-18: Ernst Buschor, *Greek Vase-painting* (New York: Hacker Art Books, 1978), plates 57, 69, 122, 231. Figs. 19-21: Peter Gorsen, *Sexualästhetik* (Reinbek bei Hamburg: Rowohlt, 1972), pp. 181-183. Fig. 22: Georges Wildenstein, *The Paintings of Fragonard* (Garden City: Doubleday, 1960), Catalogue number 342. Fig. 23: Capon and Yve-Plessis, *Les Théâtres clandestins* (Paris: Plessis, 1905), plate 6. Fig. 24: Jacques Boncompain, *Auteurs et comédiens au XVIIIe siècle* (Paris: Librarie Académique Perrin, 1976), plate 4. Fig. 25: Private collection. Figs. 26-27: Nicolas Edme Restif de la Bretonne, *Monument du costume physique et moral de la fin du dix-huitième siècle* (Neuwied sur le Rhin: Société typographique, 1789). Figs. 28-29: Georges Wildenstein, *The Paintings of Fragonard* (Garden City: Doubleday, 1960), plate 86 and p. 263. Figs. 30-33: Private collection. Fig. 34: Robert B. Douglas, *Sophie Arnould, Actress and Wit* (Paris: Carrington, 1898). Figs. 35-38: Private collection. Fig. 39: Karl Toepfer.